Chasing
Peace

Chasing Peace

A Story of Breakdowns, Breakthroughs, and the Spiritual Power of Neuroscience

TOM ROSSHIRT

THE OPEN FIELD / PENGUIN LIFE

VIKING
An imprint of Penguin Random House LLC
penguinrandomhouse.com

The Open Field / A Penguin Life Book

THE OPEN FIELD is a registered trademark of MOS Enterprises, Inc.

Designed by Alexis Farabaugh

Grateful acknowledgment is made for permission to reprint the following:

Lyrics from "I Will." Words and music by John Lennon and Paul McCartney.
Copyright © 1968 Sony Music Publishing (US) LLC. Copyright renewed.
All rights administered by Sony Music Publishing (US) LLC, 424 Church
Street, Suite 1200, Nashville, TN 37219. International copyright secured.
All rights reserved. Reprinted by permission of Hal Leonard LLC.

Excerpt from *Unlearn Your Pain* by Dr. Howard Schubiner.
Copyright © 2010 by Howard Schubiner. Used with permission.

Library of Congress Control Number: 2024018199
ISBN 9780593653289 (hardcover)
ISBN 9780593653296 (ebook)

Printed in the United States of America
1st Printing

MARIA SHRIVER
PRESENTS

THE OPEN FIELD

A PUBLISHING IMPRINT

BOOKS THAT RISE ABOVE THE NOISE AND MOVE HUMANITY FORWARD

Dear Reader,

Years ago, these words attributed to Rumi found a place in my heart:

Out beyond ideas of
wrongdoing and rightdoing,
there is a field. I'll meet you there.

Ever since, I've cultivated an image of what I call "the Open Field"—a place out beyond fear and shame, beyond judgment, loneliness, and expectation. A place that hosts the reunion of all creation. It's the hope of my soul to find my way there—and whenever I hear an insight or a practice that helps me on the path, I love nothing more than to share it with others.

That's why I've created The Open Field. My hope is to publish books that honor the most unifying truth in human life: We are all seeking the same things. We're all seeking dignity. We're all seeking joy. We're all seeking love and acceptance, seeking to be seen, to be safe. And there is no competition for these things we seek—because they are not material goods; they are spiritual gifts!

We can all give each other these gifts if we share what we know—what has lifted us up and moved us forward. That is our duty to one another—to help each other toward acceptance, toward peace, toward happiness—and my promise to you is that the books published under this imprint will be maps to the Open Field, written by guides who know the path and want to share it.

Each title will offer insights, inspiration, and guidance for moving beyond the fears, the judgments, and the masks we all wear. And when we take off the masks, guess what? We will see that we are the opposite of what we thought—we are each other.

We are all on our way to the Open Field. We are all helping one another along the path. I'll meet you there.

Love, Maria S

For Molly, Nick, and Ben
The best people who ever happened to me

Perhaps the most important revelation in human split-brain research is precisely this: that the left cerebral hemisphere of humans is prone to fabricating verbal narratives that do not necessarily accord with the truth.

Antonio Damasio, professor of psychology, philosophy, and neurology and David Dornsife Chair in Neuroscience at the University of Southern California

The left brain weaves its story in order to convince it and you that it is in full control. . . . It is really trying to keep our personal story together. To do that, we have to learn to lie to ourselves.

Michael S. Gazzaniga, professor of psychology at the University of California, Santa Barbara, and founder of the Centers of Neuroscience at the University of California, Davis, and at Dartmouth College

CONTENTS

Chasing
Peace

CHAPTER ONE

The Self-Image
Model of Happiness

I hate it when life tells me I'm not who I think I am.

And it's the best thing that ever happens to me.

Maybe to you too?

What's the most precious dream you've ever had, maybe so bold you'd be embarrassed to admit it—becoming a professional athlete, writing a hit song, running a Fortune 500 company? Or maybe falling in love, getting married, and raising a family?

Whatever your dream is, or was, can you remember a moment when that dream took a hit, maybe a mortal blow, and in the midst of the loss, you didn't make excuses, you didn't cast yourself as a victim, you didn't hurt the person you blamed for your pain—instead, you saw that there was a clash between your self-image and reality, and instead of revising reality to suit your self-image, you revised your self-image to meet reality, and not with grievance but with grace?

In my view, that was a moment of triumph.

The feelings of peace and wholeness we seek through "success" are hiding in the death of dreams that are too small. We break through only after we break down, and we break down only after we've spent years building up.

This is not a book about quitting on your dreams. It's not about giving up on the highest image of who you want to be. It's about what happens when you pursue a dream with passion, see the dream fail, then look into the darkness and see the light.

When I was a sophomore in college, a friend and I hiked up the side of a mountain, sat down for lunch, and read to each other from the dialogues of Socrates. The old philosopher was put on trial for either the most subversive crime ever or the greatest civic gift possible, depending on how you see it. Socrates was accused of being a doer of evil who corrupts the youth. Actually, his "crime" was seeking out Athenian citizens who were seen to be wise and, through public debate, showing them they were *not* wise. The young people loved him. The elders sentenced him to death. Phaedo describes the scene in the prison cell as Socrates drinks the poison, lies down, and waits to die. He closes the dialogue by saying, "Such was the end, Echecrates, of our friend; concerning whom I may truly say, that of all the men of his time whom I have known, he was the wisest and justest and best."

I read those lines aloud and fell silent—electrified. From that moment, I was consumed by a desire to reach the end point of moral development—by whatever name you want to call it. I decided to major in philosophy. I took courses in religion. I read books on Gandhi. I started to meditate. I did ten-day retreats. I visited Zen temples in Japan. I went to a hermitage in Sri Lanka. I began a doctorate in human development. The search consumed me. When I was read-ing or meditating—time disappeared. I hadn't eaten, but I wasn't hungry. I hadn't slept, but I wasn't tired.

But the most important thing I see, looking back nearly fifty years, is not that I found a passion but that I made it into an identity. My interest was genuine, but I used it to try to be better than others. And there was an unconscious social calculation for me in choosing the self-image of a spiritual person. I'm very competitive, and I be-gan to see people my age becoming successful. They were running for office, starting businesses, performing in symphonies—and I wasn't. So I took refuge in spirituality. This allowed me to say to the people living in my head: "Sure, you're a Rhodes Scholar–Olympian with a book on the *New York Times* bestseller list, but I'm a spiritual person who's transcended competition. So, I win."

And my spiritual boasts were not easy to test. It's not like I was saying "I'm the best left-handed bowler in Indiana." I made it hard for others to hold me accountable. *Of course*, I wasn't a saint—this was obvious to everyone. But I was *going to be* a saint. (Though this wasn't obvious to anyone.) I was on my way. Which means I had one more element in my self-image that I had to cling to desperately: "I'm getting better"; or another version of the same conceit, "What I'm doing is working"; or—even worse—"I've figured everything out!"

My spiritual self-image wasn't the only identity that was precious to me. From early childhood, I started trying on identities for the buzz they gave me, and I held on to the ones that worked—good reader, gifted writer, strong chess player. At some regrettable point, I took on the identity of being super-reliable. It's not that I "was" those things but that I got high if others saw me that way, and I got hurt if they didn't.

All these idealized images of myself—from meditator to writer to "totally reliable"—flow together into a story I tell others about myself and hope they tell back to me. My story is just my self-image in motion—my fantasy of how it all works out for me.

And it's surprising to me how people and events can still affect my mood by affirming or challenging my story and the beliefs that make it up. Without ever planning it or consciously choosing it, I tied my happiness to a story of who I am. If someone contradicts my story, I get angry. If someone honors and affirms my story, I respond with the false grace of an addict who just got a fix.

I believe that most of our struggles for happiness can be seen inside this frame, which, for this book, I'm going to call the self-image model of happiness. This is the implicit model of most self-improvement literature—you achieve happiness by deciding who you want to be and becoming that.

One of the most memorable and influential descriptions of this model was articulated by Stephen Covey in his book *The 7 Habits of Highly Effective People*. In chapter 2, titled "Habit 2: Begin with the End in Mind," Covey invites us to picture ourselves at our funeral and asks us, "What would you like these speakers to say about you and your life?"

> That, he says, is the criterion by which everything else is examined. Each part of your life—today's behavior, tomorrow's behavior, next week's behavior, next month's behavior—can be examined in the context of the whole, of what really matters to you. By keeping that end clearly in mind, you can make certain that whatever you do on any particular day does not violate the criteria you have defined as supremely important,

and that each day of your life contributes in a meaningful way to the vision you have of your life as a whole.

To begin with the end in mind means to start with a clear understanding of your destination. It means to know where you're going so that you better understand where you are now and so that the steps you take are always in the right direction.

I loved this book. I studied it. I marked it up. I quoted it. I lived by it. It was a brilliant expression of what I believed. It was also a precise distillation of the scripture of our culture. Be who you want to be.

After testing this approach for many years in this and other forms, I've come to the view that this is outstanding advice for achieving excellence in sports, business, entertainment, politics, or virtually any pursuit we take on *but one*—it can help us achieve everything but peace.

PEACE AND HAPPINESS

Peace is different from happiness. Happiness is a material pursuit. Peace is a spiritual state. Happiness is getting what we want. Peace is wanting what we get. Happiness is becoming who we want to be. Peace is becoming who we are.

This is how I'll use these terms in this book. Happiness comes when my self-image and the story I see for myself line up with the world—the precious moments where there is nothing I want that I don't have. Peace is the same feeling—there is nothing that I want that I don't have—but it's not tied to events. It's a state of mind, so it can go on and on.

True happiness includes peace. If happiness doesn't include peace, it's just a good mood. When I use the term *happiness* in a spiritual sense, I mean happiness through peace.

This book is about the shift from seeking happiness by achieving the self-image to finding peace by dissolving the self-image. There are several words I use in the book to refer to the state we enter as we surrender the self-image—*peace, joy, grace, love*. This state is where I believe we're all headed. But I don't think that seeking peace and joy and grace and love is how most of us start out. We first seek happiness by creating a story of who we want to be and trying to achieve that in the world. At least that's how it was for me.

When I look back on my greatest happiness and sadness, they correspond with my success or failure in sustaining my story of myself. When I've been able to live up to my self-image and be recognized for my gifts without straining over the effort, I've felt happy. When my self-image gets overwhelmed and I appear to be those things I hate and have worked hard to avoid, I get depressed.

And this is the most embarrassing insight: the deep cause behind my story-making—and the happiness and sadness that comes with it—is nothing more than my longing to be special. That's all. I'm just a little boy trying to live a story that makes me the hero so I can be loved.

It doesn't matter what the identity or the story is, my motive is to be separate and superior (and special and secure). When I took on the self-image of being "spiritual," I was trying to put myself above people who sought fame or wealth or power. I thought, "I'm laughing my way past that material-success trap they're wasting their time on."

No, I wasn't.

Some years ago, I asked a friend of mine to read Richard Rohr's book *Falling Upward*. I loved the book, and I wanted to see if it resonated with her. She read it and didn't say anything, so in an act of spiritual espionage for which I feel no contrition, I glanced through her copy to see if she'd made any notes.

She had marked one of my favorite passages. Richard writes: "If we seek spiritual heroism ourselves, the old ego is just back in control under a new name. . . . Any attempt to engineer or plan your own enlightenment is doomed to failure because it will be ego-driven."

My friend had underlined these words, and in the margin had written "Tom."

I laughed with the joy of a man whose flaws are known and still feels loved. In fact, my friend had once said to me, "Maybe you should go to a therapist and see if you can find out why you need to be so special and why you always need to be improving." She was wise enough to see that the two were related—and that a passion for self-improvement isn't always a sign of health or a path to happiness.

The content of my self-improvement aims and dreams might be different from other people's, but the structure is not. If I take "I want to be a saint" and replace it with "I want to be a senator," the pattern is the same. No better. No worse. No matter what name I give to my ambition, I am on the same path, in one form or another, as anyone who's ever chased peace.

And because our journeys are the same, at least in their structure, I think we can help one another. That is the point of this book. We all build ourselves up in life. We're born to it. It's how we make our way in the world. But what we build up eventually breaks down. It has to—reality doesn't treat our conceits kindly.

The outcome of our lives, I believe, comes in how we handle the breakdowns—and whether we see them as a chance for a breakthrough. Looking back, I can see that the time I spent working at the White House was the high point of success for my strategy of seeking happiness by fulfilling the self-image. It was also the beginning of the breakdown, and the breaking down was a blessing—because it was not "me" who was breaking down; it was the self-image strategy for happiness that was breaking down, and that breakdown cleared a path to peace.

BREAKING DOWN THE SELF-IMAGE

Today, I still carry a lot of identities in my head, but I still am most attached to "spiritual person." And my aims and goals are as embarrassingly audacious as they were when I was young. I want to be able to respond with love in any situation—to answer ill will with goodwill, to absorb pain without passing it on, to come closer to meeting the most outrageous demand ever made of human beings: "Love your enemies."

The project feels more practical and accessible to me when I cast it in the words of theologian and Catholic priest James Alison, who says, "Love your enemies; it's the only way to get the bastards out of your head."

I have found that the most helpful frame for growth for me—one that helps me see when I'm stuck and when I'm free—comes from adding another element to the concept of self-image, and that is the shadow. The "self-image" is who I claim I am, and the "shadow" is who I insist I'm not. I soothe myself and situate myself in the world by telling myself, "I am this and not that."

This mechanism—creating a self-image and a shadow, then defending the self-image and denying the shadow—is often the way I get through the day. But it dooms me to conflict because I'm deny-ing part of who I am. (When I hear, "Be your *best self*!" I think, "Okay, but what am I supposed to do with all these *other* selves?")

Only when I fully admit the shadow (in both senses of the word *admit*—to confess and to include) can I find peace. This model par-adoxically makes spiritual growth a matter of self-aggrandizement, so to speak—making myself bigger and bigger until "I am this, *and* I am that." I am everything—especially those things I insist I am not. Perhaps this is the state of mind that prompted the Roman African playwright Terence to write, "I am human, and I think nothing hu-man is alien to me."

Years ago, I dreamed I would write a book with the triumphal narrative "I have figured it out! Here's how I found peace—and here's how you, too, can find it!" Mercifully for all of us, I don't have the facts for that story. I'm writing a book in the middle of the battle—talking about where I'm free and where I'm still stuck in "self-improvement," which is something in between a scheme and a scam. For me, it's really self-*image* improvement—creating an ever more glorious persona, imagining a future where people will pay homage to my self-image, and I will win the "turn the other cheek" prize at the Enlightenment Awards Dinner.

Continuous monitoring of the many precious measures in my self-improvement protocol, "Did I exercise, meditate, eat well, sleep enough, meet my deadlines, and get things done?" keeps me locked in self-absorption and swings me back and forth between gloating and feeling guilty. I need to review how I've done to know how I feel. This is a defensible approach to achievement in many fields, but for someone seeking peace, it's a trap. I know because I'm writing to you from inside the trap.

Thus, the title *Chasing Peace*. I love that phrase because it's a joke on me. Peace is chasing me, and it can't catch me because I can't stand still, and I can't stand still because I'm chasing peace. When I shared this title with a friend, he said: "Ha! Like furiously seeking a state of calm!" Exactly. I have spent my life chasing peace as if it's a loose dog that's running away, and it's running away because I'm chasing it. And I can't stop chasing it because I hate the way I feel when I'm still. I don't mean the stillness of sitting in meditation. I mean the stillness of not making progress, not being productive, not getting better. I can't *stand* that stillness.

I would not have come by anything interesting to say about chasing peace except that I failed for forty years to find it, then I found it—or started to let it find me. I have never been happier or laughed louder or longer. Things I used to hate I now absorb with a shrug. Anxious states of mind come much less frequently, with less intensity, and don't last as long—because I have figured out how I've been feeding them and am now slowly starving them. When dark thoughts come, bringing their dark feelings with them, I know what to do. And some dark thoughts and feelings never come at all anymore.

Before I describe the breakthrough—what led to it and what it's like—let me offer some context on breaking down. My breakdown wasn't a result of picking the wrong goals and not recognizing it until midlife. I didn't decide as a kid that I wanted to be rich and famous, only to achieve my goals and find myself unfulfilled because I had sought the wrong things. That's not my story.

My breakdown came from the constant battle of trying to defend my inflated self-image. I broke down from the strain of telling a story of who I am and trying to get others to tell it too. I was striving to be everything on my list of identities, and the effort to be anything—even in the name of noble self-improvement—is exhausting. That constant battle broke me down. That's the background on my breakdown.

Here's the foreground: On a Monday afternoon in November 2018, I was in an apartment in northern Virginia, on the phone with a psychiatrist who was reviewing my brain MRI. I had moved to Arlington—a thirty-minute drive from my home—on the advice of several doctors. Depression, anxiety, brain fog, memory issues, neuropathy, and a host of other symptoms had worsened over the years—and then spiked after we did a renovation on our home. The paint on the walls and the stain on the floors triggered my symptoms and made me dizzy, and I moved out temporarily—leaving behind my wife and kids and the dog—so I could try to get a handle on my health.

Unfortunately, in the eight months I'd been in the new place, things had not improved for me—even with the low-chemical-content building materials and the saunas, the air purifier, the supplements, and all the other diet and detox tricks I was trying. In fact, my plan had failed. I wasn't any closer to moving back home, and when I did visit home to test it out, I got dizzy. I missed my kids, my wife, my neighborhood, and my life, and I felt like my family was moving on without me. I was running out of hope, and I was praying this doctor could help.

"Have you had a head injury—sports or car accident?" she asked. I'd been asked the same question six months before by a psychiatrist who'd read a different scan. I described some head-banging moments in soccer and on the playground, nothing serious, and she told me I was showing some asymmetry that suggested head injuries. The injuries make the blood-brain barrier more permeable, she explained, so if you're exposed to mold or other substances, it's easier for them to get in the brain. She told me that my working memory could be wiped out fairly easily. I asked how that could happen, and she said by anesthesia getting through the blood-brain barrier.

She asked if I'd been diagnosed with Lyme or coinfections, which I hadn't, then she told me my amygdala was swollen, at the 98th percentile. The amygdala is the brain's fire alarm, she said. It should go off only for a fire—but when it's at the 98th percentile, it could be set off by something harmless, triggering a fight-or-flight response, and making me more reactive to everything. She spent most of the time going over my brain, area by area, noting the atrophy, and she closed by saying: "To sum up, the MRI is highly abnormal. Not good, you understand. And luckily, I'm not with you in person to tell you this."

I wanted to make sure I had heard that right.

"You're glad you aren't delivering this news face-to-face?"

"Right," she said, "because I'm telling you very bluntly. This is sad. No way to really mince words here."

I got off the phone and sat quietly for a while. I was glad she was candid, but I was hurt by her tone. She had encouraged me to go on a protocol that I'd already tried, and she made it clear she didn't want me as a patient. Both points were depressing. But my dominant reaction was anger at myself, triggered by her report that my "fire alarm" could be set off by almost anything. If I am so reactive that I have to leave my home and isolate myself because of a mysterious stress-based illness that affects no one else in my family, then what was the point of all that meditation; all those silent retreats; all those stupid, pointless visits to this temple and that hermitage?

That question was not coming to me for the first time; it came to me all the time. But it was such painful proof of my failure that I never raised it with anyone but myself. Except once. I was on a retreat with a medical doctor from the University of Wisconsin, the kind of guy who could make anybody open up, and I remember telling him: "I've been meditating forever, and you know what? If you stood me in a lineup of a dozen people and put us through experiments designed to irritate us and then asked a panel of observers to identify the guy who's been meditating for forty years—no one would pick me, the rigid German with the Irish temper."

It was hard to confess that I had spent all my adult life chasing peace and in the end wasn't much different from the way I was at the start. But I shared my shame with him because I wanted to know if he thought I had wasted my time.

He flashed me a smile of fatherly affection, raised his finger for emphasis, and said, "Never devalue the work you do before your breakthrough."

When he said that, I dismissed it as kindhearted consolation offered to a loser. But I've since changed my mind. A few days after the MRI analysis, I began to feel a wave of peace. And paradoxically, it didn't come from seeing a path to health. I had reached the *end* of my path. I didn't know what to do. I had nowhere to go. I didn't want to quit, but everything I'd tried had failed. So, I stopped. There was no activity. There was stillness. And in that stillness, grace had an opening. Or perhaps I was opening to grace. Three weeks later, I got the phone call that led to my breakthrough.

BREAKING THROUGH THE SELF-IMAGE

The call came from a woman who ran a support group for people with chronic symptoms like mine—everything from mold illness to chemical sensitivity, fibromyalgia, chronic Lyme disease, anxiety, and chronic pain. These illnesses often cost the sufferers their jobs, their savings, their spouses, and their homes because they get so reactive to their environment that they have to withdraw from life.

The woman told me she had checked with members of the group and they were happy to have me, but they wanted me to understand that the group does not talk about new supplements or medicines or air purifiers or in-home saunas or the best new tea or how to find a "clean" living space; they talk about neuroplasticity and rewiring the brain's response to triggers. If I wanted to take that approach, I would be welcome in the group.

"Neuroplasticity" refers to the brain's ability to adapt to its environment. If we can trace the source of a physical pain or illness to neural pathways in the brain, we can treat the body by changing the brain.

I had heard about neuroplasticity, but not as a practice. This particular approach discussed by the group was developed by a woman named Annie Hopper who reacted so strongly to so many elements in her environment that she went to live on a houseboat, where she read books on neuroscience and developed an approach that cured first her—and then others. The cause, in her theory, was a limbic system stuck on high alert, constantly sending out messages of danger and flooding the body with cortisol, adrenaline, and norepinephrine. The more activated the threat detector, the more threats it detects, which is why people stuck in this pattern run into more and more triggers, leading not just to isolation but to anxiety, depression, and a host of other ills.

I read the book, joined the group, ordered the videos, attended the workshop, and a few months later, I moved back into my house. I dropped the supplements, the air purifiers, the saunas, the restrictive diets, and the rest. This breakthrough was the mother of all my other breakthroughs. I had made the shift from believing and obeying my false and fearful thoughts to questioning them and defying them.

It's hard to rely on words to convey the impact this approach has had on my life. I would just say that—in terms of joy increased and suffering reduced for time invested and money spent—nothing I had ever done came close to it. When I completed the workshop, I had never felt happier, every relationship was better, and I had never laughed so much in my life.

After I moved back home, I explored more approaches to self-directed neuroplasticity, learned about others, and practiced approaches from different teachers. As I mentioned above, neuroplasticity means that the brain is designed to be changed by experiences—namely, thoughts, beliefs, and emotions. "Self-directed neuroplasticity" means doing practices that favor the thoughts, beliefs, and emotions that change your brain in the way you want. In the words of one of my teachers, if you change certain habits, "your brain has no choice but to change."

The practices I've sampled are all grounded in the same insights—the central role of fearful thoughts in causing physical and emotional illness and the ability of certain practices to weaken or dissolve those thoughts and the feelings that come with them. In this book, I'm not telling a story about one practitioner or one approach. The expanding insights of neuroscience are generating waves of change grounded in scientific truths whose full application, when it comes, could be staggering. To paraphrase research psychiatrist Jeffrey M. Schwartz, "Your mind can change your brain."

The neuroplastic approach is not currently widely understood or accepted, but it's gaining followers. In late 2021, a study, published the next year in *JAMA Psychiatry*, highlighted the power of a neuroplastic approach in healing back pain, and a *Washington Post* article by social historian and science writer Nathaniel Frank put it this way:

> The view that chronic pain originates in the brain—that it's fundamentally a psychological phenomenon, and can be eliminated by altering thoughts, beliefs and feelings rather than by changing something in the body or flooding it with chemicals—has long been controversial and is still largely dismissed as New Age hooey or offensive victim-blaming. But what started out as a hunch by health-care practitioners on the fringe is finally being proved true by science.

In this back-pain study—a randomized controlled trial conducted at the University of Colorado at Boulder—66 percent of the patients who'd been suffering for years with chronic back pain declared themselves nearly or fully pain free. A separate study published at the same time by Harvard-affiliated researchers showed comparable results.

The method used in both studies was a practice designed to reduce fear—and reducing the fear reduced the pain. These findings support the claim that chronic pain often originates in the brain and is not a result of tissue damage. The *Post* article notes that A. Vania Apkarian, who runs a neuroscience pain lab at Northwestern University, can predict which subjects will develop chronic pain by looking at images of their brains, not their backs.

The ability to heal chronic pain and other illnesses is hugely significant—but this is just the beginning. The coming applications of neuroplasticity can go deeper than healing physical and emotional ailments—unless by "healing physical and emotional ailments" we mean healing suffering itself.

The link between thoughts and suffering has been posited by spiritual teachers for more than 2,500 years, and the art of dissolving thoughts that cause suffering has been taught as well. So, neuroplasticity is not an invention of science. It is a reality of nature that is now being confirmed by science, explained by science, validated by science, and in the future can be applied more broadly through innovations inspired by science.

Self-directed neuroplasticity turned my life around. This is the breakthrough—the art of changing the thoughts and feelings that cause our suffering. Not just the thoughts and feelings that lead to back pain but also the thoughts and feelings that build the false image of who I am and tell me I have to defend that self-image if I want to be happy.

I used to believe that if I understood clearly who I wanted to be and worked for a long time to achieve it, then I could *make myself* into that person, and that would give me love, respect, and peace.

I was wrong. I don't mean to say that there aren't some lives that are happier than others. And I do believe that a person whose self-image is supported by circumstances without much strain on their part is a happy person for as long as it lasts. I also believe this approach can lead to great accomplishments. But it is not a way to find peace. Peace comes not from fulfilling the self-image but from dissolving it.

As I mentioned at the start, there are two basic approaches to seeking peace: getting what you want and wanting what you get. The first is chasing peace; the second is finding it. The breakthrough is moving from the first approach to the second.

The principles of neuroplasticity are the heart of the shift. Before the breakthrough, I was trying to defend and preserve the self-image. Since the breakthrough, I've been cutting off the fuel that sustains the self-image.

The secret is knowing that a feeling of fear always needs a fearful thought to feed it, and a fearful thought always needs a fearful feeling to drive it. If we can disrupt that two-way network, the fear starts to dissolve. When fear dissolves, the self-image dissolves too—because the self-image was created to defend us from fear.

That's a big part of my practice—in the midst of a dark feeling, finding the thought that feeds the feeling, then starving the thought of the fear it needs, sometimes by laughing at it. "Giggling at yourself is the best therapy," James Alison once told me. Then he added, "The devil can't cope with humor."

This is one of the approaches I use. But no single practice or approach will work for everyone. We each have to find a method that works—and we may switch our practice from time to time. To find our way, we have to go through a lot of trial and error, and we don't live long enough to try everything. We need to learn from other people's errors—and their successes. We're at our best when we're helping one another figure things out—reporting dead ends, detours, breakdowns, breakthroughs, shortcuts, blind spots, and things that backfired.

That's why I have always felt a compulsion to write down the things I do in case they work. I think we owe it to one another to share whatever helps. In this book, I am adding my notes and practices to the conversation—I hope they will help others, and I'm confident the feedback will help me. We're in an age of change, with a more profound understanding of a way out of suffering than we've ever had, with innovations that could change the world by changing us. We need to stick together, share what we know, and help one another find the way. We were born for such a time as this.

CHAPTER TWO

The Beginning of
Breaking Down

I n the summer after I finished third grade, I watched on TV as
Senator Daniel Inouye of Hawaii gave the keynote address at
the 1968 Democratic National Convention.

I didn't know anything about Inouye at the time. If I noticed
during the speech that he gestured only with his left hand, or that
his right sleeve hung empty at his side, I don't remember it. Only
later did I learn about his courage in battle. All I knew about him
that night was that he could electrify my eight-year-old brain by saying this: "In closing, I wish to share with you a most sacred word of
Hawaii. It is *aloha*. To some of you who have visited us, it may have
meant 'hello.' To others, *aloha* may have meant 'goodbye.' But to
those of us who have been privileged to live in Hawaii, *aloha* means
'I love you.' So to all of you, my fellow Americans, aloha."

That was the first speech that ever inspired me. When I became
a speechwriter myself, I carried that memory inside me. "This is

what a speech can do. This is what a speech *should* do. This is what *I* should do."

Even now, when I write a speech, especially if it's a speech for a big occasion, I picture a triumphal outcome of people moved to tears, cheers, laughter, and applause. That's the story in my head. That's what my self-image wants. It doesn't matter who is giving the speech; I have to be the secret unsung hero. (People will sing songs about how unsung I am.) If the speech fulfills my hopes, I'm *delighted*. If it fails, I get angry—and look for someone to blame.

One of the last speeches I worked on at the White House I wrote with Sandy Berger, President Clinton's national security advisor. He was giving a short talk at a White House staff farewell party in a tent on the South Lawn in January 2001—a week or two before we'd all be gone.

It was a chance for Sandy to say "thank you" to the president for his contributions to foreign policy, with an emphasis on how much the people of the world loved him. We had just seen thousands of people flood the streets in Vietnam to get a glimpse of Clinton. In Ghana, five hundred thousand people had come to hear him speak. During his visit to India, a famous columnist and novelist had written: "India is mesmerized by Clinton. He's cast a spell. Even the sanest of people have lost their reason." The president had won friends for the United States all over the world, and Sandy wanted to pay tribute to that.

His remarks were short. But the speeches before Sandy's ran long, leaving people drained and drifting toward the food at the edge of the tent when it was Sandy's turn to speak. The words flowed well, but people weren't paying attention, and I got furious and stormed out of the tent. An hour later, a colleague who'd been at the event saw me and said, "What a surprise!"

"What surprise?" I asked.

"Fleetwood Mac!" he said, looking at me oddly.

Stevie Nicks and Fleetwood Mac had been standing behind the curtain that Sandy was speaking in front of. A few minutes after Sandy's speech, the curtain dropped, and the band performed "Don't Stop"— the Clinton 1992 campaign anthem. That was one of the higher prices I paid for one of my touchy-speechwriter temper tantrums. Three and a half years of White House stress had begun to break me down.

THE SELF-IMAGE STRATEGY FOR HAPPINESS

No matter who we are or what job we have, our self-image is getting affirmed and wounded every day. Some days burnish the self-image, some days batter it, and some days do both. But outside the daily fluctuations of the self-image, there is a larger trajectory, running over the course of years, that tracks the rise or fall of the self-image and can tell us whether we're still building up or have entered the phase of breaking down.

I don't believe that it's the self-image alone that is building up or breaking down; what's breaking down is the self-image model of happiness—an often-unconscious strategy for seeking happiness that is made up of three parts: (1) forming a positive self-image or story that makes me feel good, (2) trying to get people to tell my story back to me, and (3) trying to live up to my story without exhausting myself. When this system is working, I am getting what I want in life, including a feeling of purpose and belonging. I believe that this is generally what we call happiness, and as I said earlier, most of the self-improvement literature lies inside this model.

This larger strategy for seeking happiness is either working or failing, building up or breaking down over a period of time—and here's how we can tell which one is happening:

I'm building up (the strategy is working) if my story is getting bigger and bolder, there is more validation and support for my story from the people I care about, and I don't feel much strain in keeping up the story: I'm not drinking or taking drugs to boost my mood, I'm not exhausting myself with work, I'm not lying to make myself look good, and I'm not obsessing over diet and exercise or relying on other tricks and tactics to keep up appearances.

I'm breaking down (the strategy is failing) if my story is getting harder to defend; it's being challenged, so I have to fight for it; I feel anxious, exhausted, and depressed; and I get angry with the people and events that contradict my story. I might even be breaking down if my story is getting bigger and bolder and I'm getting lots of support for my story, but I'm feeling anxious and depressed and exhausted because it's getting harder and harder to live up to that story.

A decisive factor in whether I'm building up or breaking down is how I feel. The self-image model is a strategy for peace and happiness, so the test of how it's faring is personal: Do I feel happy? Do I feel peaceful? It's not only what I produce that tells me whether I'm building up or breaking down—but what it takes to produce it, what it takes *out of me* to produce it. An artist might be at the peak of their fame and on the edge of despair. The self-image might be rising while the person is collapsing.

So, a key measure of breakdown is "Do I *feel* broken down?" Am

I exhausting myself to produce what I do because it would humiliate me to produce anything less? Is my self-image, in other words, turning into an abusive boss?

The breakdown of the self-image model of happiness starts with the breakdown of the self-image itself. And the self-image *has* to break down because the self is a false construct—which we can learn from a study of Hinduism, or Buddhism, or Jungian psychology, or a variety of neuroscientific perspectives, or, more significantly and fruitfully, a lifetime of introspection.

If we pay attention, we can see that the more pressure that's put on the self-image, the more certain it is to break down. The higher the standards, the higher the stakes, the greater the power of the people watching—the more stress will be placed on the self-image. And the stressful forces that break us down are patient and persistent— they don't usually break our self-image in two. It's rarely so dramatic. Instead, they make constant demands so that we spend all our energy defending the self-image, and that effort saps the life force of the person behind the image.

PERFECTIONISM—BEING *PERFECTLY* MY SELF-IMAGE

When someone first asked me if I had impostor syndrome at the White House, I was *offended*. "Are you saying I'm not good enough?!" "Impostor syndrome" means feeling I'm in a place I don't belong, in a job I don't deserve, and I'm about to be exposed and fired.

That wasn't me. I *totally* belonged. That was the story I was telling myself. But here's another story: A few days after I started the job, I was supposed to get in a motorcade that was leaving from the

South Lawn, but I didn't know how to get there, so I asked a colleague for directions. He said, "Go across West Exec into the West Wing, take a left at the VP's office, and walk down the hallway past the Oval . . ." and I stopped listening because I was thinking: "Are you *crazy*?! If I walk past the Oval, the Secret Service will tackle me!"

That's how much I felt I belonged.

So how did I deal with the impostor syndrome I didn't know I had?

I worked overtime in overdrive every day to prevent the mistake or mediocrity that would prove I didn't belong. It started with frenzied research. I became best friends with the librarians in the Old Executive Office Building. I would gather hundreds of pages of book excerpts and old speeches and put them in fat binders. I'd read them all, mark them up, code them by section—always searching for the fact or phrase that would stand out—and I'd delay writing the draft so I could do more research. Then I'd write draft after draft, never letting anyone see anything until it was superpolished, then follow with obsessive proofreading and compulsive fact-checking, always scanning the horizon for threats and rewriting the draft to defuse them.

This was my approach to the silent voice inside telling me I didn't belong: I took a hike up the steep mountain path of perfectionism— desperate to reach the summit but terrifying myself over the tiny margin for error and the huge cost of failure.

Back then, though, I couldn't have said any of this. Perfectionism was a force I didn't understand and couldn't name. I just thought I was being the way people are supposed to be if they're not losers.

Perfectionism, at least my practice of it, is driven not by my fear of making a mistake but by my fear of shattering my self-image as the guy who never *makes* mistakes. So, a minor error is a disgrace. A missed deadline is a scandal. And my brand of perfectionism combines the terror of error with the need to amaze. Everything is all-important. When I send you a draft, I'm not asking for edits; I'm asking for applause. If you say, "This is a good *start*," you will depress me. If you say it's "great," I'll say, "How great?" If you want me to go away unwounded, it's best to say, "This is breathtaking."

Perfectionism is my drive to *perfectly* embody my self-image—to be "who I really am" in my most exalted formulation. Perfectionism is part of a warning system that triggers a surge of energy to suppress any evidence that I'm not who I claim to be.

If anyone challenged my approach back then, I would have denied any psychological motive and insisted that I *have* to be perfect—that's the job. Any thought that I should drop the mask and be who it was I was trying to hide was decades away. I wasn't ready. I was still building up the self-image, still needing it—still in many ways getting what I wanted from it. I had only the thinnest awareness that I was deeply insecure, and because I wasn't aware of it, I was governed by it. I was one hundred percent dedicated to defending the self-image and denying the shadow. And denying the shadow is hard work.

I was in a continuous state of high alert, always preparing for a sudden call or meeting with anyone who would give me a stream of information I would have to write in a speech. I never went anywhere without a reporter's pad in my jacket and pens in my pocket. I had such compulsive anxiety about being caught without pen and paper that I would see a pen on my desk and put it in my pocket—no matter how many pens I already had. Even now, more than twenty-five years later, I am often carrying anywhere from three to eight pens in my pockets, and I've lost countless pairs of pants to ink stains.

My compulsions would spike when I was preparing the vice president for media interviews, especially for joint press conferences with foreign leaders. I lived in terror of seeing the VP stumped by a question I should have prepared him for. So, I would go on an endless dive into my imagination to come up with questions a reporter might ask.

One night I was in Switzerland preparing a memo for the VP, who had a joint interview the next day with British prime minister Tony Blair at 10 Downing Street. The venue made me more anxious than usual, and my compulsions set in. "What if they ask *this* question?" And I added that question and wrote an answer. Then I thought, "What if they ask *that* question?" And I added that question and wrote an answer. I couldn't stop. On some questions, I emailed White House colleagues for answers. I kept this up until three or four in the morning. No one was awake to tell me to go to sleep. The next day, during our prep session, I handed this fat memo to Gore, who looked at it for a minute, tossed it aside, and did a great job in the interview. Thanks to me.

Another attack of perfectionism pushed me to memorize the names of the leaders of all the countries in the world. In October 1999, General Pervez Musharraf launched a coup in Pakistan, installing himself as head of state. Musharraf was on the front page of US newspapers for two weeks straight. At the time, George H. W. Bush was emerging as a front-runner for the Republican nomination and was asked frequently about the coup. When he kept referring to Musharraf as "the General," some of the press started suggesting maybe Bush couldn't remember the name. They had some fun with it, and I thought, "Things are going to flip, and the press will come after Gore with a *You think you're so smart?* question." Then I thought (because this is how I think): "Hell, I'm the VP's foreign-affairs spokesperson. I'm the easiest target. I'll come walking out of the Starbucks at Seventeenth and G and run into a CNN reporter asking me, 'Who's the leader of Burkina Faso?'" So, I memorized everybody's name. And nobody asked.

LOSING MY SELF-IMAGE—LOSING MY COOL

Amid the steady stream of anxiety, there were some moments when I lost my cool—and they were always tied directly to defending my self-image.

When Al Gore announced he was running for president in the summer of 1999, AIDS protestors interrupted his speech with the chant "Gore's greed kills!" They claimed Gore was threatening South Africa with trade sanctions to keep the South Africans from making affordable AIDS drugs—*and* that he was doing it in exchange for drug-company campaign contributions.

I had traveled with Gore to meetings in South Africa, so I talked with staff, gathered the memoranda of conversations and the internal memos, and met with the protestors at the White House. I said: "My brother died of AIDS before there were any AIDS drugs. I saw him go from diagnosis to death in five months. I support this cause. But what you're saying about the vice president is unfair and untrue. I have the documents here to prove it, and I'm asking you to stop."

There were about two seconds of silence in the room, and then a young protestor gave me an icy look and said, "Change the policy."

For protest tactics, that was as good as it gets. Target a person with the power to help you achieve your goal, tell a story that threatens the image that makes him appealing to the people he needs, make it clear he can redeem his self-image by doing what you want— and make sure as many people as possible are watching.

The cause was just. The US global policy on pharmaceuticals was indefensible. It still had not been updated for the age of AIDS. Change had begun but was moving too slowly. During this time, Gore had been pressuring the US government for change, not the South African government. And that gave me a two-part job: work with staff to speed the policy change and work with reporters and protestors to make Gore's record known to the public.

Two months after the protests began, an article appeared in *The Wall Street Journal* with the headline GORE HOPES NEW AIDS PACT WILL HELP SHAKE PROTESTORS. I had spent a lot of time talking to the reporter for the article, and I read it eagerly. But before I was done reading, I called the reporter, shouted into his voicemail, and slammed down the handset, shattering the phone. (My colleagues collected the pieces and presented it to me as a gift in a shatterproof plastic case.)

There wasn't a single thing in the article that was wrong or unfair. In fact, it made points that other reporters had not acknowledged— that Gore had been working to help South Africa get cheap AIDS drugs for nearly a year before the protests began and that a leader of the protests said they were targeting Gore because he had the power to help fix the problem and not because he was causing the problem.

But here's the line that drove me nuts: "South African and US officials say that the pace of negotiations quickened considerably after ACT UP began its protests in mid-June."

That's what set me off—and it was absolutely true. Why did it hurt to read what was true—that the protests got action? I wanted Gore to get credit for working to fix the problem before the protests began. And I didn't want the protestors to be able to say that the change came only from their pressure.

Millions of lives were at stake and progress was being made, but I was obsessed with my self-image, wanting to be seen as someone with the moral character to be on the right side of this issue and the professional skill to get the story we wanted in the news.

The same year, with my self-image at stake, I made another angry call to a newspaper.

In the spring of 1999, Gore made a call to Russian prime minister Yevgeny Primakov during the Kosovo war. It was a tense call between two rivals on opposite sides of a conflict. NATO forces were bombing targets in Belgrade and Serbian forces in the field. Russia was hotly opposed to the bombing. The purpose for the call was classified, but I still had to brief the press. So, I called reporters in the afternoon and related some unclassified points that were made in the conversation. Then at midnight, a *Washington Post* reporter called me back and said, "Why did you tell *The New York Times* things you didn't tell me?"

He read to me from the *New York Times* story with the headline US ASKS RUSSIA TO PLAY A MEDIATING ROLE IN THE KOSOVO CRISIS. I was alarmed. That wasn't true. That wasn't the point of the call, and that wasn't the headline we wanted. I called *The New York Times*, found an editor working the late shift, and told him: "That's not what I told your reporter. It's not what the call was about. You need to change the article."

The editor got off the phone, called the reporter, and then called me back. "She says you're not the only person she talked to, and she's not changing it." I got scared. This was a sensitive communication between adversaries at a time of war. My job was to brief the press. If my briefings led to a wrong story that complicated efforts to achieve our aims, then I would be responsible.

When the editor told me, "We're not changing it," I pushed back a few times, and when he wouldn't budge, I said, "This is my *job*!" with a tone of panic in my voice. The editor laughed out loud. I got off the phone, left a voicemail for the White House senior director for Russia, and went to bed worried.

In the end, the story caused no harm, and a few weeks later, we did ask Russia to mediate, which helped lead to the end of the war. All that was good news, but in the narrow world of my self-image, the even better news was that I wasn't the idiot who delayed the end of the war by doing a bad job briefing the press.

Here is what is striking to me, decades later, about these two stories: They both end with scenes of my calling a newspaper, whipped up with anxiety, and whining, "You're not writing the story I want!" And they both found their way into a book about the futility of chasing peace by trying to force the world to write the story I want.

WHEN THE STORY SAYS WHAT YOU WANT IT TO SAY

Despite the stress, I never really considered leaving the White House before the end of the administration. The lows were tough, but the highs were addictive.

In 1998, I flew with Vice President Gore to Charlotte, North Carolina, for a meeting of the Transatlantic Business Dialogue—a gathering of US and European leaders. On the way down, the VP was looking over his remarks and asked me to get feedback from Larry Summers, who was on the plane. Summers would soon be named secretary of the treasury and shortly after become president of Harvard. I walked the draft back to him, he made some edits, and I carried the speech back to Gore, who accepted the changes. A few hours later, in the middle of Gore's speech, a colleague walked up to me and whispered, "Larry Summers loved one of your lines; he was *beaming.*" I said, "What line was that?" He said the United States couldn't be "the importer of only resort." I laughed and said, "That wasn't my line; that was *his* line."

I don't think it matters how lofty you are—hearing your own words spoken in public can get you high.

The biggest high for me came on a four-stop, weeklong trip to Europe with President Clinton in the summer of 2000. I was writing remarks for the last two stops: President Clinton's Kremlin press conference with President Vladimir Putin and an open-air speech to tens of thousands of people at Saint Michael's Square in Kyiv.

I spent the early stops hiding out in my hotel room working on the Ukraine speech. It had consumed me for the last two months. I had a binder of several hundred pages of material for a ten-minute talk. By the time we arrived in Moscow, the draft was being passed around, and we were down to the last edits. I was pleading with Sandy Berger to let me include a line in Ukrainian. He was open to it, but I had to make the case. It was a bit risky—What if people didn't get it? What if it didn't mean what we thought it meant? What if the president pronounced it wrong and it confused people?

These were good questions, and I gave the best answers I could. I was working with the interpreter, asking her to help me find a famous line from the national poet Taras Shevchenko that matched our message. The point of Clinton's speech was to honor all that Ukraine had done and endured; to note that communism had lost but freedom had not yet won; and to promise the Ukrainians that in their fight for democracy, America would be on their side.

I didn't want a slow, dull, predictable approach: "As your national poet Taras Shevchenko has written . . ." I wanted a short, striking line that everyone would know.

We were down to the last day, and opinions were mixed. As a number of us camped out in a room at the Kremlin during the Clinton-Putin meetings, the deputy national security advisor read the draft and said dismissively, "I don't get it—we're saying Clinton is a closet Ukrainian speaker?"

During a break in the meetings, I made my final appeal to Sandy. I told him the interpreter said it would work. She would coach the president on pronunciation, and I was confident it would make people remember the speech. He said, "Okay, let's do it."

When President Clinton took the stage in Saint Michael's Square, he said:

> I am honored to have laid a wreath of flowers at the memorial to the millions who perished in the forced famine of the 1930s. Ukraine has endured oppressors who carved up your lands, banned your books, starved your children, purged your writers, enslaved your workers, plundered your art, stole your soil, and forbade you even to talk about the tragedy of the famine.

Today, the oppressors are gone. Stalin is gone. The Nazis are gone. The Soviet Union is gone. . . . But you, the people of Ukraine, you are still here, stronger than ever . . . reclaiming your land, uniting your people, restoring your culture, and raising your children in freedom.

Then the president listed the challenges and exhorted the crowd, "Do not give up. Keep on fighting. *Boritesya poborete.*" And the crowd roared at that famous line, which means, "If you fight, you will win."

The lead of the Associated Press story read, "To the surprise and delight of many Ukrainians, President Clinton addressed them repeatedly Monday in their own language, borrowing the words of beloved national poet Taras Shevchenko."

"He chose the key words to say," a woman told Ukraine's One Plus One TV. "He told us to fight . . . and I heard there is freedom waiting ahead."

This response was the biggest high I could hope for—and it lingered for days, and when it began to dim, I got an email from a National Security Council director who was a top White House advisor on Ukraine. He wrote:

> Tom, I got two phone calls at home last night from senior members of the Ukrainian-American community who were beside themselves with glee over the President's speech in Kyiv. One told me that people were pulling it off the internet and were calling around to friends, reading passages to each other over the phone. Support from the Ukrainian-American community is important for our policy in Ukraine, and you made a tremendous contribution. Congratulations, and thanks.

That is why I wanted this job—for the chance to make an impact. And I would love to claim all kinds of noble motives, but I have to acknowledge the supreme motivating power of the feeling I have when the world tells me I'm the person I want to be.

In fact, the only times in the White House when I was happy and lighthearted and free of the drive to prove myself came right at the close of a successful event. I would be swimming in peace and satisfaction, my self-image fulfilled for a moment. Then the drive to prove myself would rise again. Success didn't calm me down. It set me up. The highs created a new level of expectation that I had to meet or get depressed. That's how it was—if a speech didn't make me high, it brought me low. My outsized reactions weren't something I outgrew. On the contrary, I kept winding myself tighter, all the way to the end.

SIX STATES OF BREAKDOWN

When we're in the process of breakdown, there are actually three related things that are breaking down: (1) Our self-image is breaking down—as the evidence mounts that we're not everything we say we are; (2) our body is breaking down—from the strain of defending and promoting the self-image; and (3) the self-image strategy for happiness is breaking down—the strategy that says the best way to be happy is to try to become who we want to be in the world.

This strategy for happiness is iconic. It is so embedded in our culture and our unconscious that we never critique or question it. It's celebrated and promoted by marketers who sell us on a self-image so they can then sell us what we need to *achieve* the self-image. But this strategy is a dead end—it can never lead to lasting happiness.

That's why the breakdown is good news—because the pain makes us pay attention to what's going on. Breaking down happens to all of us. Whether we're losing the battle to fulfill our self-image or exhausting ourselves in trying to win it, we all break down. But we don't always break through. This book is about flipping breakdowns into breakthroughs by surrendering the self-image that once was moving us forward, but now is holding us back.

As I've looked back at my own life and read about the lives of others, I've identified six states of breakdown of the self-image. Each state of breakdown is a distinctive experience that I've wrestled with and suffered through. They do not always form a progression. They can come in any order at any time, and we can be in more than one at once. The six states are anxiety, depression, addiction, illness, crisis, and grace. Each is a slightly different form of the conflict between self-image and shadow—except for grace, which flows in during a pause in the battle between ego and shadow or comes at the very end, when the ego and shadow dissolve into each other.

Anxiety is often the first sign of breakdown. It erupts when the shadow threatens and we quicken our efforts to defend the self-image. Our first response is to try harder to make the mask work. We haven't usually suffered any lasting scars or injuries at this point, but we're called into anxious service to make sure the self-image doesn't slip.

Depression slithers in when the shadow overturns our self-image and we feel defeated. We are either not who we thought we were or not who we wanted to be. It can be a dangerous time because we've lost the soothing power of the self-image, and so we will seek a consoling remedy elsewhere, sometimes in the self-image that we're a victim and that someone else is to blame. Or we could seek solace in . . .

Addiction, which becomes an especially inviting option when we're anxious or depressed. The heavy pressure on the self-image can lure us into substance abuse to give us energy and restore our confidence so we can believe that we "really are" who we're pretending to be. Or we can fall into addiction to soothe ourselves because we feel wounded and defeated.

Illness can come with any of these states, either because I'm fighting so hard to be my self-image that I exhaust myself and get sick, or I get sick from other causes, which threatens my self-image because I can't do what I used to do. Being sick makes me feel weak, which is an assault on my self-image and a hindrance to being who I want to be.

Crisis occurs when the pain of holding on to the self-image in the face of reality is so great that I'm forced to either surrender my self-image or lie more aggressively. One type of crisis comes when I know the change I have to make (go to Alcoholics Anonymous, for instance, or perhaps come out of whatever closet I'm in). Another type of crisis comes when I know I have to change, but I don't know *what* to change or how to change it. This is the state that sometimes gives rise to . . .

Grace. This is where events unfold beyond all planning. We do things that are out of character and outside our repertoire and think, "Where did *that* come from?!" This may be the beginning of the end of the self-image driving our lives—or it may just be a moment of grace that leaves us as suddenly as it comes—often during a moment on the edge when we face injury, illness, or death. When grace enters, whether through an eclipse or collapse of the self-image, we're acting outside our story and are moved by unselfish motives. This is a sign—or at least a hint—that we're taking a step into the second half of life, which is what I mean when I say "breakthrough."

The passage from the first to the second half of life is a core theme in literature. It's the focus of Richard Rohr's book *Falling Upward*. It's a central teaching in mythology; it's an essential concept in spirituality; and it's a foundational element in Jungian psychology. Jungian therapist June Singer writes:

> While the first part [of life] is directed toward achievement, the second part is directed toward integration. Where the first part is directed toward emergence as an individual, earning a living, rearing a family, establishing a home, the second part is directed toward achieving harmony with the totality of being. In the beginning, the ego arises out of the depths of the unconscious. In the end, the ego surrenders to those depths.

The purpose of this book is to use the concepts of self-image and shadow and the six states of breakdown to offer a precise description of the passage from the first half to the second half of life, so we can see what's happening when we're breaking down and flip the breakdown into a breakthrough.

What I'm calling "breakthrough" is the birth of the spiritual life, a movement away from the material life, the shift from defending the self-image to dissolving it. When I'm no longer trying to be anything, I'm not trying to deny anything either, which allows the self-image and shadow to merge and vanish. Jungian expert Robert A. Johnson says that the only word in the English language adequate for describing the synthesis of self-image and shadow is *love*.

When I look back at the White House through this lens, I see that it was the opportunity of a lifetime for me. Yes, I was privileged to work at a high level for causes I believed in. But the infinite benefit came from the intensity of the place. The high-stakes scrutiny of my work by the president, the vice president, the press, and the public put my self-image to a rigorous test every day, and the energy I spent to defend that self-image and the self-image of the people I worked for tipped me into breakdown and set me on a path to breakthrough.

CHAPTER THREE

Anxiety

On February 14, 2002, in the middle of Valentine's Day dinner at home with my wife after the boys were in bed, the phone rang. It was a call from a new West Coast client. I had just joined two close friends, White House speechwriters Jeff Shesol and Paul Orzulak, in starting a writing and strategy firm called West Wing Writers, and I was super eager to impress this guy.

"Hey, hope I'm not interrupting anything," he said.

"Not at all," I lied.

"My boss is leaving tomorrow morning on a trip, and she'd like to see a draft before she goes. Any chance you could send it tomorrow by the start of business?"

That was a big switch and a harsh request.

"No problem," I said.

I talked for another thirty seconds, hung up, and started hating myself. I had about eight hours of writing to do to finish the draft.

But instead of working from nine to five the next day, I had just agreed to work from nine to five that night.

Why did I say yes? I was anxious. And I was anxious because my self-image was at stake. I was just getting to know this client, so I was pitching myself as an iron man. "I can do *anything*. No one can outwork me." And whenever I put forward that image of myself, people in my world will take me up on it.

I ended our dinner early, sat down at my computer, and began writing.

That's how it was in the early days of our firm. Jeff, Paul, and I were determined to get the business launched with only cell phones and laptops—using no office, taking out no loans, giving away no equity, and suffering no loss of income.

We were *swamped*, and we were burned out when we started. When I left the White House, my dream was to work alone in a small room on easy assignments with soft deadlines and no one talking to me. They would just write notes, slip them under my door, and hurry away.

That's not how it played out. There was never an easy assignment, and the work was in some ways as high stakes as it had been at the White House—every speech had to be great because our clients could drop us at any time. This was not a season for drawing boundaries.

I didn't even have the *vocabulary* for boundaries. As a technical matter, it would not have been hard to train myself to recite the words "I would *love* to help you out, but I have other commitments, so we're going to have to stick to the original agreement." But I could not have said that any more than I could have said, "I'm a spoiled, pampered wimp, and I won't do what you want."

If I got a non-emergency "stay up all night" request today, I would laugh and answer with an affectionate "no." But back then, it was completely outside my power to say no because it was core to my self-image to say yes. The harder the request, the more I wanted to say yes so I could prove that I was tough.

THE SHADOW

Anxiety is proof of a self-image under threat. And when my self-image is threatened, it is always threatened by my shadow—which is just another name for shame.

The concept of the shadow is central to the work of Carl Jung, whose analytical psychology has been influential in fields from anthropology to literature to religious studies. The shadow—as June Singer writes in her book *Boundaries of the Soul*—"consists of all those uncivilized desires and emotions that are incompatible with social standards and with the persona: it is all that we are ashamed of."

The self-image (or "persona," in Jungian language) is all the things we insist we are, and the shadow is all the things we insist we're not. The shadow poses an ever-present threat that a hidden truth about ourselves will emerge and unsettle the self-image in a way that will humiliate us.

The concept of shadow is so instinctive that a toddler can navigate it, and so deep that the most profound spiritual teachers wrestle with it. Jung says that it's easier to grasp the concept of shadow than other psychological concepts. "With the shadow," he writes, "we have the advantage of being prepared in some sort by our education, which has always endeavored to convince people that they are not one-hundred-per-cent pure gold. So everyone immediately under-stands what is meant by 'shadow,' [it's the] 'inferior personality.'"

When we start to understand the shadow, we know enough to feel the danger and start *denying* the shadow. Even as little kids, we have a deep instinct for physical and emotional safety, and we start doing threat assessments. I remember reading a fairy tale to my son Ben when he was four, and at the end of the tale, he asked, "Are wolves nice, or are they mean?"

"Well, wolves can be mean."

"Do wolves stay where they live?"

"Yes, wolves mostly stay where they live."

"Where do they live?"

But even a few years before assessing the threat of wolves, Ben understood the threat of the shadow and how to disown the person he didn't want to be. In the middle of a difficult stretch of toilet training, he waddled into the room and said, "Mama, somebody pooped in Benjamin's diaper."

I don't think it's possible to overstate the psychological need we have to push out the shadow so we can be who our self-image tells us we are. Our self-image creates a world where we feel significant and safe, even superior, and we *need* that world, or we would not have created it and cultivated it.

Stripping away someone's self-image can expose them to shame, and that can get them killed. As an example, let's go a little more deeply into the story of Socrates and recall how he got his reputation for wisdom and how that led to his death.

Socrates explained at his trial that his friend Chaerephon went to Delphi and asked the Oracle if anyone were wiser than Socrates. The prophetess at the temple answered that no one was wiser.

This statement bewildered Socrates because, as he told his accusers, "I know that I have no wisdom, small or great." So, Socrates set about questioning the wise men of Athens to find someone who was wiser so that he could refute the Oracle. But he kept finding that the people presumed to be wise were not truly wise. He described one of his encounters with a "wise man" by saying: "I tried to explain to him that he *thought* himself wise, but was not really wise; and the consequence was that he hated me, and his enmity was shared by several who were present and heard me. . . . This inquisition has led to my having many enemies of the worst and most dangerous kind."

As the "wise men" of Athens saw their cherished self-image shredded, they thought: "We have to get rid of this guy." And that is the blueprint that can explain pretty much every dissident killed or jailed by every dictator in history.

Of course, I would like to identify with Socrates, but I would be more honest if I identified with his killers. As I think back on the times I felt angry with people, it's obvious that I was angry because they interfered with my self-image and my story of myself. People don't even have to know me to inspire my anger. They just have to interfere with my story, which is my sacred plan for who I want to be and how I want the world to behave.

We invent our self-image and our stories as a form of refuge from the pain of life. They are carefully constructed to be soothing. When we reach for "alternative facts," we're looking for the facts that support a soothing story of ourselves. That's why "rational" debate does so little to change our minds. Because we cannot be persuaded to drop our story if it returns us to the pain we adopted the story to escape.

At the core of every such story is "I'm a good person. I belong. I deserved to be loved. I'm special. And I'm right." This is the alpha and the omega—the story that the other stories emerge from and converge with. And the shadow is every message that undercuts this story: "You're disgusting. You're beneath us. You're ruining us. Get out of here." When my story isn't fulfilled and the world is not honoring me and my alternative facts cannot soothe me, then my next alternative set of facts becomes a story about the villainy of the people I blame for my pain.

When we have our culture-war debates on immigration, abortion, guns, or climate (I'm not referring to policy debates, which are different), we're basically just using policy terms to mask our real messages:

"I'm a good person; you're a bad person."

"No, I'm a good person; *you're* a *disgusting* person."

"No, you're a despicable and evil person."

"*You're not even* a person; we'd all be better off if you didn't exist."

We're a bunch of people shouting at one another, "Get out of here. You're ruining our country. You don't belong!"

Henri Nouwen, the revered theologian, published a book titled *The Inner Voice of Love,* which he said was "my secret journal . . . written during the most difficult period of my life." In it, he wrote to himself, "Not being welcome is your greatest fear."

That's it. And our shadow is where we hide everything that makes us feel unwelcome.

The self-image and shadow have such an overpowering pull on us that they're often the best tools people have for manipulating us—advertisers go mad with their efforts to shape our self-image and sell us ways to achieve it—clothes, cars, trucks, hair, makeup, jewelry, diet, nutrition, exercise. Be the *real* you. The *best* you. The *new* you. The luxury lifestyle? I *deserve* it!

Manipulating others with the self-image also works much closer to home. As parents, we use the self-image all the time to control our kids—just as our parents did to us. In fact, we pass our shadow down to our kids, generation after generation, because we're terrified that our kids will express and expose our shadow, so we make sure our shadow is their shadow too.

My mom had a tactic she would roll out whenever I got in trouble and started embarrassing her in the neighborhood. She would sigh deeply and say in a slow, sad, world-weary way: *"Just* when I *thought* you were *beginning* to *show* some *signs . . ."*

This tactic was effective until I was fifteen, when the electrifying pleasures of adolescence became more compelling than my mom's approval—and then I had to play hide-and-sneak so I could keep Mom's approval and still do what I wanted.

The desire to get along with our parents, our teachers, and our friends *requires* us to hide our shadow. My son Nick showed me his grasp of this when he was fourteen and said, "Dad, if I said everything I thought, I'd be living on the street."

It's risky to express our shadow, but it can be liberating to hear someone else express it. One Sunday at Mass, when Ben was about four, he said aloud during the Offertory, "They say the same thing every week; it's so *annoying!*" Everyone but his parents laughed. We held our laughter until we got to the car.

When Nick was five years old, I took him trick-or-treating, and I was embarrassed that he didn't say anything when the people offered him candy—not "Trick or treat" or "Happy Halloween" or even "Thank you." So I told him between houses, "Nick, next time, just say something nice, like 'Those are spooky decorations' or 'That's my favorite candy.'" At the next house, the door swung open, a large woman leaned forward with a tray of candy, and Nick said, "You have really big pumpkins!"

Okay, Nick, never mind.

We also have a collective shadow, of course, which includes things we all secretly agree to keep quiet about so we don't embarrass a powerful person. I had an experience of the collective shadow during Nick's graduation from sixth grade. We were sitting in folding chairs on hot asphalt, in ninety-five-degree heat, hearing four kids give stilted, poorly recited speeches. I was irritated—and not because there were four kids giving stilted, poorly recited speeches, but that my kid was not giving one of them.

"How did they pick the speakers?" I asked my wife.

"They had every kid write a speech, and the teachers chose four."

"What did Nick write about?"

"He wrote about how the old principal was so much better than the new principal."

I'm betting the selection committee enjoyed Nick's speech before rejecting it.

For most of my adult life, I never actually saw my self-image. I didn't recognize the shadow as a *threat* to my self-image, and I didn't see my anxiety as a response to the shadow. I was embedded in perfectionism without seeing the *cause* of the perfectionism or what it was I was trying to perfect. And, consequently, I didn't see that my perpetual state of anxiety was something I was contributing to. I saw my behavior as a sensible response to the world out there. My breakthrough emerged only when I began to see that I was operating inside the instinctive, semiconscious set of behaviors that I have named the self-image model of happiness—which I now want to explain further.

THE SELF-IMAGE MODEL—TWO CONCEPTS

The self-image model of happiness, as I began to describe it earlier, is an approach to happiness that consists of three actions: (1) cultivating a self-image or story that gives us feelings of love and belonging and meaning and purpose, (2) getting the important people in our lives to tell that story about us, and (3) trying to embody that story more fully. When we're able to manage these three tasks, we're happy. When we're struggling to manage them, we're anxious. When we fail to manage them, we fall into depression or addiction or illness.

In this chapter, I want to describe two features of the self-image model that help explain the link between the self-image and anxiety and the other states of breakdown. The first feature is what I will call false triumph.

"False triumph" occurs when my self-image aligns strikingly with the world. Suddenly, by some combination of work and luck, I am who I've been longing to be—and the evidence is everywhere. I close the big deal at work. I get the job I wanted. I'm marrying the love of my life. I'm on top of the world.

Happiness, as we tend to talk about it, is made up of moments such as these. So why call it false? It's false because it's not final. It's dependent on external events in a changing world. Everything in the self-image model that passes for happiness is a buzz held in place by a fleeting truce between self-image and shadow. The point is not to put this buzz down but to put it in its place. It's not peace. It's *chasing* peace.

It's also a false triumph because it's deceiving. When the world suddenly supports my story, I think I've figured it all out; I have mastered life. I feel smug, and I start giving everyone advice. I have fallen for this again and again and again. Every time I've found a new book, a new practice, a new diet that works for me for a while, I never wait to see how long it lasts, I tell everyone immediately, "You've got to try this; it's the best thing ever!"

My son Ben won his mom's everlasting gratitude one day when I approached him and said: "Ben! Let me teach you a new meditation; it's the best technique I've learned in forty years!" Knowing my pattern, he said, "If you still think that in five years, come back and see me."

The second feature central to the self-image model is equilibrium. Here, too, life and circumstances support the self-image, which gives us a feeling of happiness. But this happy feeling is different from that of the false triumph—which tends to be more striking and more fleeting. Equilibrium is a steady state where the self-image is supported and not easily threatened. I can keep the self-image intact without much effort or strain. Equilibrium, like the false triumph, can give me a sense that I've mastered things and am in control. This is what we generally think of as happiness. It's possible to create a life that is happy in this sense—and the feeling of happiness is real, but it's still grounded in the self-image, and it's still at the mercy of circumstance.

This equilibrium feature of the self-image model of happiness helps explain one of the happiest times in my life. I was in eighth grade, living in prerevolution Iran with my family, attending a school called Iranzamin, which enrolled students from more than sixty countries. I was in my third year in Tehran and felt very much at home. When I look back at those times—through the lens of the self-image—I'm struck at the alignment between the way I wanted to see myself, the way I was seen by my friends and family, and how little effort it took to sustain my self-image.

My Farsi was strong, which won me some good regard from my Iranian friends. I had been elected president of my class, which was kind of cool for an American, because the school was 60 percent Iranian. I won the fifty-meter butterfly for my age group at the international-school swim meet. I won the school's chess championship, which was a big deal because I was only in eighth grade and the school was K–12, and also because it was the year after Bobby Fischer defeated Boris Spassky in Reykjavík for the World Chess Championship, and my school was chess mad.

Things were going well. Perhaps the most amusing bit of good karma came toward the end of the year. There was an American military presence in Iran at the time, and the American community established a cotillion, a traditional program originating in the US South designed to teach social graces and ballroom dancing to young kids. In May, there was an end-of-year dance held in the Intercontinental Hotel. There were contests for each dance style, and I won the modern-dance competition with a young woman named Tori. After we won, we were given a minute on the floor to dance together as a couple, and I noticed in the middle of the dance that a few athletic-looking guys had entered the room and were leaning against the wall watching us.

After our dance was done, my friend Keivan came up to me and said, "*Santos is in the hotel!*" Santos was the best and most famous soccer club in the world at that time, largely because of its global star Pelé, who had been the lead player on the Brazilian team that won the World Cup in 1958, 1962, and 1970. Santos had just arrived in Tehran in the latest stop on their Asian tour.

Keivan and I spent some time talking to the players who'd come in the hall. When we asked for autographs, one of the players made out an autograph to me, writing, "To the best dancing." When his teammate signed, he saw it and scolded the first player for his poor English, then wrote, "To the best dancer." After these two soccer gods agreed on the right language to describe my prize-winning dancing, we asked, "Where is Pelé?" And they took us to a hidden dining area with a lone table where Pelé was eating a meal with one other guy, and we interrupted his dinner to ask for an autograph, which he graciously gave us.

That's how life was for me in the spring of 1973. It matched the feeling of the Santana song, popular at that time, "Everything's Coming Our Way." That was the most complete and effortless happiness of my life. In fact, in Iran, where they had a popular national lottery, they used to call the lottery winners "Champions of Luck." During that time in my life, I was a champion of luck.

Then my luck ran out.

A few months after meeting Pelé, I met Max Armor. Max was the aging, bulging, balding gym teacher and freshman football coach at Lyons Township High School in La Grange, Illinois. I was late to gym class on the first day of school because I got lost in the huge building that housed half the 5,200 students who went there to school.

"Where's your form?!" Coach Armor bellowed, picking on me, the ninety-two-pound boy who came in late.

"Um, what form?"

"The one they gave you at orientation!"

"I missed orientation."

A crowd of boys gathered around us—laughing at Coach Armor's comments, hoping to make the freshman football team.

"Why?!"

"I was out of the country."

(Big mistake!)

"Out of the country? Where *were* you? JAPAN?!"

"Switzerland."

"SWITZERLAND?!—what were you doing there—learning to *yodel*? You'll be yodeling before *I'm* done with you!"

That was my orientation.

LT was a fantastic school—great resources, teachers, tradition. But it was a self-image challenge for me. Most everything that I was good at and got credit for a few months before was mocked or ignored in my new community. And then there was the torture of gym class. I was small for my age and young for my grade, and after every gym session, I had to strip naked and go stand under the showers. It was an embarrassing scene repeated several times a week: two hundred bigger, older boys and one hairless tot.

When I look back on it now, I can't help but laugh. But at the time, the self-image reversal pushed me into anxiety and put me on a path to addiction.

FLIPPING BREAKDOWN INTO BREAKTHROUGH

This self-image model of happiness explains both the happiest and the hardest times of my life. For me, these periods fall into three broad categories: (1) the times when I was inhabiting my self-image easily and being acknowledged for it, (2) the times when I was straining to prove that I was who I wanted to be, and (3) the times when I couldn't hold the story together and felt defeated.

This last category, when the story can't hold, paradoxically includes the most blessed moments—moments that teach us that the self-image model is futile because it's built on a plan to force the world into the story we want—and that plan *must* fail. But we must *see* it fail and see *why* it fails before we can move on to something that *can't* fail.

Unfortunately, to actually see the self-image model fail *as it's failing* is difficult to do because that experience always comes with suffering, and the suffering is confusing. It doesn't just feel *bad*; it feels *wrong*, and if it feels wrong, we believe we can't be on the path to anything good.

This is the paradox of spiritual growth—and also the danger. We have to suffer before we can wake up and solve the problem of suffering. Yet when we're suffering, we might conclude that we're on the wrong path when we're not. *The path goes through suffering.* But it's hard to see that—especially early in the journey.

So we end up going back and holding on to the self-image instead of moving forward and letting it go. Of course, we can't let go of the self-image until we see that we're holding on to it. And it's hard to see we're holding on to the self-image, because we can't ever see it directly—we can only detect it. We know it's there, because of the emotional reactions we feel when it meets the world in different ways.

When I've watched my reactions enough to become aware of my self-image, I see that I play a lead role in my own suffering. I can no longer blame my pain on people being jerks—or life cheating me— or someone not supporting me. I see that my suffering comes from the tension between my self-image and my reality, and I am the author of my self-image. There is no more empowering truth for anyone seeking peace. If my suffering were caused by the world, I would be helpless to stop it. But if it's caused by my own thoughts and mental creations, then I have the power to end it.

I'm more likely to become aware that I'm seeing the world through my self-image when I have a clearer picture of what my self-image is, a familiarity with the kinds of events that threaten my self-image, and an understanding of the defensive actions I take in response. As soon as we notice that the world we see is a function of what we're seeing *through*, we can start exploring the thing that we're seeing through. That is the search for the self-image and shadow.

This search isn't easy. "No one can become conscious of the shadow without considerable moral effort," Jung says. And the search for the self-image and the shadow is not a slight shift in the pursuit of peace and happiness; it's a complete change of direction. If we take Father Thomas Keating's definition of repentance—which is "to change the direction in which we're looking for happiness"—the change of direction from fulfilling the self-image to letting go of the self-image is a form of repentance.

IN SEARCH OF THE SELF-IMAGE AND SHADOW

The effort to become conscious of the shadow is inseparable from the effort to become conscious of the self-image. They're in a continuous dance, each reacting and responding to the other. We can't see either directly. We detect them only by watching our emotional responses. And some of the best approaches to discerning the two come from searching through moments of joy and pain. We can see outlines of the shadow in moments when we feel threatened. And we can see outlines of the self-image in moments when we feel happy—because the light is shining on the parts of us we want the world to see.

Here are some questions that can help us learn about the composition of our self-image and shadow.

THE INDIRECT QUESTIONS

- What are you most proud of? What kind of flattery are you most susceptible to—and from whom? Have you ever received a compliment that was so satisfying it made you laugh out loud? Have you ever received a compliment that made you weep? It seems to me that if someone delivers a compliment that makes me do either, they've exactly identified a cherished aspect of my self-image. If you look to others to see what flattery makes them laugh, you can learn a lot. But be kind. It's a little bit like spying on someone's inner life.

- What hurts you most? Can you recall a criticism you've heard that stuck with you for a long time because it hurt so much? Can you recall a fight you had that you keep having in your head, thinking of the things you should have said? Can you boil it down to one thing the other person said that hurt the most? What is it? And what image of yourself did it dethrone?

- Who is your audience? A self-image is always adopted with an audience in mind—the people you need, the people you want to impress. If something happens to *affirm* your self-image, who is the first person you want to tell? If something happens to *undercut* your self-image, who is the first person you want to tell—if anyone? (If it's the same person, you're lucky. You have a great friend.)

- Who are you trying to *recruit* to your audience—people you want to reach with any news of you achieving your self-image? What does this say about how you want to see yourself and how you want to be seen?

- Can you think of a time when you freely admitted something embarrassing and another time when you denied the same thing? What accounts for the difference?

- What was the most embarrassing moment in your life—or at least one of them? What made it embarrassing? What is the embarrassing moment you have worked hardest to prevent? Why is it so important to prevent? Can you think of people who wouldn't be embarrassed by what would embarrass you? What do you think accounts for the difference?

- Think of a time when you had a big reaction to a mild setback. Run through the scene. Visit all the thoughts that surround it, and ask yourself: Which thoughts hurt most? What does that tell you? (Richard Rohr writes, "When you have a strong emotional experience out of proportion to the moment, your shadow self has just been exposed.")

- What is it that is true about you, that other people often freely admit about themselves, but you would never be willing to admit about yourself?

- What do you measure to track your progress? What are the performance marks that make you feel proud if all is going well and make you feel guilty if things are going poorly? They could relate to your diet, fitness regimen, meditation practice, health measures, or "getting things done." How obsessively do you measure these things? Can you put into words the thoughts you have when you're doing well by these measures? Can you articulate the thoughts you have when you're *not* doing well? What would happen if you stopped measuring these things for a week or a month? What's the image of yourself that would be threatened if you stopped?

- Can you think of a moment when you said to yourself, "I am never going to let that happen *again!*" What was the event? What did you hate about it?

- Can you think of a moment when you said, "I *hate* myself?" Step back into that scene. What was happening? Explore all the thoughts that led to that feeling. What thought hurt most? What did it hurt?

THE DIRECT QUESTIONS

- What would you say are the most precious elements of your self-image?

- What are the most glorious chapters that are still to come in your story?

- What would be the most triumphant end of your story— and the most disastrous?

- Who are the people who make you want to hold on to your mask? Why?

- Who are the people who make you feel you can drop your mask? Why?

- Who bugs you the most? Which of their qualities really gets under your skin? (If they get under your skin, they get under your mask.)

Exploring the joys and pains of the past are good ways to train ourselves to see the self-image and shadow. It helps us understand our emotions, not by asking "Who did what?" but by asking "How did events affirm or undercut my story—and how did I respond?" This can help us start to see the self-image model.

WHAT ARE YOU TRYING TO DEFEND?

In 2018, when my health was near its worst, I contacted a therapist and asked her if I could join her therapy group. There was no room at the time, but a year and a half later, after I had started my new practices and felt I was on a path to health, the therapist sent me an email saying a space had opened up. I thought about it for a while and then decided to join. I had never been in group therapy, and I wanted to find out what it was like.

I was nervous on the day of my first session. I arrived a bit early and chose the middle seat on one of the couches, figuring that the senior members would prefer the seats on the end, next to the arm rests. I didn't want to sit in the favorite seat of the dominant member—whoever that turned out to be. Two men who were longtime members of the group had also arrived early and began asking me questions in a polite and curious way. I started by giving short answers, wondering to myself "Is this part of the session? Have we begun?"

As they kept asking questions, my answers got longer. Soon we were clearly into session time, but the therapist, who was present along with three women members of the group, had not started the meeting. I was wondering, "Is this how they deal with a new member—they spend the first session questioning him?" Then, six or seven minutes into the session, another woman entered, saying, "Sorry for being late," and took a seat on the end of the couch nearest the therapist. I was now launching into the story of my life, and the new arrival took turns looking at me and looking away. After a few more minutes, she pivoted toward me, leaned forward, and said with irritation, "Here's some feedback: *Get to the point!*"

I was hit with a stun gun. My brain froze. Seconds later, as my surprise began to pass, my sole instinct was to keep my footing—and keep from being shamed. I sat for a few moments saying nothing, and then asked, "What do you want to know?"

"Why are you in therapy?"

"To be challenged."

"What does *that* mean?"

"I want to be challenged the way you're challenging me now—you don't get directly challenged that much in normal life."

"Use I; don't use You, she instructed me, citing a point she frequently pressed in group, whose effect on me can be seen in the pages of this book.

"*I* don't get directly challenged that much in normal life," I revised.

She and I went back and forth for a few more minutes and then some group members challenged her for the emotional charge in her questions, which she acknowledged.

She was a formidable group member, who combined the instinct for the right question with the guts it took to ask it. I made it through the first session, but I felt I had been shamed—that I got pushed around and should have done a better job standing up for myself. I carried that scene in my head for months, telling myself, "I should have said *this*," "I should have said *that*."

One day, maybe four months later, on the morning before a session, I was hit with a wave of anxiety, imagining an attack coming from her—and I began thinking up one-liners I could use to make sure that this time I would win the exchange. After a few lines came to me, I thought, "These are good. I should write them down and memorize them so I'll be ready."

As I started to write, a thought stopped me. "You're being so *defensive*. What are you trying to defend?" And slowly the answer emerged—I'm trying to defend my idea of myself as a smart, confident, quick-witted person who can't be pushed around. And then the thought came, "But you're just defending your ego—how can you dissolve your ego if you're defending your ego?"

And it occurred to me that in so many tense moments of life, I'm torn between two motives—defend the ego or dissolve the ego, try to be separate and superior or try to be one with everybody.

I saw which motive was driving me, and I let it go. I didn't prepare any talking points, and I went to group, had a good session, and came away with two thoughts. First, if I had prepared and memorized my talking points, I would have entered the room in a combative mood and would have been more likely to have had a fight.

Second, I saw something deeper about what I was trying to defend. My biggest fear was *not* that she would sting me with a question and I wouldn't have an answer and I would feel defeated and shamed. My biggest fear was that she would sting me with a question and I would feel defeated and shamed *and* I would blow up and attack her and *try to shame her*—and shatter my self-image as a calm, wise, kind, spiritual person. It turns out I wasn't afraid of *her;* I was afraid of *me.* I was afraid of my own shadow.

It won't surprise anyone who's spent time in group therapy that I came to see her as my teacher, because she pushed me in ways that gave me lasting insight into my shadow side—into my fear that I would blow up in a way that would prompt people to say, "Yeah, we always kind of knew he was a fraud."

THE WORLD'S BIGGEST SECRET

On that Valentine's Day years ago when I ended my dinner so I could write all night and impress a client in the morning, I could not have explained the process that controlled me. To me, the action was all external. I didn't see that I was defending a self-image, that I was afraid of my shadow, and that I was the creator of both.

The self-image and shadow flourish in darkness. They depend on secrecy. But it's not just secrecy about the things that could unsettle our self-image; it's secrecy about the process itself. We need to keep it a secret from ourselves that we only *appear* to be driven by external motives and principles, but we're *actually* driven by the need to protect the self-image and deny the shadow. We can't see or talk about this process, or it will be exposed and disempowered.

In 2022, I saw a news item that startled me because it blurted out the secret. A High Court judge in London ruled that the contents of the will of Prince Philip, the husband of Queen Elizabeth II, would remain secret for at least ninety years (in contrast to the wills of nonroyals, which are open to public inspection). The judge wrote: "The degree of publicity that publication would be likely to attract would be very extensive and wholly contrary to the aim of maintaining the dignity of the Sovereign." He then added, "There is a need to enhance the protection afforded to truly private aspects of the lives of this limited group of individuals in order to maintain the dignity of the Sovereign and close members of Her family."

Washington Post reporter Karla Adam then added, "While it is not unusual for a senior royal to seek this kind of privacy, this was the first time that a judge had published the reasons for allowing the exception."

This was stunning to me because while the judge dutifully kept the *first* secret, ensuring that we not really know what was going on with Prince Philip, the judge failed to keep the *second* secret—which requires that he be silent about the purpose for the first secret. Instead, he essentially conceded that the dignity of the Royal Family depends on our not knowing what's really going on.

To perpetuate the tradition that some people are intrinsically more entitled to dignity than are others, we have to hide a lot of stuff. Because the truth is we all have the same basic patterns and rhythms, similar vices and virtues, a desire to be loved and not to be judged, so we know what would happen if we read the royal wills. We'd take exquisite delight in the mischief and misbehavior they tried to hide, and we'd say "They're just like us!"—which is precisely what the monarchy cannot allow. When the judge says "the dignity of the sovereign," he really means "the illusion that the Queen and her family are intrinsically deserving of their privilege," which means that they are far better and above the common run of humanity.

That's just false. And that explains the need for the jewels and crowns and pearls and palaces and all the hushed traditions. They are fantastic masks. And we *believe* the masks. So we sustain the masks. They owe their power to our response. The monarchy would end tomorrow if we suddenly all saw it as silly. But we can't see it because we're awed by the masks.

George Bernard Shaw, whose play *Pygmalion* became the basis for the musical *My Fair Lady*, makes the point in one of Eliza Doolittle's lines. You might remember remember that the play is grounded in a wager Professor Henry Higgins makes with his friend Colonel Pickering that with three months language training, he could pass off Eliza, a flower girl, as a duchess at an ambassador's garden party. After Eliza successfully appears at the garden party, *and* a dinner party, *and* an opera, Higgins exults in his triumph. But Eliza later recasts the accomplishment by saying, "Really and truly . . . the difference between a lady and a flower girl is not how she behaves, but how she's treated."

These images—lady, flower girl, queen, or, in my case, iron-man speechwriter—are real to us as long as we *believe* they're real, and we believe they're real until we see that we make them up. We are the authors and inventors of the self-image and the shadow. And for the self-image and the shadow to survive, we need to keep the process a secret from ourselves. Our unconscious cooperation is the only fuel the process needs to go on forever—dragging us through our lives without our consent.

The only way we end it is if we move from unconscious cooperation to *conscious noncooperation*. When a thought emerges from the shadow to unsettle my self-image, I make no anxious response. I don't resist. I don't defend. I do nothing. If I can pull this off, then the thoughts that stand guard over the self-image stand *down*, and the shadow begins to seep in, and I slowly become free.

The voice in my head—the one that criticizes me, scares me, shuts me up, puts me down—has only one tactic that gives it power, and that is to frighten me with my own shadow. But when the shadow dissolves, this voice goes with it. And then no one outside me has power over me—because an outside accuser gains power only by forming an alliance with my inner accuser, which is gone.

As the shadow dissolves, we still make mistakes, and we still apologize earnestly for any harm we cause. But we do it lightly, with regret but no shame. It can be very frustrating for someone who's trying to shame you if you admit every point they're making but do it in a lighthearted way—because they don't just want you to admit wrongdoing, they want to make you feel bad, and if you won't do it, they're disempowered. People will use your self-image and the threat of your shadow to control you. If you show that you cannot be manipulated by the threat of shame, you become free and unpredictable and dangerous.

It all emerges from making conscious the unconscious process of defending the self-image and denying the shadow. That is what it means to wake up—and anxiety is often the first call to wake us. Anxiety is like an alarm clock that beeps softly at first, steadily getting louder, begging us to wake up and see what's going on. In our semidormant state, we keep trying to turn off the alarm before we wake up.

But it doesn't matter how many times we hit the snooze button. We can't sleep forever, because reality will never leave our false views alone. It will play havoc with them until, for the sake of peace, we give them up and seek happiness, not through fulfilling the self-image but in losing it. That is the spiritual purpose of anxiety. When anxiety alone is not enough to wake us up, things escalate, and events not only threaten our self-image but overthrow it. That is depression, which we talk about in the next chapter.

CHAPTER FOUR

Depression

I woke up terrified. The room around me oozed a weird gray haze, and I couldn't see the time on the clock. It seemed about three in the morning, and I was too scared to go back to sleep or stay where I was, so I got dressed, left the house, and walked a mile down the hill to the hospital.

The emergency room physician checked my vitals and gave me a bed for the night, telling me my doctor would arrive in the morning.

Dr. Kato was not surprised to see me. I had been coming to him regularly for asthma and bronchitis, which flared with stress. That morning, he told me I had a rapid heart rate and palpitations, but otherwise I seemed fine. He prescribed Valium, and he sent me home saying that I needed to rest.

I was twenty-two, had just graduated from college, and was six months into my new life as an English teacher in Japan. There was nothing in my environment that I could point to as a cause of depression. I admired and enjoyed everyone I met: the women administrators at the school who helped me with my Japanese; the charming grandmother who gave me lessons in table manners; and the relentlessly cheerful Noriko, the school director, who welcomed me at the airport with the gift of a book titled *Japan: The Coming Social Crisis*.

"My wife's English is very bad," said Noriko's blunt husband, Mitsuo, as he reviewed my gift. Mitsuo and Noriko had founded the school where I taught. They hired me to come teach English, and they treated me like a member of the family. They signed me up for lessons at a karate dojo. They took me to early morning meditation at Engakuji Zen Temple in Kamakura. They even bought a car for me to drive to my classes, and when I smashed the fender, they added more insurance and said, "Feel free to bang it!"

Everyone was so courteous and generous that when I began slipping into depression, I wondered, "What is *wrong* with me?!"

In fact, my life wasn't what I had expected. I felt isolated. I wasn't working alongside other teachers. I wasn't near a university. There was no school building where people gathered. I met my students in small groups in private homes, and the children I taught were five to eight years old and spoke only a bit of English. When I asked the kids, "What is your name?," one boy said, "My name is six years old." Another kid said, "My name is Takahito," with excellent pronunciation. But his name was Seiji. The kid who answered before was named Takahito, and Seiji was repeating the correct answer he had just heard.

The kids were adorable and affectionate and funny. But I saw each one for only an hour a week and couldn't get to know them. The school wasn't really a community. I was living alone in the home that housed the school offices, dealing with my isolation by meditating, reading about neuroses, and drinking liter bottles of Coca-Cola while recording my laments on cassettes that I mailed back to my soon-to-be ex-girlfriend in America. On stressful days, I would find the chocolate umbrellas I kept as treats for my students and eat all the umbrellas as fast as I could.

The emergency room visit was a blow for me. I had to face the possibility that I wouldn't make it. I had arrived in Japan with a two-year teaching contract and the feeling that I could go anywhere in the world and learn the language and make it my home. That wasn't happening, and the prospect of leaving Japan before the end of my contract struck me as a huge, embarrassing failure.

So, I wrote a long letter to Father John Dunne. Father Dunne was a deeply beloved theology professor at Notre Dame. By the time he died in 2013, he had taught more students than anyone in the history of the university. He was legendary for his wisdom and kindness, and I had audited his class my senior year. In my letter, I told him: "I know that growth can come through pain, but can growth come through *this* pain? How can I tell if it's helping me or hurting me? I need to know—should I stay or should I go?"

He wrote back a letter filled with love, but little guidance. He talked about Simone Weil, said he would pray for me, and said, "There is grace for you in the void." That's the problem with wise people. They never tell you what to do.

I then found the name of a Spanish Jesuit priest who was a therapist at Sophia University, a Jesuit University in Tokyo. He was willing to see me for free—which was all I could afford after spending all my yen calling my soon-to-be ex-girlfriend in America.

I poured out my project to him. I was drawn to the spiritual life.

I had come to Japan in part to learn about Zen. I thought it would be a time of joy and growth, but I was hit with a depression that I had never known before, and it rattled me.

I told him I have this dynamic side that is adventurous and competitive and wants to achieve and stand out and be separate, and I have this passive side that is more peaceful and accepting and more focused on belonging. I'm overwhelmed now, I told him. The dynamic side is making me miserable. I want to change. I want to become more passive, more accepting.

He smiled and said, "But you're activating your dynamic side to cultivate your passive side."

DEPRESSION AND THE SELF-IMAGE

I stayed in Japan another four months after my emergency room visit. I made some changes in diet and exercise to manage the stress. I read about depression. I traveled more often to Tokyo to spend time with people I knew. But in the end, I gave up. I left the school after nine months and went back to the United States, where I stayed in my parents' home for a few months and then moved to Chicago, where I had grown up and where I knew lots of people.

The moral of that story for me, which I'm still learning, is that the confident, adventurous young graduate who went to Japan was not a freestanding, separate individual but a function and creation of the college scene I had lived in—a familiar and comfortable environment where I saw a hundred people I knew and liked every day. When I was taken out of that environment, I became weak, anxious, sickly, and depressed. It's hard to know how needy I am until I'm not getting what I need. I had no idea that my happiness was tied to my story of who I was; that I needed an environment to *support* that story; and that I had left that environment behind, back in the United States, in college.

I got depressed because my self-image was defeated. So, I went back to a place where my story was affirmed. What I did *not* do to ease my depression—because I just couldn't see it—was to ease my grip on my story. Or question the criticisms I had made of myself for not achieving my story.

I want to pause here briefly to make the point that while the dark thoughts of a defeated self-image are tied to depression, I don't want to suggest that people in severe depression should stake their treatment on efforts to change their thoughts. They should avail themselves of every treatment option possible—and working with thoughts and self-image can be part of that.

One of the joys of my post–White House life was coming to know Mike Gerson, President George W. Bush's chief speechwriter and a *Washington Post* columnist until he died in 2022. We were introduced by John Bridgeland, one of Mike's closest friends and chief domestic policy advisor to President Bush. For a few years, I joined Mike, John, and our friend Tim Shriver for monthly lunches in a restaurant a few blocks from the White House. The four of us also shared a memorable retreat together, accompanied by our master facilitator, Ted Wiard, and we learned a lot about one another's lives. Mike had suffered a heart attack when he worked at the White House. He suffered from cancer and Parkinson's disease as well. In fact, in a story John told at Mike's memorial service, one night during our retreat, we gave Mike our coffee orders for the next day, knowing he loved to make early-morning visits to Starbucks. The following morning, as he handed out the drinks with a trembling hand, he said with a grin: "It takes a lot of chutzpah to ask the guy with Parkinson's to bring the coffee."

Mike also suffered from depression and had been hospitalized for it just before he gave a talk at the National Cathedral in February 2019. In that talk, Mike explained depression in these terms: "The brain experiences a chemical imbalance and wraps a narrative around it. So, the lack of serotonin in the mind's alchemy becomes something like, 'Everyone hates me.'"

During this time, he said, he kept a journal, and at the low point of his depression, he wrote to himself: "You're a burden to your friends. . . . You have no future. . . . No one would miss you."

"These things felt completely true when I wrote them," he said. But he added, "In my right mind . . . I know that I was living within a dismal lie."

On his own, Mike had worked out the elements of a practice I was later taught by a spiritual master: write down the painful thoughts, question them, and see that they're lies.

PROGRAMMING OURSELVES

As I see it, everything we do is a search for happiness—or a search to ease our pain. When we form a self-image, this is what we are doing, even as little kids. We start out looking for unconditional love, and we don't get it, so we begin to calculate: "What are the conditions I need to meet for getting love, or at least a feeling of connection, or at least a buzz of belonging?"

We may be little kids, but we're smart as hell. So, we start noticing the identities that make us feel good. The point is to find a way to prove we're special, and that search is based on our belief that we can't be who we are and get what we need. So, we try to be somebody better.

When I was sixteen, I was taking a ride on the South Shore Line from northern Indiana into Chicago, and a little girl was sitting next to me working on a coloring book. I said, "That looks great! Are you going to color this part green?" She looked at me with condescension and said, "I'm *creative*. You're not *creative!*" I don't know where that little girl is today, but I bet she'd be crushed if a friend said to her, "You used to be so creative. What *happened*?" These thoughts about our identity are a lot easier to put in our heads than they are to get out.

As children, though, we're not consciously deciding who to be. Our brain is just taking in data: "I do this, and I feel good; I do that, and I feel bad." If a set of circumstances leads to a happy feeling, the brain stores it and seeks it.

Over time, the thought "This makes me feel good" becomes "This can make me happy" becomes "This is what I need to be happy." Then if I don't get it, I'm not happy—not because this is what human beings need to be happy but because this is what I told myself *I* needed to be happy.

A few years ago, I was on a plane trip to see my dad. I was in an aisle seat, with an irresistible view of the computer screen across the aisle. At the top of the page, my fellow passenger had written "Goals" in large type and bold font. After a few minutes of fighting the urge to spy, I gave in. I found his goals fascinating, and I wrote some of them down.

He had written:

- Bring peace to work and home.
- Loving kindness meditation.
- Buteyko breathing method.
- Achieve 1 percent fitness level.
- Do radical longevity program.
- Live to be 150.
- Sell business.
- Build net worth to 20 m.
- Reintroduce endangered species.

I was drawn in by this list because it's the kind of list I would write—big principles and practices mixed in with audacious goals across every phase of life. The more insecure and needy we are, the more extravagant we need to make our self-image to get the level of "specialness" we need to feel okay. If we're more secure and less needy, we don't need to have a crazy self-image to redeem or justify ourselves.

That wouldn't be me. I saw myself in his goals and in the activity of writing them down. As I reflected, I realized that when I put together a list of goals, I'm not just creating a program for myself; I'm programming myself. I'm telling myself that achieving these goals will make me happy. I'm not seeing or questioning the premise that I get happy by setting goals for who I want to be and achieving them; I am *buying* that premise. So, I'm not just writing a program; I'm writing a program for happiness.

Given that the stakes are so high, I also create measures, metrics, and submetrics so I can check my progress on the goals. The guy on the plane and I have some different goals, but I'm pretty sure our pattern is the same. That's why I wish I could follow his story, watch the flow of his life and the path of his growth. It's the story of us. We all have programs for happiness. We all program ourselves. And programs are hard to change.

THEN THE EXACT SAME THING HAPPENED

Three years after I left Japan, I traveled to Sri Lanka to stay in the mountain hermitage of a Buddhist monk. I had been practicing Vipassana meditation at a center in Massachusetts, and I made a friend there from Montreal whose brother was a monk in Sri Lanka. I wrote a letter of inquiry to the monk, and he invited me to stay at the hermitage. When I left for Sri Lanka, I thought I might never come back.

I was given a little room at the hermitage, meditated in the hall, took cold showers, went on long walks, and followed the monk every day on his alms rounds where he would beg for food for his midday meal. I soon imagined myself calling a friend at the school where I taught and saying, "Empty my apartment, sell everything and keep the money; I'm becoming a monk."

Then, in the middle of a ten-day course I was sitting with the monk, I got slammed with more fear and depression than I'd ever known. I talked to the monk about it and then just decided to double down. I got up earlier, meditated later, and tried to sit longer without changing my posture.

I completed the course and had a day or two of peace and then the fear and depression roared back. I tried meditating for fewer hours a day, but that didn't help, and the monk advised me to leave the hermitage for a while. I took a three-hour train ride to Kandy and spent some days there trying to calm myself down. But reading about the civil war in the north, or learning about the arrest of a driver with 1,200 pounds of explosives in the back of his truck outside the presidential offices, didn't ease my anxiety. I was experiencing the same kind of depression I had in Japan, and I didn't see how to soothe it or how to stand it—so I decided to leave Sri Lanka and come home after five weeks.

My time in Sri Lanka shared some elements with my stay in Japan: I was far away from home; I was isolated; I was in a humid environment that triggered my asthma and allergies; I was blasting myself with Primatene Mist. But the most obvious and overarching common feature of both experiences is that I arrived with a lot of confidence and enthusiasm and left early feeling defeated—with my self-image badly in need of revision or repair. I remember telling my mom, "I failed as a monk," and I told a colleague, "I ran into a barrier I did not know was there."

I healed in the same way I had healed after Japan. I went back to where my story worked—or at least wasn't contradicted every day. To see that I was creating a story that was causing my suffering was far beyond me at the time. So, I never really was able to see the thoughts that formed my story and were the basis for my misery: "I should be a monk." "This is the only way for me to be happy." "I need to try harder." "If I were tougher, I could do this." Any one of these thoughts would have been a good entry point for flipping the breakdown into breakthrough—if only I had questioned them. But I believed and obeyed them all—so the story remained supreme, running my life from behind the scenes. The only way to recover was to return to a place where the story wasn't tested.

MINIDEPRESSIONS

I believe that our depressions have a spiritual purpose. They move us closer to breakthrough—closer to the moment when we can see that the suffering comes from clinging stubbornly, defiantly, angrily, and fearfully to our story, or attacking ourselves for not fulfilling our story. Sometimes it's easier to see the pattern in discrete events rather than in long, drawn-out experiences.

My brother John is the sweetest, gentlest big brother in the world. But when I was thirteen years old, he crushed my dreams of being a soccer star—defeating me in a penalty-kicking contest and leaving me face down on the ground, sobbing over my lost greatness.

I *had* to be great at something, and I had picked soccer. It was a naive ambition, given my modest athletic skills, but I had very few options for greatness—and I had an angle that I thought might work. I had just returned to the Chicago area after our stay in Iran, where I played soccer every day. Soccer wasn't a big deal in the United States at the time, and I thought I would be better than the kids who mostly played other sports. It was a thin scheme. My friends in Iran, who'd played soccer since they could walk, taught me as best they could, but they had found in me a charity case of high cost. When my eighth-grade classmate Hassan put me in as goalie during our game against the ninth graders, it took the older kids two minutes to score on me and three minutes to score again. I got pulled.

A sweet girl from my math class came over to console me, "Tom, if you get so upset over a little thing like a soccer game, how will you deal with the big things?" But while she was being kind, I heard two kids offering an analysis of the second goal, "Tom shaped his arms into a basketball rim, and the ball went through the middle!"

Nevertheless, I thought I could be a bad soccer player in Iran and be a good soccer player in America—like taking advantage of a favorable exchange rate. I was trying to find a little image for myself to give order to my world, so I awarded myself the identity of "good soccer player."

Since then, I had been guarding the perimeter, patrolling the border between good and bad, between me and not-me. I told myself the story: "I am a good soccer player. John is a bad soccer player. He is bad. I am good. See how different we are? Very different."

Then I challenged John to a penalty-kicking contest one day after soccer practice just to prove my point. Oops. My story lost. My heart was broken. My life was ruined. Bad beat good. Up became down. I lost control of the border between me and not-me—and I had to start looking for another fake ID.

Of course, I kept playing soccer for as long as I could find a team that would have me. But as I look back, it's now clear from my huge reaction to that mild setback that a wise set of eyes inside me saw that my big dreams would not be supported by my modest skills.

At age thirteen, there was no chance I could have seen the role my defeated self-image played in my depression, but when a similar event occurred forty years later, I did see it—at least a little.

In the spring of 2015, I went to a retreat in the California redwoods where we were asked to bring a "sacred object" and tell others about it as a way of introducing ourselves to the group.

I spent ten hours preparing a two-minute talk.

Why? Because it wasn't enough for me to give a good talk or even a heartfelt one. I had to stun the crowd into silence, giving them no option but to halt the exercise, give me a standing ovation, and present me an award for Best Speech Ever.

Instead of awed silence followed by an awards ceremony, my talk was followed by a woman whose sacred object was a rubber chicken she squeezed when she was stressed. That was her talk. And the crowd *loved* her. Another guy talked about his spirit animal and had the place rolling in laughter. One woman held up an image of a broken heart and said, "When our hearts break, they break open." And everyone's heart broke open with hers.

None of those speakers had a script. They just talked and connected. Not me. I wrote my talk and polished it and memorized it and recited it.

I know what a hall feels like when a speech hits home. I didn't feel it, and I was devastated. There were three people sitting across from me who I wanted to impress, and it scalded me to see them moved by other speakers. Oddly, though, I can't say they didn't like my talk—because I didn't see their reaction. I didn't even look at them. It's hard for me to look at people when I'm trying to remember my lines, so I looked down, or up, or off into space. I really wasn't talking to anybody.

When the event was over, I felt angry and embarrassed and headed off to lie on the ground and stare at the stars and think, "These are *not* my people!"

For years I'd been going to silent retreats. For me, talking retreats were for people who couldn't handle silence. But within hours, this place had stirred me up and made me want to leave. What was I doing at a talking retreat?! I was *performing*—posing as an expert, trying to impress, hoping to arrive at the event by helicopter while others came in cars.

My talk wasn't bad. It was maybe even good. But it didn't out-shine the other talks, so to me it was a disaster. Luckily, I summoned the courage to stay. (Actually, it wasn't the courage to stay that kept me there. It was fear of the embarrassment in leaving.) And over the next few days, I thought about what had happened. I had treated the talk as a competition when the point was to connect—and people don't connect by reciting lines to one another. They connect by opening up, sharing an emotion, a goal, a loss, or a flaw that unites them with others. That's the connection that a rigid self-image often blocks. I had to be *separate* from others—and better. I was a speechwriter. So my talk *had* to be better. If my talk wasn't better, then who was I?

If I had been able to talk *about* my self-image instead of *from* my self-image, then I might have found the guts to introduce myself as a guy who is desperate to impress. Or I might have given my talk and then said, "I spent ten hours writing this talk, and I recited it instead of telling it because I wanted to hide behind it—because the talk I wrote is polished, but the guy who wrote it is not." I *might* have said that, but I didn't, because I wasn't willing to be wounded—and that's what got me hurt.

My real sacred object, I later realized, the most precious thing that I brought with me to the retreat—was my self-image. Of course, the secret to protecting the self-image is to make sure it's never tested, except when it's sure to triumph. But if I have the image "I'm a great speechwriter" and I introduce myself at a retreat by giving a speech, then the image is at risk. With the help of some reflection and some friends at the retreat, I saw how my self-image drove me to obsess over the speech and how it led me to suffer over it afterward.

THE HEALING POWER OF LITTLE HUMILIATIONS

If there is a lesson I take from these stories, it's that we learn and grow from moments of conflict where we see we're not who we think we are. Richard Rohr writes in *Falling Upward:* "I have prayed for years for one good humiliation a day. In my position, I have no other way of spotting both my well-denied shadow self and my idealized persona."

"If you can begin to 'make friends' with those who have a challenging message for you," says Richard, "you will usually begin to see some of your own shadow. If you don't, you will miss out on much-needed wisdom."

That's, of course, what a humiliation does. It tells us, "You think you're this, but you're actually that." The little humiliations that wake us from our delusions are vital for our health and growth— which means it's helpful for us to be around people who don't see it as their duty to affirm our self-image. I may not have had enough of them, but I've had some—and they deliver experiences I never forget.

When I was hired to write for the president, I told a close friend: "I'm a speechwriter for the president of the United States!" She didn't react, so I said it again, and she said, "You seem impressed by this."

Another time when I was reflecting on my growth and how much calmer and more accepting I was, a colleague said, "One thing you can't say, Tommy, is that you know better than others what you're like to work with."

Ben's girlfriend came to stay with us one summer, and after a few days she told me, "I asked Ben what his dad was like, and he said, 'We're both into meditation, but he's not as discerning.'"

(Ben walked into my bedroom once when I was doing a new type of meditation. He watched me for a minute and then left, saying, "You're getting ripped off!")

When I taught high school, my daily life was filled with little humiliations. One Friday afternoon in the spring, I gave a test during my last class of the day. Test day was usually a good day because I didn't have to prepare a lesson and so could sit at my desk and do what I wanted. But it was a good day only if the kids kept busy after they finished their tests. So, I wrote the homework up on the board, and I told the kids, "When you're done with your test, start on this homework."

After forty minutes or so, Silas was the first to finish, and he put his test face down on my desk and went back to his seat. After a few minutes, I noticed he was reading a magazine. "Silas," I said, rapping my knuckles on the blackboard. "Do the homework." He sulkily closed the magazine and reached under his desk to get his textbook. By this time, other kids had finished their tests, put them on my desk, and started the homework. Not Silas. He had taken a binder out, then hidden his magazine inside the binder. When I saw it, I stood up, walked over to his desk, took his magazine, and said, "Do the homework," then went back to my desk.

At this point, we had the attention of the whole class. Silas stood up, walked over to *my* desk, placed his hand on the stack of completed tests, thumbed through them a few times and said, real slow, "What's the matter, Mr. Rosshirt? It's the last class period on Friday, and you just . . . can't . . . bring . . . yourself . . . to start grading these tests?"

I laughed out loud and handed Silas back his magazine, consoling myself that I had created a classroom environment where it felt safe to challenge authority.

One of the most powerful messages I've read on the importance of being challenged came from Robert A. Johnson, who wrote a series of short books on Jungian psychology, including my favorite, *Owning Your Own Shadow.*

In his book *He*, a treatment of masculine psychology, Johnson writes about the mother complex, which he says is a man's "regressive capacity which would like to return to a dependency on his mother and be a child again. This is a man's wish to fail, his defeatist capacity, his subterranean fascination with death or accident, his demand to be taken care of. This is pure poison in a man's psychology."

To me, the wish "to be taken care of," which Johnson says is "pure poison," is synonymous with the desire to have our self-image affirmed. If the idealized mother is the essence and image of comfort, then surrounding ourselves with people who tell us our story is the comfort zone. Going out of your comfort zone means going where your self-image or story is not noticed or honored or affirmed— either because your story doesn't make you special or because the elements that make up your story aren't valued.

The path to breakthrough means leaving the comfort zone and never returning—because the story no longer gives comfort, or, at least, not the comfort you need or seek or get stuck on.

TRYING TO EASE THE PAIN OF DEPRESSION—AN OPTIONS MEMO

There is a pattern to the depressions, the minidepressions, and the little humiliations I've described in this chapter. And there is a pattern to the way I've tried to recover from them. The injuries and recoveries are all grounded in the self-image model.

When I was in Japan, away from my cozy college home, my self-image was defeated, I got depressed, and I went back to where my story worked. When I was in Sri Lanka, I did the same thing. I went back to where my story worked. The self-image pushes us to try to create a world around us where our story doesn't get contradicted. We sometimes call that home. I went back home.

In addition to homecoming, I responded to depression by making some amendments to my self-image. I tempered my view that I could go anywhere and do anything and make any place my home. I also surrendered bit by bit to the idea that I was never going to be Pelé. I went from "Okay, maybe I can't be great, but I can be good" to "Maybe I can't be good, but at least I can make the team," and from "At least I can make the team" to, in college, "What is my name doing here on the list of cuts?"

(I still have dreams about seeing my name on that list, and those dreams compete for frequency with finding myself naked in public; taking a final exam for a class I never attended; and getting ready to play guitar before a packed concert hall and realizing I don't know how to play guitar and wondering if there is still time to learn.)

I also responded to depression by playing the victim. After I got dropped by my first serious girlfriend, I couldn't bear to explain events by tampering with my sacred story—that I was a great guy. So, I soothed myself by creating a negative story in my head about the guy who replaced me.

Of course, playing the victim is soothing. When the self-image feels defeated, it's a relief to be able to blame someone—to be the guy who got screwed rather than the guy who screwed up. But playing the victim means creating a villain, and that's addictive and dangerous—because it means defending the false story of myself by adding a false story about someone else.

All these responses to depression involved trying to build the self-image back up by returning to where the self-image was affirmed; or making small, grudging, forced changes to the self-image and holding on for as long as I could; or adding the story that I was a victim. Sometimes I also added a positive element to my self-image—adding a skill that could help me through. I added the skill of managing, the skill of coping, the skill of finding the environment where the self-image could survive and building it back up again, but I did not add the skill of breaking through.

It wasn't until I was suffering the depression that led me to move out of my family home and into an apartment that I responded to the breakdown with a breakthrough. It was the deepest depression I'd had. The darkest moment came one afternoon when I felt that I was never going to get back home, nothing I was doing was working, and my life was moving on without me. I was lying on blankets I had spread as bedding on the kitchen floor because I couldn't take the chemical smell of the carpet in the bedroom—and I just stared at the ceiling, sobbing, saying over and over: "I never wanted this. I never wanted this. I never wanted this."

During this time, I would burst into tears imagining my kids finding out that I was dead—not because I was planning my suicide but because I knew I couldn't keep feeling the way I was feeling and live long enough to die a natural death.

Unlike with past depressions, though, my way out wasn't to protect my story by going home. I couldn't go home. So this time I didn't change my environment to support my story. I changed my story. That is what self-directed neuroplasticity makes possible. We don't have to fulfill the story, prove the story, insist on the story, or be a servant of the story: we can edit the story—and not just by adding new thoughts to outshout the old thoughts but by editing, even deleting, the old thoughts that tell us "This is who I am. This is what I need to have. This is how things have to be."

No matter who we are or what stage of life we're in, reality will at some point cause depression in us, making us suffer by defeating our self-image. The pain will get our attention and force us to act. If the pain is great enough, we might see the role of our story in our suffering and start to break through.

If we don't see the role of our story, we will think the action is all external, and we will try to make a change in our surroundings, or blame someone for the defeat of our self-image, or double down on our false stories, which will only make the pain grow. That sets us up for addiction, which is a natural response to anxiety and depression.

CHAPTER FIVE

Addiction

Before the guests arrived at the wake, my brothers and I stood in front of the open casket of our brother Matt, who had just died of AIDS at the age of twenty-three. We looked on for a time in silence, then my brother Dan, on my left, said, "Why do his hands look all screwed up?" And my brother Dave leaned in from the right and whispered, "Because he's *dead*!"

We exploded in laughter. That moment of emotional blasphemy came when we were deeply in need of the soothing relief of a dark joke. It also felt okay because Matt was the most irreverent and amusing person we knew. If he'd been able to speak, he'd have said something worse.

Matt had an addictive personality. When he was in the hospital after he'd been diagnosed with AIDS and was trying to recover from pneumonia, he ordered one Dixie cup of ice cream after another and ate them in between his cigarettes—smoking in defiance of the nurses' warnings about blowing up the hospital by lighting up near oxygen.

Renee, Matt's friend from their college days at Georgetown, came to visit him when he got out of the hospital. My mom asked her not to give him any cigarettes because he was still feeling the effects of pneumonia. But as soon as Mom left the house and Matt and Renee were alone, Matt said from his wheelchair:

"Renee, grab me some cigarettes; they're in the cupboard over the fridge."

"Matt, I can't. I told your mom I wouldn't."

"Renee, she's never going to know!"

"Matt, I'm your mom's guest. I *promised* her."

"Renee, stop being ridiculous."

"Matt, stop pressuring me."

"Renee—are you going to *deny* your *dying* friend his *one* request?"

"Go to hell, Matt."

"Sorry," Matt said lightly. "I had to try."

Matt had gone to Georgetown because he wanted to get involved in politics. In a caper he never fully explained, he leaped over the White House fence the night Reagan defeated Carter, and was arrested by the Secret Service. He was then mercifully released to the custody of a Georgetown priest, who bored Matt with questions about the deep meaning of his drunken stunt. He was kicked out of college his sophomore year for failing grades after spending every night in the bars.

Matt was younger than I was by three years, but in some ways he seemed my elder—first, because he was smarter and a better writer; second, because he took me to my first AA meeting; but finally, I think, because he would listen to me talk about my crises and help me understand that they weren't crises. I heard the same story from a high school friend of Matt's who almost drowned in Lake Michigan during her first epileptic seizure. She was mortified by the seizure, terrified of having another, and said Matt was the only classmate who made her feel normal. Thirty years after he died, Matt still comes to her in her dreams, she told me, listening, smoking cigarettes, and telling her everything's going to be all right.

When Matt was twenty-one, he told me he was gay. I was visiting him at the University of Texas at Austin, where he had transferred after Georgetown, and he wanted to introduce me to his partner, so a little background was in order. I was totally surprised—both that he was gay and that he had taken so long to tell me. We went over all the false stories he'd told me of his pseudo-hetero-romances, and I laughed at how stupid I'd been. I asked whether he was going to tell Mom and Dad, and he said, "No. I'm sure they could handle it. I just don't want to handle them handling it."

About a year after that, Matt started feeling sick. He dropped out of UT. He was rapidly losing energy, and he resorted to amphetamines to try to restore his old sense of self. He called me from a state hospital after checking himself in for detox. "Why didn't you go to Mom and Dad?" I asked. "I'm trying to have this breakdown as cheaply as possible," he said.

Just prior to detox, down on his money and between minimum-wage jobs where he kept getting fired for falling asleep, Matt had sold his blood at a plasma center and received a letter telling him that he had tested positive for HIV. He kept the news to himself for months.

As Matt was dying, I spent time going over old memories, trying to understand his life, and I remembered a scene from our childhood.

I was eight, Matt was five. Three or four of us boys were crowded around the bathroom sink one night, brushing our teeth before going to bed, and one of my brothers playfully shoved me and said, "Get away, you homo!" I giggled and said, "I'm not a homo; *you're* a homo!" and shoved him back. We had no idea what a "homo" was. It was a word one of us heard at school.

Years later, Matt told me: "It's terrible when you find out you are what you hate."

ADDICTION AND BELONGING

The self-image is a social-bonding tool. We create our story and defend it because we believe we need it to belong. If we can't find a self-image that makes us popular and we can live up to, we're going to be more prone to addiction. And when the self-image is false and the truth is dangerous, the threat of addiction is greater and deeper. I read Matt's journal after he died. It was, in parts, a chronicle of his efforts to overcome his addictions. In one entry, after he described another failed effort to quit doing drugs, he wrote: "Good night, weakling."

In a TED Talk presented in 2015 that has more than ten million views, Johann Hari highlights research that blows up a lot of our beliefs about addiction. Hari notes that many of our assumptions stem from experiments done in the twentieth century that give rats a choice between plain water and water with heroin or cocaine. The rats chose the drugs, got addicted, and died.

But in his talk, Hari cited the work of a professor of psychology named Bruce Alexander who created what he called "Rat Park." Rat

Park was filled with rat delights, such as cheese, tunnels, colored balls, and lots of sexually available rats. The rats in Rat Park were given the same choice of beverage: plain water or water with heroin and cocaine. And they chose the plain water.

The rats in the prior experiments were isolated. They were in empty cages. They had nothing to do but be depressed or get high. So, they got high. The rats in Rat Park were already high with activity and community, so they rarely used the drugs, and never got addicted to them.

Hari then tested the same insights against examples of human addiction and found that the same truth holds with humans. Human beings have a need to bond, Hari summarized. When we're happy and healthy, we bond with one another. When we're "traumatized or isolated or beaten down by life," we are going to bond "with something that will give you some sense of relief."

"The opposite of addiction is not sobriety," Hari concludes. "The opposite of addiction is connection."

This sounds wise to me. But what if we're trying to connect with others by putting forward a story that disconnects us from ourselves?

FIGHTING ADDICTION IN A CLIMATE OF DISCONNECTION

One hot August day about ten years ago, I was sitting at a table with a friend who leaned forward and said in a whisper: "See that guy over there? He cut off his wife's head with a sword."

Then my friend went table by table and told me about the murders each of these guys had committed. It was visiting day on death row. There were eighteen to twenty guys out of their cells visiting friends or family, all wearing orange jumpsuits. I was visiting with my friend and former soccer teammate, John, who had been convicted of a drug-induced murder and sentenced to death.

John was one of the most popular kids in high school, good athlete, good-looking, lots of girlfriends, well-liked by everyone, always upbeat. But his happy-go-lucky persona hid the hell of his home life. He grew up in a den of addiction. His dad—who John later found lifeless on the floor of his garage, dead from a lifetime of drinking—installed a keg in the basement of their house when John was a kid, and John started taking sips at age six. His mom tucked John into bed at night, often smelling of alcohol. John's older brother was found in his trailer in his fifties, dead from cirrhosis of the liver. His older sister was hit by a car and killed while crossing the street carrying an eighteen-pack of beer with a blood alcohol content of 0.44 percent.

John's other sister was scheduled to testify at a hearing where John was trying to get his death sentence overturned. The court had heard days of testimony from experts about how addiction had devastated John's family. His sister then drove into the courthouse parking lot, rammed a police cruiser, and was arrested for drunk driving in the middle of the afternoon. She never testified, but John's lawyer said, "That was testimony enough."

When John was in high school, his dad divorced his mom, moved away, and "never paid a dime in child support," John said. They moved into a much smaller house, and "with Dad gone," John told me, "my home lost its dignity and became 'the party house.' My mom would let anything go on."

John managed to get admitted on scholarship to the boarding school we attended together. When classmates who lived far away asked to come home with him on weekends, he was terrified. "I wanted to hide my family from my friends," he said. At the same time, when he was at home amid the mess and it was time to return to school, he felt guilty for leaving.

John managed to keep it barely together into his thirties. He made it a long way on charm and good looks and good luck. He had a great job at a movie studio, then he lost that job, and, in his words, "things started to fall apart." He told me, "I just know in my heart that if it wasn't for being whacked out on crack for two weeks prior to that fateful day, I never would be here."

After he got fired from the movie studio, he struggled for income. He got a job as a handyman and came to love the family he worked for, who liked him a lot. Then one day, frantic for money for more crack, John went to the home where he worked to ask the man for an advance. He wasn't home, but his wife let John wait on the porch. There was a lunch tray outside. John brought it inside to give to the woman, and for reasons he still can't explain, struck her with it, knocking her unconscious. He ransacked the house, searching for anything of value.

When the husband came home, John panicked, grabbed the nearest weapon he could find, and hit the husband too. The man cracked his skull on the floor and died. The wife survived and called the police. Hours later, sitting in a car in a drive-through banking lane trying to pass a stolen check, John heard dogs bark and glass crash as police officers smashed the car windows and put their guns to his head.

When I first visited John on death row, I told him I could stay only until lunch. That was a lie. I just didn't know how weird it would be to sit across from him at a little table for six hours straight, the full length of visiting hours, so I gave myself an out. But when lunchtime came, I said, "John, I can stay." And on every visit after, I would come in the first hour and stay till the last minute. We even had a little game. When it was time to go, we'd start to pray, reciting the Lord's Prayer and the Twenty-third Psalm, and the guard who came to clear out the visitors always gave us a respectful distance and an extra minute to finish our prayers.

On that first visit, John told me every detail of the day of the murder and described his regret, his guilt, his shame, his remorse. He couldn't believe I had come to see him. He couldn't believe anyone would. And that's what kept me spellbound with John—his descriptions of his guilt, his efforts to do good, and his accounts of the scenes of death-row life.

He told me how it felt when "the entourage in white shirts" paraded past his cell, stopped at cell 17, and said, "It's time," before escorting an inmate to the death-watch cell near the execution chamber. I asked him, "John, what do people say when a guy is walked out—'Goodbye'?!" John said, "Everybody shouts: 'Stay strong, brother. Stay strong!'"

John wrote me once, "The worst possible news came three days ago." I thought it would be about his death-penalty appeals. But no. He had received an emergency phone call from his sister saying his mom had died, which left him simmering in guilt for the humiliation he thought he had created for her and feeling ashamed to know he couldn't go to his own mother's funeral.

In 2019, John's death sentence was vacated, and he was given a life sentence and transferred to a maximum-security prison, which was actually more dangerous for him because he and other inmates were out of their cells much more than when he was on death row.

Soon after his transfer, John had looked into the face of an inmate who was being stabbed in the chow line. He told me of one inmate who was raped in his cell, and the next day came up behind his rapist and stabbed him through the heart, killing him. "Everyone here has a weapon," he told me. "At night, when the cells are locked, you can hear the sound of inmates sharpening their knives."

I've spent a lot of time thinking about John, and addiction, and spiritual growth. His addictions raged after he lost his job, leading him to go crazy on crack, commit murder, and end up in a violent prison. So how did he deal with the disconnection that led to addiction after he ended up in a much worse environment than the one that led him to addiction in the first place?

In John's case, I think he began to heal the disconnection within himself. It seemed to me that he immediately dropped the "Everything's great!" persona that I met in high school and that had carried him through his arrest—and replaced it with something more real. He had to. John has a team of twenty-five friends from high school who send him money and letters and pay him visits. I don't think he would have been able to keep a circle of friends on false premises. He had to be real.

He told me in the first letter he sent me from prison: "I sincerely apologize to you for the position I'm in. We all look forward to hearing success stories from our classmates. I'm embarrassed and ashamed at the disgrace I'm bringing to you and everyone else."

Then, face-to-face, he told me, "It's hard to talk about anything real in here. People don't admit they did anything. They're all 'innocent.' They deny it all. They blame everyone but themselves for the fact that they're here." He said, "Rosh, I deserve to be here."

Then he reflected for a moment on his conversations with inmates and said, "You know, I think their lawyers won't let them admit what they've done because if you admit anything, people here can go tell the warden in the hopes of getting themselves a break—and what you say can come back to hurt you if you're working on appeals."

When John's sentence was commuted to life, he was hoping he could get a job in the prison, something he couldn't do when he was on death row. If there ever came a chance for parole, John wanted to be able to say that he'd been doing something useful, like tutoring inmates for their GED. But John wasn't allowed a job because he was considered a security risk, having been on death row. Then, through a break, he got a job in the chapel, and I was thrilled for him. But on my next visit, he told me: "I don't like the guys with the chapel jobs. They're posing. They act all pious. In my wing, I'm living with murderers, but we don't pretend to be better than we are."

I asked him how he thinks about the future, and he said: "I can't take on the future. I have responsibilities. I have to be a good brother to the guys around here, a good role model to the young prisoners, a good correspondent to you guys. If I spend my time worrying about the future, I won't be able to do any of that. I'm worried about a young kid in the cell next to me. He's only been here a few years. He's twenty-three. He's fighting depression, and I want to try to help him because the inmate on the other side keeps telling him, 'There's no hope. There's no hope in this place.'"

I was struck by the bond John felt with the people who were suffering, but the biggest surprise for me came when he said he wanted to reach out to a guy we knew who was convicted of murdering his wife. I told him, "John, your friends have sympathy for you because you're a good guy who got addicted to crack, committed murder, admitted his guilt and his shame, and has tried to redeem himself by the way he lives. That guy is guilty of the premeditated murder of the mother of his children, which he then denied and tried to cover up. How can you have any sympathy for him?"

"Because I know what it feels like when that door clangs shut."

I never heard John fault anyone for what happened to him. He didn't make himself the victim. He talked about his family, but he never blamed them. And John's story reinforces for me that mending the self-image is where the growth is. When we quit drinking and doing drugs, we still have to deal with what made us want to drink and do drugs in the first place. That work is with the self-image; it's inspecting the stories we've been telling ourselves and throwing out what's not true.

I am struck by the match between what I have heard from John and what I have read from Shaka Senghor, who spent time in prison for killing a man and wrote the stunning book *Writing My Wrongs: Life, Death, and Redemption in an American Prison.*

Shaka says he came to see that "I was responsible for my thoughts and the feelings that they produced. It didn't matter what other people had done to me; ultimately, I was responsible for my anger, and for the actions that I took in response to it. . . . I knew in my heart that if I wanted to make things right with others, I had to make them right with myself."

MY STORY

There are very few alcoholics who can resist telling their story of addiction—and I'm not one of them. My story starts with Grandma, Helen Hurley Moynahan. Everyone in my family adored and feared

Grandma (except my dad, who just feared her). She was formed in an unruly family. Her dad was born in Ireland, completed his studies for the priesthood, and took the traditional cash gift his parents gave him for the purchase of his vestments and bolted for America. So, my line of the family owes its life to a sin against the Church.

Grandma was the only girl in a family of nine kids, many of whom became alcoholics, and one of whom helped open one of the first casinos in Las Vegas. He would come to visit with cash gifts and tell my parents: "Don't put it in the bank."

Grandma's alcoholism was, my mom told me, "the best kept secret in La Grange," which meant that everyone knew and pretended they didn't know. She had quit drinking years before I was born, but the flavor of her addictive personality remained. She was very decisive about what should be done and how it should be done. I remember hiding in shame under her kitchen table as she scolded me for skipping out on my chores: "You're just a shirker in my book, Tom Rosshirt. Just a *shirker*." (Careful, Grandma. You could end up in *my* book.)

"Helen terrified me," my cousin Tricia told me fifty years after Grandma died. But, wow, she could make us feel like heroes. That was an early buzz of mine—getting Grandma to love me. And my trick was saying to her, "I'm going to be a priest, Grandma!!" She *loved* that, and she loved seeing the stars I got for memorizing my prayers and the scapular I got from Monsignor O'Brien for going to morning Mass more than all those lazy kids who stayed at home eating Cap'n Crunch and watching morning cartoons while I went to visit God.

Of course, like any kid, I was torn between the buzz of being good and the buzz of being bad. So after I got caught—again—stealing money from my mom's purse to buy candy for the big kids so they would be my friends, I asked Mom if she thought I could still make it to heaven. In fact, from the beginning, I seemed to be calculating how bad I could be and still not go to hell.

With this temperament, my addictions were on a fast track from the start. Grandma would come to our house and give each of us a pack of gum. I would be chewing all five pieces in minutes, and she said, "If you chew it all at once, I won't give you *any!*" Not sure what the lesson was there. But gum and candy were early addictions. I ate so much candy that my teeth turned to sand—almost. I do remember going to the dentist constantly to get fillings and then leaving there and going straight to Vann's drugstore a block away to stock back up on candy.

When I was ten and we were traveling in Europe, my mom got the idea it would be cute to serve us kids a little wine at lunch. I drank mine and then snuck the wine that had been poured for each of my brothers. By the time the food came, I was drunk.

As a freshman in high school, I was drinking beer, getting high on pot, smoking cigarettes despite my asthma, and drinking the vodka of a friend's mom after school. By sophomore year, I was trying LSD and PCP. I also did some downers one time when my parents were out of town. I remember thinking, "I don't feel anything; I better do some more." I woke up the next day like a zombie—*and went to school!* My friends said: "You're moving like you're ninety years old. Stay home, man!" I had zero street sense—I was okay with doing handfuls of downers from an unknown source, but I couldn't skip school, that was crossing a line.

Then came the summer of mescaline. I bought 125 hits from

some guy in the woods and did them with friends. One night, when I was tired of getting drunk on beer, I drank a pint of whiskey and woke up the next day wet with my own vomit and urine. I smuggled my sheets into the washing machine while my mom praised me for washing my own linens. "You're really growing up!" she said proudly.

The summer of mescaline included getting hired at my first job—washing dishes at the Howard Johnson's on La Grange Road for two dollars an hour—and getting fired from my first job (for not showing up to wash dishes at the Howard Johnson's on La Grange Road for two dollars an hour).

Alas, the summer of mescaline turned into the fall of getting arrested for pot and flunking out of school. My addictions went into remission when I went to boarding school, partly because of the tight control, but also because of the connection I felt with the students and the teachers, especially Mr. Kirkby—who had the love and the skill to both hold me accountable and win me over.

My drinking stormed back during my sophomore year in college in Austria, where the academic load was light and there were no consequences for drinking myself blind. Again and again, I staggered home drunk just as the birds were starting to sing.

All my friends drank a ton then, too, but I seemed to drink more, and every time I drank, I got drunk. No amount was enough. That carried over into my junior year back on campus at Notre Dame. One Saturday in winter, after a long night of drinking, I got the idea that I should drop in to see my girlfriend in Farley Hall. It was past 2:00 a.m., and I was drunk enough to think she'd be happy to see me.

Problem was, at Notre Dame, guys can't be in the upper floors of a women's dorm after 2:00 a.m. on the weekends. But I had a plan.

I stood outside the entrance to the dorm, and as someone walked out, I stumbled through the open door, hoping to go unseen. I would have had a better chance of sneaking in a horse.

Two people at the security desk yelled at me, so I ran down the hall and out the other door and back to my dorm, where my rector saw me sprint into the lobby—drunk, breathing heavily, without a coat—in February in South Bend.

I went to my room, and a short time later heard a knock at my door. I opened it and found two uniformed cops from ND security, and a kid who smiled at me sheepishly and said, "That's him."

They took me down to security, asked me questions like "Do you know where you are?," and then released me.

I had to meet with the dean of students, and my "punishment" was to see an alcohol counselor—a wise and kind woman who saw me once a week until I graduated. I came out of my first meeting thinking: "I'm an alcoholic. I'm *special*." I told my story to my girlfriend, who said, "Wow. I thought you were just being a jerk." I said, "We can't rule that out."

I watched my drinking for more than a year, keeping it somewhat under control. But a month before graduation, I was back to my old patterns—waking up three days in a row not remembering what I'd done the night before. So, the next night, I went out to a bar with friends, ordered a Coke, and never drank alcohol again. Two years later, after tapering off my drug use, I quit all drugs too. It's an unusual story of quitting, but it worked in part because I had no doubt that I was an addict, I felt no shame about the addiction, I had no denial about the danger, and I got one lucky break after another that supported me in my sobriety.

RUNNING HOT

Matt and John were especially susceptible to addiction—Matt because he was growing up gay in the 1960s and John because he grew up in a den of addiction. Both faced extra social pressure to put forward a story that was false. But I had a white male, heterosexual, privileged, stable, cozy life, and still I was super addictive. What was *my* excuse?

I didn't have to go to more than a few AA meetings before I heard people say that their first drink was bliss. A lot of people have the same message, and it sounds something like this: "When I had my first drink, I felt calm, confident, and playful for the first time in my life. It was like I suddenly felt at home." Drinking had the same effect on me—it turned me from gloomy introvert to garrulous extrovert. It made me think I'd found the answer. In fact, if I'd been able to figure out how to go through life with the happy buzz of five beers, I never would have bothered with meditation.

That's the story for a lot of us. One of the striking features of a room of alcoholics is how grandiose our ambitions are, and I have a theory about this: we're so anxious that we need an especially lofty self-image to calm us down. "I don't want to just *belong*. I want to be *cherished*, and for that I need a heroic self-image." Of course, a heroic self-image is harder to achieve, which creates more anxiety about achieving it, which tempts me to drink to soothe the anxiety.

I never said I wasn't messed up.

Eckhart Tolle remarked in one of his retreats: "Many very sensitive people become addicted to drugs at a young age because the world to them is painful, and they can't stand it, and they believe they need to dull the pain."

My addictive tendencies perhaps came not only from the stress of a disconnect between the story I was telling and the story I was living but also in part from a body that was overreacting to my environment. I was definitely a sensitive kid, both physically and emotionally. A few days after I was born, I came home from the hospital covered in eczema. I developed asthma at a young age. I had an anaphylactic reaction to nuts when I was six and went to an allergist, where I tested positive to nearly every one of forty allergens. My parents put an electronic air purifier in our home. When the gerbils died, they were not replaced. No dog or cats for us kids, and I remember as a little boy standing out by the street in front of our home talking to Mr. Christmas Tree, who got hauled out of our house on December 26 to minimize my exposure. I felt guilty about it, so I went out to keep him company and tell him I was sorry.

Emotionally, I was prone to wild temper tantrums as a kid, and my mom asked the pediatrician if she should warn the kindergarten teacher before I showed up at school. I was an obsessive rule follower (until my addictions made rules inconvenient), and I was socially anxious, especially desperate to avoid situations where I felt I didn't belong.

When I was a kid going to Cubs games at Wrigley Field with my friends, we sat in the cheap seats. By the eighth inning, when the rich people left their box seats and headed home, my friends would say, "C'mon, let's go sit near the dugout." I would join them, but I hated it. I worried that I would suddenly feel the grip of an usher's hand on my shoulder. "Hey, kid. Show me your ticket!"

My anxiety wasn't just about box seats at a ball game. It applied widely to life. I lived to avoid those moments. I never wanted to be questioned, challenged, or told I didn't belong. And I was largely able to live my life in ways that gave me adventure and opportunity and kept me from being challenged. And *still* I had an emotional system that simmered so hot with insecurity that I became an addict to calm it. In fact, if I hadn't lived a life of privilege that protected me from the charge that I didn't belong—alcohol, drugs, and anger might have ended my life long before I reached the age I am today.

THE ORIGINAL ADDICTION

Any mind that is running hot will seek something to cool it, and candy and gum for a kid and drugs and alcohol for a teen offer something soothing. But underneath all that, and driving it, is the original addiction—the addiction to the self-image, or, to be more precise, the addiction to thinking, worrying, and obsessing about our self-image and our story. "What's going to happen to me? What does this mean for me?" Our addiction to the story of ourselves is the addiction that underlies and sets in motion all other addictions, and—if cured— would cure all the other addictions as well.

Killian Noe is the founder of Recovery Café, a network of more than sixty centers across the US that serve people who suffer from homelessness, substance abuse, and mental health challenges. When I asked her to read a draft of this chapter, she sent back a message that is too precious to paraphrase. She wrote: "Underneath our addictions are the lies we tell about ourselves—both positive lies and negative lies. Lies that are illusions about how special we are and lies that are illusions about how terrible we are. Surrendering our self-image means surrendering both. Usually, the illusion about how special we are is a reaction to the lies about how terrible we are. They are related, and in a dance with each other."

Thinking I'm great is my response to thinking I'm a loser. Whether we want to be a saint, a senator, the president, or the pope, the mechanism of self-image addiction explains our obsessive effort to choreograph that dance between the me I long to be and the me I am terrified to be.

A few years ago, I was on the beach and fell into meditating. And then I thought: "Wait! I should get my phone and set it for thirty minutes and meditate till it rings because then the meditation will count."

My meditation will *count*, ha! What does *that* mean? It means it will count toward fulfilling my story. What story? The story of what I need to do today so I can achieve the story of who I want to be tomorrow. And if I do whatever it is I need to do and mark it down and measure the time and make a note of it, then I will get a little buzz in my brain because the stuff I did *counts*. What's the point? Who even asks? My brain just gets a little buzz whenever I think I'm achieving my story. The point isn't even the story. The point is the buzz. That's the purpose of the story—the story controls the buzz, and the buzz tricks us into thinking we're on the right track.

When we're addicted to our story, we need constant updates to stay informed on how we're doing, so we tune in continuously to the news of ourselves: "What just happened? How does that affect me? Whose fault is that? What are they saying about me? How are they treating me? How am I doing? How do I look? What's going to happen to me? Have I eaten right, slept well, worked out, done my chores, called my mom, paid the bills, answered emails, said my prayers?"

And these updates let me know how I am allowed to feel. This is the mood-setting algorithm. I run all the data through the screen of my story—and I adjust my mood to align with how I did today, and how it looks like I'm going to do tomorrow.

The Tom News Channel is on in my head twenty-four hours a day. And I don't just watch. I am the anchorperson, the reporter, the viewer, the sponsor, and the subject of the news—all in one! I set the scene, report the story, watch the story, and I react to the story by coming back for more story. It's my job to report the news, so I must *follow* the news, which means I have to keep checking and checking and checking—the day, the time, the weather, my weight, the number of steps I've walked. Because I need to know how I'm doing in achieving my story of myself.

If we could see a transcript of our thoughts, we would easily see how addicted we are to our story and all that affects it. It drives everything. For everyone. And while we tend to miss how much joy and peace and freedom it costs us to live this way, we *also* miss how much suffering the self-image addiction causes for society.

The most powerful people in the world are often desperate self-image addicts. They are deeply addicted to a glorious story of themselves, and they work aggressively to shape the world to support their story, often with no concern for the people injured in their drama. This can lead to "success" for the addicts, but when there is no limit to what they will do to achieve their story, it opens the door to evil.

In the lead-up to World War II, when the president of Czecho-slovakia signed a communiqué allowing German troops to occupy his country, Hitler "could hardly contain himself," according to historian Alan Bullock. "He burst into his secretaries' room and invited them to kiss him. 'Children,' he declared, 'this is the greatest day of my life. I shall go down to history as the greatest German.'"

The scale of Hitler's sickness was historic, but the pattern is universal.

ESCAPING ADDICTION

The way out of addiction is not just to stop doing the things we're doing that could kill us—although that's a first step. It's not even to find connection, although that can soothe us and take some of the intensity out of our addictive urge. The deepest way out of addiction is to ease our addiction to the story we think we have to live. This is spiritual work.

In 1961, Bill W., a cofounder of Alcoholics Anonymous, wrote a letter to Carl Jung to tell him that a conversation Jung had had with an alcoholic patient of his became "the first link in the chain of events that led to the founding of Alcoholics Anonymous."

Years before, in the 1930s, Jung had told his patient, Roland H., that there was no medical or psychiatric treatment for his alcoholism. When the patient asked whether there was anything outside medicine or psychiatry that could help, Jung said there might be help in the form of a spiritual experience, but he cautioned that such experiences are rare.

Roland H. then left the care of Dr. Jung, found the company of people who practiced prayer and meditation, and had a spiritual experience that allowed him to stop drinking. Roland H. then shared his experience with others, including Bill W., who was also suffering from alcoholism, and that led to the founding of the AA fellowship.

In his letter to Jung, Bill W. said that William James's book *The Varieties of Religious Experience* gave him the realization that most conversion experiences "have a common denominator of ego collapse at depth."

Jung wrote back warmly, confirmed his conversations with Roland H., and then noted that he had not said to his patient all he thought at the time because "I had to be exceedingly careful of what I said. I had found out I was misunderstood in every possible way." Jung wrote that Roland H.'s "craving for alcohol was the equivalent, on a low level, of the spiritual thirst of our being for wholeness, expressed in medieval language: the union with God."

That goal of wholeness, Jung wrote, can be reached "by an act of grace or through a personal and honest contact with friends or through a higher education of the mind beyond the confines of mere rationalism."

In my view, Jung and Bill W. seem to be equating four concepts: religious experience, ego collapse, union with God, and overcoming addiction. These four concepts are to me synonymous with a fifth concept: overcoming the self-image.

My brother Matt began moving toward wholeness, finding the courage to delete the lies in his self-image before he died. My friend John moved toward wholeness in prison, owning and sharing openly the darkest truths about his life.

If we can give up the self-image and embrace everything our story keeps out, addiction can be the breakdown that leads to breakthrough. Or we can keep posing as someone we're not, soothe ourselves with addictive tricks, and likely find that illness comes next.

CHAPTER SIX

Illness

When I was eight years old, my mom was taken to the hospital. It was her first attack of ulcerative colitis, and we kids were scared. But my dad and my aunt Jane—who was not my real aunt but my mom's best friend and my best friend's mom and my godmother and the sweetest soul I ever knew—told me that Mom would be fine.

Then Grandma came over and yelled at us for being bad and causing work for Mom and making her sick. When Mom came home a few days later, I went to her and said, "Mom, Grandma said we were bad kids and made you sick."

She burst into a long peal of laughter, pulled me close, said that we were great kids, that we didn't make her sick, and she was going to be fine. I was comforted by her words, but even more by her laughter. Nothing signals the message "Everything's going to be all right" more than a mother's mirthful laugh. Luckily, for me, the memory of that laughter stayed in my head until I was old enough to look back and figure out what was so funny.

It's Grandma. The Grandma I introduced to you in the last chapter. Mom and Grandma were different souls. My mom once told Aunt Jane, "I don't tell the boys not to stomp in puddles, because I want to be obeyed." Grandma wanted to be obeyed, too, but she didn't customize her instructions. Once, after causing tension again in one of the parish committees at Saint Francis Xavier Church, Grandma heard about it from our pastor Monsignor O'Brien. "But I have to be myself, don't I?" she asked. "Yes, Helen," the pastor replied. "But do you have to be all of yourself, all of the time?"

Yes. Yes, she did.

One morning before 8:00 a.m., Aunt Jane got a call from Grandma. "Jane," she said, "do you know where Alana is? *I cannot reach her!*" Jane, thinking that Grandma would be impressed, explained that my mom was at the Stone Avenue train station raising money for charity from morning commuters. Grandma was irate, saying that my mom had recently had a cold, owed her family her first priority, and had no business being out raising money on this cold, rainy day.

Years after Grandma died, my mom explained, "My mother called me every morning, asked me what I was doing that day, and criticized my list." And at least once in a while, if Mom didn't pick up the phone, Grandma called Aunt Jane—and Mom momentarily became the sister Jane never wanted to have.

A few years after Mom first got sick, when her health had stabilized, my dad, who was an attorney at Amoco, was offered a position in Iran that would run for three years. My mom's health was a sticking point. How would her ulcerative colitis respond to the stress of the move, the new culture, the new doctors? She decided it was worth the risk to make the move, and it turned out that her colitis went into remission during the years we were there. When I later asked her the reasons for the remission, she said, "I was seven thousand miles away from my mother."

Despite how it may sound, we all loved Grandma madly. She was a big mama bear protecting and policing her brood. It was lonely for her when we were in Iran. People in town would see her, and she'd say, "I hope I make it till they get back." When the family arrived home after our three-year stay, she fell immediately ill. I had stayed behind in Europe for the summer, and I called her and said, "I can't wait to see you, Grandma," and she answered, "It's great to hear your voice, Tom." She died a few weeks later. My mom gave me the choice of staying where I was for the rest of the summer or coming home for the funeral. I came home.

GETTING SICK

Defending a self-image can wear you down and make you sick. Or as psychologist Rheeda Walker writes, "Keeping up personas can send you to an early grave." Mom was a perfectionist, and some people offered her rewards for playing that role. In the early part of her life, she took the bait. In the early part of *my* life, so did I. My body held up longer than my mom's did, and I had a different illness, but in the end, I broke down physically too.

For eight years after I left the White House, I worked at West Wing Writers, writing speeches and doing strategy for a range of clients. One of the challenges of serving those clients was that none of them knew or cared what other projects I had. It wasn't their job to keep me from doing three urgent, high-intensity deadline projects all at once. That was my job—and I didn't protect myself.

Starting the business was stressful, but I was still in my forties, and I didn't get sick or have any worrisome symptoms or feel at all that I was breaking down. I just felt superanxious about delivering excellence on deadline over and over again.

When I approached my fiftieth birthday, though, things started to change. I got overwhelmed with the administrative aspect of the work at West Wing, so I left the firm I had cofounded and went solo, working from home, a move that a close confidant warned me was a blunder, and I immediately and massively missed the company of my partners, who were also my closest friends.

In the two years after I left the firm, my mom died of cancer, my best friend moved away, my top client scaled back our work, and my dog, Walter, who kept me company sitting on the couch during my long hours of writing, died at age four. I was living a stressful, isolated life and eventually woke up one morning with an explosive outbreak of anxiety, depression, brain fog, and memory issues, which sent me on a long, weird medical odyssey that eight years later would lead me to my breakthrough.

Two days before the outbreak, I had a tooth drilled down to make a crown, which I did without Novocain because I wanted to be tough, and I got a scratched cornea and went to the emergency room at midnight because I thought it was something worse. They put dye in my eye, followed by an anesthetic, followed by an antibiotic, then I went home and woke up three hours later in a terrifying fog. Later that day, I was driving on a road and thought, "How did I get here?" The next day I reached into the cupboard and pulled out a sealed dish with leftover vegetables that should have been in the fridge. Then I went to the doctor.

TESTS AND TREATMENTS

I first went to see my no-nonsense, longtime doctor, who said, "I don't see anything wrong with you." She didn't dispute the symptoms; she just didn't know what would explain them. So, she sent me to a neurologist.

The neurologist ordered an EEG, an EMG, a sleep study, standard lab tests, Lyme tests, mercury and toxic-metals tests, a brain MRI, a spine MRI, and a neuropsych exam.

The tests said I had moderate obstructive sleep apnea, so I got on a CPAP device. My EEG came back abnormal with a "slowing of the temporal lobes." My EMG came back with polyneuropathy. Lyme was negative; same with the heavy-metals test. (Though specialists in Lyme and heavy metals often respond to a negative test by criticizing the test; over the course of eight years, doctors continually wanted to treat me for Lyme and heavy metals.)

The neuropsych results scared me the most. My evaluation involved a battery of quizzes and tasks done with a psychologist. When I got the results, I read that my prose recall was "average."

My performance on a verbal task demonstrated "average learning."

My auditory sequencing was "average." (I don't know what "auditory sequencing" is, but I know what "average" is, and it is not good.)

Divided attention and working memory ranged from "low average to average." Visual attention and processing speed were "mildly impaired."

Then this: "Mr. Rosshirt should remain active by participating in activities and hobbies that he enjoys for cognitive stimulation."

How old do they think I am?!

The report to my doctor concluded, "Thank you for referring this interesting patient."

Where is my mother when I need her?

I could describe the next eight years as an effort to get well. But from another angle, I was on a quest to calm down. My memory trouble, and the anxiety and depression that either caused it or were caused by it, posed a terrifying assault on my story of who I was. My plan was to return myself to the peak of my powers. That, I told myself, would make me feel better.

MY NOBLE EIGHT-YEAR PATH

The conventional doctors couldn't do anything for my cluster of mysterious symptoms. I needed exotic doctors. And I found them. When I entered the office of my first psychiatrist, there was barely room for my self-image, given the space that *his* required. I was paying him $425 for fifty minutes of his time, and I paid $5,000 on the first visit for the initial tests he recommended. I learned later that his tests didn't lead to diagnoses; they led to test *results*. And the test results didn't lead to treatments; they led to supplements, which the doctor was able to supply me at a good price, for him.

At the close of one of my visits, he said, "Your mercury levels are off the charts," then tossed me the charts. As I looked them over, I saw that all the other heavy metals I was tested for showed short lines. For mercury, I saw an ominous red line that extended all the way across the page. And we all know what *that* means!

Actually, nobody knows what that means. But I had learned in my reading that mercury could cause memory loss, dementia, neurodegenerative diseases, and other forms of hopelessness. As I was reading the chart, the doctor walked around to my side of the desk, turned on a nearby monitor, and started to show me a video of mercury killing brain cells.

I didn't have the presence to say, "Um, Doctor, you know I came here for anxiety, right?"

(And I definitely didn't have the presence to say: "Whose brain is that?!")

At the start of our next session, I asked him, "How many patients have you had with those mercury levels? What were their symptoms? How did you treat them? Did it reduce the mercury? Did their symptoms improve?"

As he was answering, I pointed out a contradiction, and he physically jumped—his body shook, and his voice took on an edge as he explained away the contradiction. You can tell when people have a monster self-image: they physically twitch when challenged.

There is a dogmatism that can take hold in the mind of a man with a theory—especially if he has staked his extravagant self-image on it, which this guy had. We all want to be special, and his medical practice was his bid to be *very* special: he believed he could find things other doctors could not find and heal patients other doctors could not heal. He got irritated with me if I stopped taking some of the supplements or if I reported I wasn't getting better. He didn't really care about *me*; he cared about proving his theory, which would affirm his self-image. It took me a while to figure this out, but when I did, I moved on.

THE PATTERN

That doctor was just the start of a complicated, confusing, entangling approach to health care that became my life for eight years. Once I got in, it was hard to get out, and there were three ingredients that made it so sticky: a sense of alarm; a theory of illness; and a totalitarian health regime.

The process starts with alarm. No one goes for this kind of care unless they're scared. I was scared because I felt my brain was slipping, and I was terrified of dementia. The fear increased my chances of interpreting my symptoms in the most alarming way. And many of the health professionals I dealt with were skillful at sustaining my alarm.

Genetic testing was especially good for this. I was told after tests that I have genes that increase the chance of having Alzheimer's, make me susceptible to biotoxin illness, make it hard for me to detox, and make me more prone to burnout. Hearing these results was like hearing someone say, "I have no cure for you, but here's some helpful information."

One of the clinics where I spent thousands of dollars sent me the following promotional email: "Alarming new research shows that having Lyme Disease increases the risk not only for mental health issues but also for suicide attempts, indicating that Lyme can have life or death consequences."

When a doctor puts a scary thought in your head, it's hard to get it out.

Years ago, when my son Nick was about six, he was reading *The Big Books of Facts* and suddenly looked scared and put the book down. I scooped him onto my lap and asked him what was wrong, and he said, "I don't like that book. It says that if my liver stops working, I'll be dead in twenty-four hours."

Nick had the sense to put the scary book down. I kept reading.

I read stacks of books on health threats, and there is a formula to these books. The opening chapters highlight a health issue, which the author declares is even more horrific than people think. They explain that we've underestimated the threat and if we don't wake up and change our ways, we're all going to die of cancer, get a heart attack, suffer a stroke, or get dementia. Then they lay out their plan of healing, with the message, "Do as I say, or you'll be sorry."

I can trace the beginning of my journey in part to one book that recommended a very specific diet. The author said that if you don't feel totally great on this diet, it could be because you've got heavy-metal exposure, a yeast overgrowth, food sensitivities, a mold allergy, or a hidden infection—and you should start exploring all of those. I did not feel totally great on that diet, so I thought, "Well, which one could it be? I better hop on the symptom checker and figure it all out—I have a lot of work to do!"

I hoped to soothe my alarm at first just by trying to find out what was wrong with me, and it took me years even to get a name. When I first read on a website a list of symptoms that matched mine, I found it reassuring. "Wow, other people have this too!" That was a relief. The label that I saw most often applied to my set of symptoms was "CIRS"—or chronic inflammatory response syndrome. Here's a typical description I found on the web: "Chronic Inflammatory Response Syndrome (CIRS) is a progressive, multisystem, multisymptom illness characterized by exposure to biotoxins. The ongoing inflammation can affect virtually any organ system of the body and if left untreated becomes debilitating".

When caregivers could name and wrap a theory around my symptoms, it generated some trust from me, and I began opening my heart to their totalitarian health regime.

Looking back, I can see that I was telling myself a terrifying story about my symptoms, what they meant, and what would happen to me if I didn't do something dramatic. I was the one who was telling myself the story, but I was often just repeating to myself what I was told by the doctors.

I ended up visiting as many as thirty different health professionals, but the nature of the journey can be captured by two that I saw toward the end—an MD and a psychiatrist.

The MD was a specialist in biotoxin illness. She looked at the brain MRI she had ordered and said: "You are smart to have come. Mold was causing you cognitive decline. And I think that eventually you would have developed Alzheimer's."

She handed me a forty-page booklet that detailed an anti-inflammatory, low-glycemic, gluten-free, low-grain, high-quality fat approach to eating that is designed for neurodegenerative diseases.

She ordered MMP-9, TGF-b1, MSH, cortisol, and MARCoNS tests just to get us started. Then she recommended one supplement after another.

"I see you're on zinc glycinate," she said. "I like zinc picolinate . . . Let's put you on some things like curcumin . . . and when you're in the sauna and you're sweating profusely, I want you to take something called GI Detox. . . . I will probably bump up your glutathione. Selenium—I think you would benefit from taking some selenium. Are you on ubiquinol . . . CoQ10? Resveratrol? All of this is going to help your mitochondria and your brain, okay?"

"Okay!" I said.

Then she recommended I move out of my house. "Go live as a minimalist," she said, "so you don't have a lot of clutter so you're not collecting dust and more mycotoxins, and keep it unbelievably clean. You don't allow anyone to wear shoes in there. While you're healing, you get your house worked on."

I told her that it would be months before I could move out and that I was not able to stay out of my basement. "You're really playing with fire when you do that," she warned me. "There's a suit you can put on. Do you have a suit? It's a white zippered suit. . . . This stuff follows you, and you have to be really smart and really careful with what you expose yourself to."

"We want to turn the switch off in you," she said, "and it's going to take time. Right now, you're responding to everything, including chemicals and all kinds of things."

Five months later, I moved out of my house and into an apartment that impressed me with this boast: "To improve indoor environmental quality, we have used materials with very low potential to emit Volatile Organic Compounds (VOC) reducing the chance of negative health effects such as headaches and allergies."

A month after I moved into the apartment, I went to a clinic, did a new series of brain scans, and talked them over with a psychiatrist. (This was not the psychiatrist who was happy she couldn't see me in person or the psychiatrist who showed me the video of mercury killing brain cells—but a third psychiatrist.)

"Your brain is not a train wreck," he said, after reviewing my scans.

(He's a *psychiatrist*! Doesn't he know my brain hears only, "Your brain . . . train wreck.")

"But it's not looking healthy either. Something has reduced activity in the very front of the brain. We use the word *injury*. Injury can mean you hit your head, had a whiplash event, or you can get injury from toxic exposure, infections like Lyme."

He went over the parts of my brain that were underactive and the parts that were overactive—including the thalamus, the basal ganglia, and the limbic system.

He then said, "If you were a typical government worker with this array of scan pictures, I'd support disability because it's not looking that healthy."

Then he suggested supplements, diet changes, and Adderall for attention deficit disorder. I pushed back on the Adderall because of a bad experience, and he said: "Sometimes, more than I'd like to admit, people don't do well on a stimulant, because they may have too much limbic-system activity, and it's a little bit like throwing gasoline on a fire."

At the end of our session, I asked him, "Do you have any idea why I'm writing the best stuff of my life with that brain?"

"Honestly, I don't," he said, "other than, I'm thinking more of spiritual issues. This may be an inflection point for you. You wouldn't naturally welcome this, but we can grow out of bad things, or maybe that's the only way to grow. I wish I could give you clear answers. I can't. I think it's best to be honest and say, 'You know, we just don't know.'"

I hadn't asked my question out of innocent curiosity. I was pretending to be a mature person taking in bad news with a light heart, but I was angry. I had been coping by clinging to the story that I was sick but would get well. He told a story that I was sicker than I thought and might *never* get well. So, I highlighted a fact that his story couldn't explain. I was fishing for the answer I got, and it was soothing—he had no idea.

I was also pointing to the only part of my story that was going well—my writing. Why did *I* think I was writing the best stuff of my life? I think that the parts of my brain that flow with insights and phrases were unimpaired, were maybe even improving. But if I could still write, then why was I scared? Because whatever it was that was giving me brain fog and short-term memory gaps could take the rest of my brain too. With all the writing I was doing for clients at work, I still had time to write horror stories for myself on the side.

SELF-IMAGE AND ILLNESS

As I was seeing doctor after doctor and trying one regime after another, the features of my self-image that made me ill were shaping the ways I tried to get well. My attitude was "I'm going to figure it all out. I'm going to master this. I'm going to figure out exactly what to do. And after I find the answer, I'm going to share it with the world, be a hero, and live belovedly ever after."

I applied perfectionism and extremism to getting well when perfectionism and extremism were factors in making me ill.

I was obsessive about symptoms, and I fell into a habit of trying to trace every dark feeling, bad mood, or anxious thought to some exposure, something I ate, some new food I couldn't tolerate. I wanted to find the source of every scary sensation and then change my habits to avoid the source so I would never have to feel that again.

This is laughably ironic because I had spent thirty-five years practicing a meditation whose emphasis was "perfect equanimity with every sensation." I had no equanimity with *any* sensation. My approach became avoidance, and with every change I made, I told my family, "*This* will fix it." Then, "This will *really* fix it." And every change I made was more disruptive to my family until I was moving out of my house.

Yoni Ashar, a neuroscience researcher at Weill Cornell Medical College, says, "When our brains are on high alert, we interpret our surroundings through a lens of danger." My brain was on high alert, and I saw danger everywhere. Fear ran my whole healing regime. I would *never* have done all that crap unless I was afraid. And because I believed that the regime was the only thing that could save me, when I slipped up on the regime, I was terrified. Fear was the driver, and fear was the result. When the biotoxin MD told me, "You're playing with fire," she was playing with fear, and it's easier to put out a fire than it is to turn off fear.

WHY DID I STICK WITH THESE DOCTORS?

As I accelerated my use of supplements and saunas, did my diet and detox regimes, deployed my air purifiers, and limited the places I would go, people close to me would look on helplessly and say or convey: "You're nuts. You can't just keep making your life smaller and smaller."

I'd justify it by saying, "Here's what I think I have . . . No, *here's* what I think I have," until one friend cut me off by saying, "We'll know what you have when what you do gets you well."

My critics weren't wrong, but they weren't totally right either—because I did all I could with what I knew. Yes, it would have been good to give up avoidance and go live a normal life, but I couldn't go live "normal" because the anxiety would have blown my head off. It's not even right to call it anxiety—it's the system going nuts. So, I did the things I did because I felt I had no choice. I didn't know of any doctors with a better record of healing people like me, and I did the more questionable things because my critical faculties were diminished by anxiety, and my analysis was contaminated by hope.

All the while, I knew my family life and marriage were at risk. One naturopath, a divorced young woman with a five-year-old daughter, was candid with me about the risks of the illness, saying, "I have what you have, and it's hard to stay married." I did enough research into my conditions to learn that people who shared my symptoms often fit a bleak profile: They lose their homes, their businesses, and their families because they can't find a place to stay where they feel okay. They try dozens of doctors and spend thousands of dollars, and they still end up sick and alone.

Moving out was supposed to be a short-term fix for me. But it was no longer short, and I wasn't getting fixed. I did drive back to my house several times a week to see everyone. I kept paying the bills and took care of some family chores. We went on vacation together, to basketball games and school events. Everyone was patient and supportive, but I was testing their trust, in part because everyone was living in the same house I was, and I was the only one with symptoms. My son Ben—perhaps saying what everyone else was thinking—told me, "Dad, the things you're doing to deal with your health problems gives off the vibe that they don't exist."

Toward the end, the isolation was grinding me down. In the fifteen months I had lived alone in that apartment, I was paid two visits—the first from a friend who told me how to fix up the place, which I never did, and the second from my kids who stopped in for thirty minutes before we headed to a basketball game. I never once saw any of my neighbors who lived near me in the building, except for the time the lock failed on my door and I sat in the hallway waiting for the locksmith to let me in. The single woman who lived next door came home while I was waiting, and we talked for a while. The next day I found a plate of cookies and a note from her outside my door. Yikes. I wrote a note in response explaining my situation, slipped it under her door, and never saw her again.

I spent my days writing, walking to get groceries, or eating a salad from across the street. I made my way by focusing on little moments of peace or progress, creating some story around them, and not pondering where I was headed. It wasn't a crisis for me yet, so long as I could still see some way to make my story turn out okay. And I was definitely still trying to get the story I wanted, still fully invested in the self-image model of happiness—believing that the only way out, up, or through was to fulfill my story. I didn't have the tools or the skill to edit my story or give up the story altogether.

I did what I could do, which was to go to the doctors who were treating people with my symptoms and move on when I didn't get well. And I chose my doctors according to their books or their websites. Through the entire eight years, until the very end, I didn't go to a single health practitioner because someone told me, "Go see her; she got me well."

As I headed toward crisis, I began to get rebellious. I resented the lack of freedom, the need for a nondairy this, a zero-carb that, and a gluten-free whatever. I was always nursing the hope that I would find the magical cure—the one simple thing that would make me Superman, able to endure all the emotional, dietary, environmental triggers and live happily immune from the irritations of life. It may be a new tea, a supplement, a special technique. One week it was vitamin D. A doctor told me I had very low vitamin D, and he gave me a prescription of a special batch from a certain pharmacist. I felt great the first few days I was on it. "That's all it was—low vitamin D. No one told me! This is the end of suffering." A few days later, the high wore off, and I was back where I was.

At another point, I thought: "I've found it! It's long, slow breathing." This is especially funny because I had done a ton of long, slow breathing before, and it hadn't changed me. But now I read it in a book, and I was convinced this new *special* way of long, slow breathing was the breakthrough I was looking for. I wrote in a health log, "Yesterday, I felt incredibly happy after only my second day of long, slow breathing!"

I wrote to a friend: "I think this is the magical cure." Two days later, after a burst of painful symptoms, I wrote: "Okay, it's not a magical cure; it's a valuable tool." Two days after that, following a burst of joyful feelings, I wrote: "Wait! I take it back. It *is* a magical cure; it's just not an instant magical cure." Two days after that, I was on to something else.

Still, I clung to the regime. If I wandered off and got a burst of symptoms, I raced back to the regime like a child goes to his mother, looking for something soothing—until, finally, I did reach that moment when a woman said to me, "Go see her; she got me well."

This is the woman I mentioned in the first chapter, who invited me to join a group and told me about Annie Hopper. Six months after I talked to her and took her advice, I cleared eighty-one bottles of supplements out of my cupboard, dropped them into grocery bags, threw them down the trash chute, and moved back home to play with fire.

THE SELF-IMAGE HELL OF ILLNESS

I had some damage to undo. Just as my self-image had contributed to my illness, my illness had shaped my self-image, and not in a great way.

When I was a senior in college, I went to New Orleans at the end of the year to watch the Sugar Bowl, the New Year's Day football game between the number-one ranked University of Georgia's Bulldogs and my Fighting Irish. Lots of my classmates were there, and I had driven over from Houston with my dad and brothers. On New Year's Eve, before the clock struck midnight, I was strolling down Bourbon Street with some friends, in a large crowd, when I saw just ahead my old girlfriend holding hands with her new boyfriend. I darted outside the stream of people and walked at high speed back to the hotel, where I entered my room, walked into the bathroom, stared into the mirror, and growled, "I *hate* myself!"

What was it, exactly, that I hated? I hated that I couldn't hang out where I was, run into my old girlfriend, say hi, move on, and enjoy the night. I hated that I ran away. I hated that I was weak.

Brené Brown, in her second TED Talk, said, "Shame feels the same for men and women, but it's organized by gender. . . . For women, shame is, 'Do it all, do it perfectly, and never let them see you sweat.' . . . Shame, for women, is this web of unobtainable, conflicting, competing expectations about who we're supposed to be. . . .

"For men, shame is not a bunch of competing, conflicting expectations. Shame is one. Do not be perceived as what? Weak."

Shame is the other side of the self-image, and weak is the other side of tough. I wanted to be tough. I've always wanted to be tough. Sadly, I wasn't well-built for it. One memory that captures this for me: I was skiing in college with a friend who did everything just on the verge of out of control. As we skied off the lift, he said, "Follow me. I know a great jump!" I skied after him, screaming into the wind: "How big *is* the jump?!"

The same story played out in numerous ways. I went to the rodeo near Austin with my brother and my sister-in-law, Sharon, whose family is fifth-generation Texan. I was loving the rodeo, but I started wheezing, sneezing, and sniffling from the horses and the hay. I made a self-deprecating joke to Sharon, contrasting myself with the men riding bulls and roping calves, and she said, consolingly, "But you're tough in other ways." I said, "No, I'm not. May I have another tissue, please?"

By the time I had developed all my symptoms, I was the opposite of tough. I was sensitive and fussy. I couldn't eat a bunch of foods. I needed air purifiers. I needed supplements. I couldn't go in certain places. I was anxious and depressed, which took away my sense of fun and adventure. All these things made me feel weak and all the things that go with weak: "I'm a loser. I'm a failure. I can't do anything. I'm never any fun." But that was not "me," I told myself.

"That's just because I'm sick." And that story was the beginning of trouble. For me to prove I was tough and not weak, I had to prove I was sick and not well.

These can be important questions around illness or injury: How do I respond when I can't do the things I used to do? What story do I tell?

The point of our self-image is to give us a buzz and protect us from shame. If the positive self-image isn't working, if it isn't credible, if people don't buy the story and tell it back to us, then its buzz is gone, and we have to seek a new story. That's where I got into trouble.

To hold on to the self-image of being tough, I had to cultivate a story of how bad things were, how difficult my life was, how much I was enduring, and how tough I was in dealing with all of it. That became my story. I organized my physical life around it and my emotional life too. There were a few people who were loving and crazy enough to listen to my whole story. I had a very long version that I told a few people. I once wrote a ten-thousand-word email to a friend. I became addicted to the things that gave me relief, and one of those things was my story of how hard my life was and how hard I was working to get better. I was just trying to hold on to some precious elements of my self-image. In healthier times, I would be telling a story that empowered me (even if a lot of it was made-up). Now I was telling a story that weakened me.

There were three types of passages in my journal entries of those days: (1) boring passages with details of my treatment and hopeful signs of progress; (2) angry passages about people I was blaming for giving me bad advice or mocking my story; and (3) a very few passages where I made fun of myself, showing that there was still a creative human being underneath the hum and drone of my dreary life.

I saw that if I tried to use "being sick" to get anything—sympathy, praise, accommodations, considerations—then the sickness became useful, and thus harder to give up. I'm not saying that people have a choice to give up being sick, but they have a choice to not make it into a story.

My story's *purpose* was innocent enough; I just wanted to be validated. "Wow, you're going through hell. Who could *do* that? You must be so *strong*." That's the little buzz I craved. But my illness was so weird and my story so strange that I told few people, and I mostly had to give the buzz to myself—collecting evidence and building the case to persuade myself I was both sick and tough.

I agreed with everyone who said: "Stop thinking of yourself as a sick person. Don't focus your life on being sick." But for me to do that, I had to be able to do all the things I used to do, in the places I used to do them, or accept the limitations without creating a story that weakened me. I couldn't do that because I didn't know how. I needed a path. An approach. A practice. A teacher. And I didn't have one.

So, I continued to cling to the story that soothed me. But as my story turned me into a victim, pushed me to blame others, addicted me to sympathy, and depended on a happy ending that wasn't happening, it lost its power to make me feel safe or protect me from shame—and left me with no new story that did.

That was the crisis, and the crisis was the way out.

CHAPTER SEVEN

Crisis

E arly on a Sunday morning in the winter of 2002, after taking Nick and Ben to breakfast at the American City Diner in Northwest Washington, DC, I drove them a few blocks to a park where we threw a ball and played on the swings. After about an hour, we headed back to the car. I had just stuffed Nick and Ben and their fat coats into their car seats when Nick started crying—he had forgot his ball.

"Man!" I thought. "Do I have to get them both out their car seats to go back and look for the ball?!"

"No," I decided, and I locked the car with the kids inside and walked back into the park, which was only twenty paces away but was around a tall hedge that blocked my view of the boys.

After a fruitless two-minute search, I headed back, and as soon as I turned onto the sidewalk, I saw a woman in her midthirties standing a few feet from the car with her hands on her hips, glaring at me with disgust.

I took the bait.

"Don't look at me like that!" I sneered at her. "I was gone two minutes to look for a ball."

She feasted on me.

"You leave two little kids alone in a car?!"

"Oh, shut up; they were never in any danger."

"What kind of father leaves his kids alone in a car?"

She turned to walk away as I got in the car and started driving home. As I passed her, I leaned out the window and said, "I appreciate your noble concern, but nobody needs you."

She answered, "Next time I'm calling the *police!*"

In these kinds of spats, the winner is the one who makes the other person feel more wounded, and she won in a knockout.

For years, I often found myself back in that memory, battling her in my head, trying to find just the right line to humiliate her. I was so consumed by that scene in those days that if I'd been dying of cancer and the kids came to my deathbed and said, "You were such a great dad," I'd have said, "*Tell that to the lady in the park!*"

Why did that scene obsess me? My self-image of being a great dad is very dear to me, at the center of my story of myself, inseparable to me from being a good person. And I had a soft but painful voice in my head constantly murmuring to me that maybe it wasn't true. Maybe I'm not such a great dad. Maybe I don't know enough about raising kids. Maybe I'm a little lazy, a little negligent. Maybe I serve myself first in all kinds of ways. Maybe my kids deserve a better dad.

That voice is so painful that I try to drown it out with my upbeat story: "I'm a great dad." But then I ran into a woman who formed an alliance with my inner accuser. My response was so strong that maybe it wasn't just about that moment with the kids in the car—maybe it was about the whole big picture of my imperfections as a parent and as a person.

There was no chance I could see or say any of this then. Even if I could have seen it, I couldn't drop the mask that protects me from people trying to hurt me when I'm facing a person trying to hurt me. So, I held on to the self-image of being a great parent. Then, some years later, I had a parenting crisis that forced me to give up some of that self-image, and the parenting crisis was a precursor to a larger crisis, which forced me to give up more.

PARENTING—A SETUP FOR CRISIS

When we use the word *crisis*, we're saying something's got to change. We can't take it anymore. If we're reading about a crisis in the history books, it's policies or leaders or events that must change. But in this book, a "crisis" means one of two things has to change—either we give up parts of our self-image or we double down to try to save it. If we can give up some of the self-image, that's a breakthrough. If we can't give it up, we return to the hell of defending our false story and try again later.

My parenting crisis, which I'll tell you about in a minute, was similar in content and structure to my crisis in life and health, which I return to at the close of this chapter. The parenting crisis was a challenge to *part* of my self-image. The health crisis was a challenge to all of it—or almost everything I believed about myself. The structure of a crisis is always the same though, and we can see it in many lesser crises that are simmering simultaneously in our lives. It helps us to see the lesser crises, where one aspect of the self-image is threatened, because it prepares us to recognize the bigger crisis when it comes.

Many of us are parents, and all of us have been children, and so we've likely all been caught up in a parenting crisis at some point. Parenting, by its very nature, is ripe for crisis.

First, anytime we hold fast to a self-image, we court a crisis, and most parents hold tightly to their self-image as a good parent. Second, when I am acting alone, I have to watch myself so I don't do anything that exposes my shadow. But when I'm a dad, I have to watch my kids to make sure *they* don't do anything that exposes my shadow. Controlling my kids to protect my self-image amounts to full-time police work, unless—*unless*—I can transmit my shadow to them. Then I have them under remote control.

This pattern is diabolical, natural, and universal. It perpetuates culture and stigma, as well as shame. It's driven by the need for belonging and the fear of exclusion. What our elders found unacceptable in themselves—because they believed it would get them shamed—they taught us to find unacceptable in ourselves. And we do the same to our kids—and for the best reasons. We don't want our kids to be excluded. And *we* don't want to be excluded. "What kind of parent would let their kid act that way?!"

My two boys have very different temperaments. When Ben was about six, he came running to me full of excitement with a question: "Dad, dad, dad," he said. "Here is my head, and here is my chest, but where is *me*?" Several years later, when the boys were about thirteen and ten, they were arguing with each other, and I asked Nick, "Are you two going to keep fighting even after your mother and I are dead?" He said, "That depends on what's in the will."

Despite their different personalities, they both rebelled in similar ways to my efforts to slap my shadow on them. I hadn't expected this. I inherited a lot of my dad's shadow and honored it faithfully. That's why we mostly got along. We hated the same signs of weakness in ourselves, and we worked hard to hide them. We had a pact not to embarrass each other—a shared shadow.

I expected the same deal with my kids. But I didn't even know it was a deal. I thought it was "the way things were." It would happen with a glance. My message to my boys was "I want you to make me proud and never embarrass me." Or, to use the remorseless phrase of an insightful friend: "I want you to look good on my résumé."

If my child doesn't accept my shadow, he *becomes* my shadow. If you don't hate what I hate, then I have to hide you. When we want our kids to make us proud and never embarrass us, we're going to be doing a lot of hiding—because there's a lot of lightness and darkness in all of us.

When Nick was about six years old, we were driving through a parking lot near the hardware store and saw a man in torn clothes holding a sign that said NEED A JOB. After we turned onto the street, Nick said, "I feel sad."

"Why do you feel sad, Nick?"

"I should have told him about Bob's Famous Ice Cream," he said.

Bob's was a local ice cream place that was run-down, losing customers, and about to close. It perpetually had a HELP WANTED sign hanging in the window. Nick's comment was touching to hear because Bob's Famous Ice Cream and the man with the sign were both down on their luck, and Nick's heart breaks for people who are down on their luck.

A few weeks later, Nick and I were walking out of church on a Sunday morning, and I was telling him about meditation. "It can help me get rid of my anger so I can be nice to you even if you're mean to me." And Nick said: "That'd be the life. I sock you in the stomach, and you give me an ice cream cone!"

This is who we are—light and dark together. Kindness and calculation in the same kid. Did I, as a dad, skillfully embrace both sides of Nick's personality to ease his conflicts and lighten his shadow? I did not. I tried to get him to express one side and suppress the other.

When people are far from us, we push the whole person to the margins. But when people are close to us, like our kids, we push just *parts* of them to the margins. That's how we signal to them that some of their qualities are unacceptable—and these are perhaps exactly those qualities we find unacceptable in ourselves. We tell ourselves we do it because we don't want our children to be excluded—and then we're the first people to exclude them. We pass our unwholeness on to them as a social necessity, as a virtue. But it's really to hide our shadow.

THE CRISIS AND RESPONSE

But our kids unsettle our shadow.

Things simmered in my house until, when Nick was thirteen, I got my parenting crisis. He was pretty rebellious in those days. The summer before, I had spent our beach vacation diagramming the book *Your Defiant Child*. Now, in eighth grade, he was skipping his homework, listening to music I couldn't bear, spending a lot of time online, and getting into trouble at school. A longtime administrator there had told me, "When students get in this much trouble this soon, they tend not to graduate from here." I'm not sure how much I was aware of it back then, but Nick was a lot like I was when I was an early teen.

One weekend, I sought parenting advice from a lifelong friend I had met in grade school who was always wise, kind, and candid. On our phone call, I complained to her about Nick's grades, the music he listened to, the things he looked at online. I expected sympathy from her. Instead, she let me complete my rant, paused for a moment, and said, "I don't know if he hates you yet, *but he will.*"

That line threw me into crisis. It was clear in an instant that my story was wrong. I didn't know what I was doing. I was not helping him thrive. I was ruining our relationship. Sometimes in a crisis, we don't know what to do. At other times, we know exactly what to do.

I got off his back. I dropped all criticism and disapproval. I tried to find something to like in everything he liked. I saw things that made me cringe and made peace with them. And if he ever said, "Hey, Dad, check this out," I came running. He wasn't easy to win over. We had a history. I said to him once, "Hey, Nick, we should go see *Invictus* when it comes out," and he gave me a suspicious look and said, "I'm not interested in bonding with you."

But I stuck to my plan. Meanwhile, and quite on his own, Nick had found a mentor at school. He won over some teachers and made some lasting friendships. All of this put him in a better mood, and he started to rally—getting better grades, doing more homework, staying out of trouble. His mentor, a teacher who had gone to the same school, said to him: "Nick, this place isn't going to change; you have to learn to navigate it." And he did.

As I watched this happen, I surrendered my idea that I could guide him well with strategic disapproval. And the positive trends forced me to consider that he might have a set of skills and an internal guidance system that would develop faster if I took a few steps back. Did my change have much to do with *his* change? I'm not sure, but it certainly made me happier and let me enjoy him more. And the change was prompted by a candid friend who wasn't afraid of puncturing my self-image as a good parent. I thanked her a half dozen times as Nick continued to rise, and again on the day Nick graduated from high school in defiance of the administrator's prediction. She always shrugged it off. But it meant everything to me.

Richard Rohr once wrote, "Suffering is the only thing strong enough to destabilize the imperial ego." Nothing could have forced me into crisis more quickly than the pain that my son might hate me. That was the one pain I couldn't bear. The only way I would have been able to manage it is if I were convinced that I was saving the child from terrible harm and hatred was the price. But that wasn't the case here. I was just putting my shadow on him.

Robert Johnson writes: "Probably the worst damage is done when parents lay their shadow on their children. . . . To give them a clean heritage, psychologically speaking, is the greatest legacy. And, incidentally, you will go far in your own development by taking your shadow back into your private psychological structure—where it first originated and where it is required for your own wholeness."

It took me a while before I felt I understood that advice. I believe Johnson is telling me to see the thing I dislike in my son and say nothing until I can seek and find the same thing in myself. Then *accept* it in myself. *Then* respond to my son, if it's still necessary. I think that's what Johnson means by telling us to take the shadow back into our structure, where it's required for our wholeness.

Of course, that's the opposite of what I did. In fact, if I had to give an analysis of the unconscious motives of my early parenting, I would say that I was trying to get my kids to be afraid of the same things I was afraid of, then they would avoid those things, and my fears wouldn't be triggered. Luckily, they weren't afraid of triggering me, so they did a good job raising me.

Ben taught me in the same way Nick had. We sent Ben to a small private high school his freshman year where they would have fewer kids and watch him more closely. He resisted it strongly. He made a point of not forming any friendships during his entire freshman year. He didn't want to put down any roots or do anything that would weaken his resolve to go to our large public high school the next year. Toward the end of freshman year, when it was time to commit for the following year, we made plans to reenroll him in the smaller school, and he erupted. It was clear the only choice was to let him go to public school, although I knew his academics would suffer.

After we agreed that he would change schools the next fall, I went to the public high school with him one morning in May to meet his new counselor and get his courses for sophomore year. The instant we entered the lobby, which was crowded with kids gathering before the opening bell, the noise and buzz filled Ben with energy. He loved the feel of the place. In the fall of the following year, when I first checked his grades online, I trembled as I looked for his math grade. The private school had held him back in math because of an entry test he had taken. I was worried about how he would do in a large class with less attention. His grade was a 98. He performed much better academically in public school than he had in private school, and he went on to study computer science in college. I had been completely wrong. But his grades weren't the only evidence of that.

That came in his junior year. I was standing in the backyard, behind a fence that shielded me from the sidewalk, as Ben was walking home from school. Unaware that he was being overheard, he told whoever he was talking to on the phone: "I thought I was happy last year. But that's *nothing* compared to how happy I am *this* year."

His mom and I mockingly congratulated ourselves for being such good parents. It was nothing but luck—and a strong-willed kid who knew what he wanted.

Parenting was a path to accepting my shadow. It wasn't anything courageous or insightful on my part. I was just being shaped by the natural forces of life. My stubborn commitment to my self-image triggered a crisis that I resolved by doing the thing that would ease my pain—dropping my insistence that I knew what was best. I realized my kids would hate me if I didn't relent, so I softened up and welcomed them, and welcomed (some of) my shadow. But I didn't do it freely. I was forced into it. I had to see that my self-image was false and my parenting was failing before I could welcome my shadow and love my kids.

My parenting crisis has an epilogue: After I completed a draft of this chapter, I asked Nick and Ben to look it over, with special attention to this section on parenting. Nick responded partly by text and partly in conversation over the next couple of days.

"You're a great dad, and it's a great book," he said. "But the way you wrote it makes it feel like we're not whole persons, just kids who presented challenges."

"But, Nick," I said. "If you had been meek, submissive, compliant kids who did everything I wanted, I never would have woken up."

"That's the issue," Nick said. "Our job wasn't to wake you up. We didn't live to make sure you fixed your issues. I'm grateful you did, but we're our own people, with our own purposes.

"Even the assertion that you made mistakes that, once fixed, allowed us to succeed is a little irritating. I understand it's the nature of this sort of memoir. This is a story about you, and it's not a story about us, right? But I just feel like we come off as something that you overcame."

This exchange startled me because it made a crucial point more powerfully than anything I had written. The moral of Nick's message is the lesson of this book: You can't know the whole truth of anything if you're looking through the lens of your own story.

I told him I was going to write another version that toned down some of my narcissism, and asked whether I could include his comments because he had made a key point of the book better than I could.

He winced, then said, "Okay."

A CRISIS OF THE WHOLE

At some point in our lives, events will not just challenge *part* of our self-image but throw our whole self into crisis. I became a witness to one dramatic example when I was a judge of the Cicero Speechwriting Awards, an annual competition launched years ago by David Murray, a godfather of the speechwriting field.

I've spent a lot of time trying to figure out why some speeches are awesome and most are not. But I never worked on the question with more intensity than during a week back in 2008, when I met with two colleagues in Washington, DC, and we sat by the Lincoln Memorial for two days, reviewed twenty-five speeches written over twenty-five centuries, and tried to answer the question, "What makes a speech great?"

The answer we came up with is—we don't know.

But we did conclude a few things: The speeches that outlasted their eras made powerful use of three elements: trust, argument, and request. And these three are interrelated. If trust is low, you'd better have a good argument. If you have a good argument, you can make a big request. And if you want to make a bigger request, it helps to have a lot of trust.

Of the three, the most important is trust. If trust is high enough, you can skip the argument and go straight to the request. Ponder that—trust can get you what you want without any argument. And if trust is really high, you can make a huge request.

That's more or less where my insight settled for six years until early 2014, when a friend of mine sent me the TED Talks of Brené Brown. At that point, I had never heard of Brené, but I was instantly astonished by her ability to compress years of social-science research into clear, succinct, pivotal insights. Here are three:

> Courage, the original definition of courage, is to tell the story
> of who you are with your whole heart.

The most accurate measure of courage is vulnerability—to let ourselves be seen.

Vulnerability is the birthplace of joy, creativity, belonging, love, innovation, and change.

As I pondered these truths, the idea jumped at me—*vulnerability is also the birthplace of trust*! And then I understood conceptually, in a way I could finally communicate, why one speech that was entered in the competition in 2013 was the runaway winner of the contest.

Speechwriter Sarah Gray submitted the talk, which she had written with army veteran Neil Colomac. Neil was with the 864th Engineer Battalion of the US Army in Afghanistan in 2007, when he suffered a traumatic brain injury from the explosions of two IEDs, spaced three weeks apart. The speech was Neil's story of his injury, crisis, and recovery.

After the second blast, Neil was medevaced to a Bagram hospital, where he had a grand mal seizure. One minute he was outside drinking a bottle of water, and the next minute, he was lying in the dirt. The doctor told Neil that seizures can be caused by traumatic brain injuries, and he sent Neil to Germany for more tests, then back to the United States to recuperate.

"I was expecting to heal and then come back to Afghanistan," Neil said in his speech. "My unit was short-staffed. They really did need me. I felt a personal responsibility for the operation and a bond with the other soldiers. I just wanted to heal as fast as I could and get back there to help."

It didn't work out that way.

"After about seven or eight months of doctor appointments, I heard the four words that broke my heart and changed my life forever. Not. Fit. For. Duty."

The words devastated him. And he was in denial. He thought about his exemplary service, his marksmanship, his award as Engineer Soldier of the Year. He hoped they would see his record, make an exception, and let him go back.

"I could still patch someone up," he said. "I can still carry a soldier away from danger."

"On the other hand, I understood . . ."

"You can't hold a gun if you have seizures."

"You can't drive a Humvee if you have seizures."

"You can't protect your fellow soldiers."

"In fact, you are a danger to them."

"You are: not fit for duty."

This is the core of a crisis—a wave of unbearable pain brought on by a shift in the way we see ourselves in the world. We swing from "I know what I'm doing" to "I don't know what I'm doing." From "I need to get back to the way things were" to "I'm never getting back." From "I can protect my fellow soldiers" to "I am a danger to them."

So, Neil looked for work as a civilian. But because of his seizure disorder, he couldn't drive, he couldn't use a chain saw or power tools, he couldn't walk on roofs or scaffolding. And he needed income immediately. He and his wife were having a new baby.

He sent out two hundred résumés, and he heard nothing for five months.

He and his wife cut down expenses. Started using credit cards to pay for essentials. Racked up huge debt. And he prayed every night, "Lord, please let me provide for my family."

Finally, tears of joy for a job at Sears—at minimum wage.

A start.

Then, he said, "What happened next is something I think was meant to be."

By chance, in processing a customer order, he met a man whose company operated the central issue facility at Fort Lewis in Washington State. He told Neil that his company hires people with disabilities, handed him his business card, and said, "Come in for an interview tomorrow."

Neil got a new job on the spot—processing and issuing parts received for the repair of military vehicles. Then he got a promotion, then another. He got a three-bedroom home near the base where he could walk to work. He and his wife paid off their credit cards. They added a third son to the family. They had the room and the income to invite another family member to come live with them.

Neil gave this talk and told his story to a group of vets in Washington, DC, who had been wounded in war, and got jobs from the same program to employ wounded warriors. Neil was asked to give a speech to pump the troops up before they talked to members of Congress to ask them to keep funding the program that employed them.

"We could just complain about how hard it was to get a job," Neil told the wounded vets, "how difficult it is to have a disability, how unfair life can be. But instead, we are making it easier for the next person who comes along."

This speech was the clear contest winner. It was the story of a man who had suffered a life-changing injury, could no longer do the things that formed the core of his self-regard, moved through the crisis with courage and humility, and then talked of his weakness to inspire strength. The power of the speech was in the vulnerability— letting down the mask and letting himself be seen at his weakest. It was the difference between showing the audience a polished self-image and showing people what's inside when the self-image fails.

It gave his talk the power of a private conversation and the feel of personal friendship. He did more than make me trust him; by the end of his talk, he had made me love him—and he did it by giving up the tricks and masks we use to get love.

AN OPENING TO INTIMACY

When we are willing to drop our self-image, admit our flaws, and confess what's failing, it leads not only to vulnerability and trust, it opens us to intimacy.

What is intimacy? I think it's what begins to unfold when you show a friend something you don't really want them to see or tell them something you don't really want them to know.

It sounds inspiring, but it's terrifying—because it threatens friendships. When we want to form a bond with someone, we tend to put forward an image of ourselves we think they'll like. But when we strive for intimacy, we're putting forward something we think they won't like—and we're hoping that they will like the courage it takes to reveal it more than they dislike what's revealed.

This openness puts us in a scary place. We reveal something that could end the friendship because it's the only way to *deepen* the friendship. And the fear of losing the friendship is justified. It may lead the other person to say, "You *what*?!" and then try to shame us.

When you admit your embarrassing desires, your selfish deeds, or your obsessive fears to someone who's not able to see the same in themselves, they may well turn on you and mock you for the truths you're admitting—and the relationship will be endangered because the reluctant partner will not let it go forward, and the bold partner cannot let it go back.

To become intimate is to change the terms of the friendship—from the bond built on a silent bargain that I will confirm your self-image and you will confirm mine—to a bond based on slowly revealing the false self to a friend.

A priest friend of mine once gave me a metaphor for marriage. He said the partners move in together and bring their trunks. Each person opens the trunk a crack and waits anxiously as the other sees what's inside. If the reactions are positive, they each open up a bit more; if the reactions are negative, they both shut down.

I love this image, especially if we include the shift that happens when we stop looking to see what's in the trunk and start watching the person who opens it. That is the transforming step—because the secrets we carry inside and struggle to hide may not be very pretty, but the person who's willing to show them is gorgeous.

MY HEALTH CRISIS AND BREAKDOWN

My crisis in parenting, which prompted me to drop some of my irritating certitudes, was a precursor, perhaps a dress rehearsal, for the larger crisis that attacked my whole sense of self.

The conceits I had to sacrifice in order to pass through my parenting crisis were powerful, but limited: "I know how to raise a child. I know how to guide my sons to happiness."

My larger self-image—from which my parenting conceits were

derived—was grounded in grander claims, not partial beliefs about who I am but core beliefs.

"I know what I'm doing. I know how to be happy. I know what to do to find peace. I know how to manage any situation. I can solve the riddles and puzzles of life. I've figured out most of it, and I have the willpower and ingenuity to figure out the rest of it."

The crisis for that grandiose self-image peaked when the psychiatrist told me: "The MRI is highly abnormal. . . . I'm telling you very bluntly. This is sad."

This is the pattern for a crisis. We hear "What you're doing isn't working" from a trusted voice on a matter of life-driving passion. That's the message—whether it's my hearing "highly abnormal" or my speechmaker-warrior-hero Neil hearing "Not. Fit. For. Duty." The message is: "Your story is finished."

Yet the crisis doesn't always lead to breakdown. We want to double down on the story and fight to save the self-image one more time. And the people around us often encourage us to just keep trying harder. Few people have the strength to be present at someone else's breakdown. In fact, the final thing the psychiatrist said to me before she ended the call was, "I think you're going to have to do the full protocol."

I told her that I had already been on that protocol for eight months, and it hadn't helped. She responded, "I'm going to have my assistant call you to get the credit card because I need to get off."

Her advice was to cling longer to the plan that failed. But I was done. My belief that "I know what to do" became "I have no idea what to do." My plan was grounded in a story, and I needed that story to be true. When it turned out to be false, I had nothing left. I had come to the end of any explainable way that I could ever recover my life.

That's when crisis can turn into breakthrough. What makes it a crisis is the pain I can't bear. What makes it a breakthrough is that I don't try to salvage the story. I drop it.

And all my stories were in crisis at once—my meditation, my health regime, my system for figuring things out and fixing them. And they were in crisis not just because they weren't working but because I no longer believed in them. We don't take up a new way until we see the old ways fail. All my old ways had failed. And when I broke down, I opened up.

In his book *He*, Robert Johnson cites the story of the knight Parsifal, who sets out to find the Holy Grail and runs into countless obstacles. At the end of the quest, he is finally ready to succeed because, in Johnson's words, he "has had the arrogance beaten out of him by 20 years of fruitless searching."

When the arrogance gets beaten out of us, grace can flow into us. "Grace" is goodness that we didn't plan or earn. It just happens for us. It's not a result of our actions; it's often a result of the failure of our actions, when, beyond all planning, a door opens, the phone rings, an insight comes, a person appears, grace flows.

Grace comes in when we let go. Letting go is the thing. Cynthia Bourgeault writes in her book *The Meaning of Mary Magdalene:* "Letting go is not in order to get something better. . . . In and of itself it *is* the something better."

Letting go lets in grace.

Grace is the next chapter. The final state of breakdown. It may be puzzling to think of grace as a state of breakdown, but we have to remember what is breaking down. It is the false self that is breaking down. It is grace that is breaking through.

CHAPTER EIGHT

Grace

On Father's Day 1986, my dad rose in the morning, got dressed, and walked into the bedroom down the hall, taking the chair next to my brother Matt's bed.

"Good morning, Matt," he said.

Matt had been in a coma for a week. He was at the end of his short fight with AIDS. There were no antiretrovirals then, and as soon as his symptoms became apparent, he faded quickly—from collapsing while taking ornaments down from the Christmas tree in late December to lingering on the edge of life in the middle of June.

My dad became a hero after Matt became ill. Dad learned all at once that his son had AIDS; that his son was dying; that his son was gay; and that his son had a partner, who wanted to stay with us as Matt died. Once Dad absorbed all this, he did his duty. He welcomed Matt back home; he welcomed Matt's partner, Michael; and he attended the meetings of an AIDS-support group, where he was often the only straight man present.

I'm sure it wasn't easy for him. He was raised in a traditional German Irish Catholic family in the Midwest in the 1930s. There was no script for this, and if there was, it wasn't kind. Dad's relationship with Matt was a little more uneasy than his relationship with the rest of us. My brothers John, Dave, and Dan and I all played the usual sports— football, basketball, baseball, soccer—while Matt was a diver, a dancer, an actor, and a gymnast, who played the piano and sang. There was a certain awkwardness to Dad's bond with Matt—maybe partly because Matt felt Dad wouldn't accept his sexuality and partly because Dad knew that Matt was smarter, more subtle, and more sophisticated than he was, and that made Dad feel a little overmatched in a game of life he still wasn't sure he understood.

But Dad opened up when Matt got sick. And that morning he said, "It's Father's Day, Matt. Your mom and I are going to go out to breakfast. Michael is here, and he's going to be staying with you while we're out." He continued, "Matt, I've been reading a book that says that when people are in a coma, they can hear you. It also says that sometimes when people are in a coma, they stay in a coma because they're not ready to die. They want to finish some unfinished business first. So, I just wanted to tell you, Matt, there is no unfinished business. I love you."

They stayed there together, Dad in his chair and Matt in his bed, for half an hour until my mom came in, said good morning to Matt, and took my dad out for a Father's Day breakfast.

An hour and a half later, as Mom and Dad returned, Michael met them at the front door, saying, "Hurry up! Come quick!"

My mom was the first into Matt's room. She saw that his color was leaving his face, and he was leaving us. She rushed to him, took his face in her hands, and said: "Oh, Matthew, my baby, I love you so much. Goodbye."

My dad, perhaps for the first time in his life unafraid of his feelings, took a seat at the bedside to be present for the passing.

THE POWER BEYOND ALL PLANNING

Most of the time in our lives, we act like we know what we're doing. We have a plan for getting what we want, and we move forward decisively. Actually, though, we know almost nothing. We enter the world with no idea where we came from. We leave the world with no idea where we're going. And we spend the time in between looking for love and frequently not finding it. It's often only when we're stung by failure or stunned by loss that we admit our ignorance and open up.

That's when we can feel the power of grace. Grace is divine energy—the ether of the spiritual world. It surrounds us, supports us, and wants to lift us—but can't break through to us until we surrender. In those moments, even if the surrender is brief, grace allows us to act with love we didn't know we had—making us better than we are. That's what happened with my dad and Matt.

OUR FAVORITE CURMUDGEON

Some years ago, when I was having a rare and cherished dinner with old friends, my godfather, Don Gralen, asked with an affectionate smile, "How's our favorite curmudgeon?" He was asking about my father. "Jack Rosshirt, now that's a genuine guy," Don had once told his son. "If he's at a party and he's bored, he'll find a chair in a corner, sit down, and start reading a book."

Yep. I went to visit Dad a few years ago, seeing him for the first time in months. I leaned over, gave him a hug, and when we released, he looked up at me and said, "Your teeth are yellow." My brothers and I remember one Sunday after Mass going to the home of friends for an impromptu gathering, arranged spontaneously after church. When we arrived, the hosts weren't yet there, and my dad turned to my mom and asked irritably, "Where *are* they?!" Mom said, "They said to let ourselves in; they'll be here in five minutes." Dad snarled, "Well that's pretty damn dippy!"

Dad was in some ways a simple guy. His happiest moment might have come when my youngest brother, Danny, playing "football" in the local rec league as an eight-year-old, took a handoff and ran eighty yards for a touchdown through a swarm of confused kids lost in large helmets. (Dan was the best athlete in our family—unless it was Matt. In my senior year playing high school soccer, I scored four goals. In his senior year at the same high school, Dan scored twenty-seven goals. But it's hard to compare players from different eras.)

When Dad felt anxious and insecure, he would preface a statement with "If you weren't so stupid . . ." When we were in a restaurant, he once told me to grab a chair that had a coat on it and was next to another diner. When I hesitated, he sneered, "Did I raise you to be *timid*?"

For decades, we kids laughingly kept alive Dad's signature high-stress order in the midst of disorder: "Do what you're supposed to be doing!" That was his inarticulate way of saying: "Please act so as to reduce my stress."

When I was in my forties and had had my fill of his scorn, I once turned on him and said, "Dad, everyone gets irritated. But when *you* get irritated, someone has to *pay*!"

The person who had to pay most often was him. When he once couldn't find the confirmation number for his flight home, he said, "I'm going to sit here and deal with my stupidity." He once said of an old friend, "She married a blundering guy like me." When I asked him what he meant, he said, "He can't talk about poetry, and he has no sensitivity."

Underneath it all, and emerging intermittently in his final years, was a man who was achingly tender. When I told him that I was working with Tim Shriver on a project to help ease the country's divisions, Dad said, "Good luck with that. You should get Jesus Christ. He's available—because no one's listening to him." When I stopped laughing, he said, "See, I can still contribute."

I once arrived to see him and said, "I was just at the cemetery to visit Mom and Matt," and he said in a soft voice, "Is there room there for me?" Another time, he asked me from his wheelchair, "Tell me why you think I will not ride a bike again."

He once said to me when I was leaving for the airport at the end of my trip, "Do you have any happy memories of your childhood?" I laughed with affection for the man who longed to be loved at the end of his life, and I told him a blizzard of stories. I said, "Remember the time when I was playing shortstop, and you came out of the dugout and waved me three steps toward second base—" He interrupted me to finish the story: "—and the next batter up lined a base hit right where you had been!"

He was frustrated living in the retirement home. He believed that if he could leave the facility, it would somehow restore his health and youth. One time, he said, "I'm going to cut your inheritance by ten percent a month until you get me out of here!" Another time, he asked me for money, and I asked, "How much do you need?" He replied, "Three thousand dollars." I said, "That's a lot of money. What are you going to do with it?" And he replied, "I have to pay some people here to look the other way while I make my escape."

Dad had a stock of one-liners he could deliver with a snarl. One lifelong friend recalled going with him years ago to hear a motivational speaker who struck a dramatic pause and said: "Most of you here will turn into what you think about." Dad leaned toward his friend and whispered, "Most of the men here will turn into women." But the one-liner I remember most was the one he delivered to my brother Dave. Dave asked him, "Do you have any favorite memories of times with your father?" Dad replied, "When he wasn't hitting me."

Dad never made any move to look into his patterns or his past. He wouldn't talk about anything painful. He once told me, "I miss your mother." I replied, "Dad, maybe you should talk about that." And he said, "I just did."

How does that man become a loving presence at the bedside of his dying child? Grace.

YOUR UNCLE WAS MY FRIEND

Even just the talk of death, or communing over those who've died, can puncture the stiff rhythms of everyday life and put us in a state of grace.

When I was at a speechwriters' conference at Georgetown University back in 2015, I was startled to see my son Ben's name on my cell phone. It was in the middle of the school day, and I never heard from him in those hours. I grabbed the phone, thinking he was sick or in trouble, and he said, "Dad, I got to tell you what just happened. I'm in geometry class right now, and my teacher called on me to answer a question, and I laughed, and she said, 'I know why you laughed—because you don't know the answer.' And I said: "No. I laughed because my name is Ben, and you keep calling me Matt."

"She said, 'Oh, I didn't even notice. I had a friend named Matt Rosshirt. Is there someone in your family named Matt?'

"When I told her I had an uncle named Matt, she asked, 'Did your uncle die young?'"

"I said yes, and she said, 'Your uncle was my friend.'"

Ben was thrilled—Matt was suddenly alive to him in a way he'd never been before. So, he asked his teacher if he could call me. After Ben and I talked for a few minutes, he put his teacher on the phone, and she and I set a date for lunch.

I was excited to meet her—learning something new about a family member who died long ago is both touching and thrilling.

We met at the restaurant, and before sitting down, she placed four photographs on the table, all candid photos of Matt taken his freshman year at Georgetown. She and I felt an instant bond. After talking about Matt, we asked about each other's lives, and she told me she had a son named Tim who had died of cancer at age sixteen. I wanted to know every detail about him. He was so peaceful and loving, she said, especially toward the end. He would say, very casually, "Mom, you can hug me here, but not there—I have burns from the radiation."

She told me that once after he called her "Mom" she told him,

"Me being your mom is just a momentary arrangement for this life. You're far too large a spirit for me to be your mother."

She told me that when he was at the end, she climbed onto his bed and hugged him and sang to him as he died.

"What did you sing?" I asked.

"'I Will,' by the Beatles."

"Could you sing it now?" I asked her.

She was a member of a church choir that toured Europe, and she sang, low and sweet:

> *Who knows how long I've loved you?*
> *You know I love you still*
> *Will I wait a lonely lifetime?*
> *If you want me to, I will*

When she hesitated in her memory of the second verse, I joined in, singing together with her, oblivious of the diners around us in a crowded restaurant. Death and the love of those who've died summons grace.

AGENTS OF GRACE

There is a quote widely attributed to Maya Angelou: "People will forget what you said, people will forget what you did, but people will never forget how you made them feel." I don't know for sure that she actually said this, because I've never seen the quote tied to a time and a place or a speech or a book. Even so, I agree with this quote and would add a point: We never forget how people make us feel, *especially* when they treat us better than we expect or better than we think we deserve. That is a form of mercy, and it has the effect of grace—a moment of healing love unearned and unexpected.

These moments can be simple—and they don't come only from people. Our dog Walter suffered kidney failure at age four. When we took him in to let him go, we placed him up on the table so the vet could find a vein. When Walter saw me start to cry, he leaned forward and licked my face.

When we lost our second dog, Chester, we put him to sleep on our kitchen floor, feeding him chocolate and bacon as the drugs did their work. I then joined the vet in carrying Chester in a bag to the car parked in front of our house, and a landscape worker whom I had never talked to before had the boldness to approach me and say, "I'm sorry for your loss." Unforgettable kindness.

On the last day of the first season of the Washington Nationals baseball team, Jamey Carroll, a second baseman, took his final batting-practice swings of the year, walked toward the stands, took a bat out of his bag, and slid it across the top of the dugout to Nick, who was nine years old. Nick put it under his seat during the game and checked every half inning to make sure it was still there.

The day after my mom died, my dad and I were out doing errands. When we returned to the house, the cleaning team had come and gone, leaving a note: "So sorry about Mrs. Rosshirt. Today cleaning for free."

When I was ten years old, I was on a state championship swim team filled with stars, including my best friend, who held several state records. I didn't belong. In one dual meet early in the season, I finished third in twenty-five-yard breaststroke—as mediocre a result as you can get. When I reached the end of the pool, my coach, a legend in the state, met me there, threw his arm over my shoulder, and walked me slowly back to our bench, past all the parents in the bleachers, talking to me about my race as if the success of the team depended on me.

These moments of unexpected kindness not only endure forever in our minds; they can *change* our lives. When Desmond Tutu died, a number of the news articles recalled his story of the time he was nine years old, walking down the sidewalk with his mother. In those days of apartheid, if a White person approached from the other direction, Black people were expected to step into the gutter to let the White person pass and then nod their heads as a gesture of respect. On this day, however, the young Tutu and his mother were approached by a white man who stepped off the sidewalk to allow them to pass, and then tipped his hat as a gesture of respect as they walked by.

The bewildered future archbishop of Cape Town looked to his mother for an explanation, and she said, "He is an Anglican priest and a man of God." At that moment, which Tutu later called "the defining moment of my life," he decided that he, too, wanted to be an Anglican priest and a man of God.

One of the great personal acts of grace I remember in my life came not to me but to someone I loved. When Matt was dying, my family was befriended by a man named Lou Tesconi, a volunteer from the local AIDS organization in Houston. Lou didn't know us. He was assigned to us. And he came to our home to visit with Matt and to offer whatever service and kindness he could to my mom and dad.

Shortly after Matt died, Lou began studies to become a Catholic priest. Within the year, he was diagnosed with AIDS and kicked out of the seminary. Lou was a lawyer by training and temperament. He appealed the judgment to a Catholic bishop who didn't challenge the seminary's decision, but instead asked Lou to found and head a ministry for people with AIDS. Lou agreed and established Damien Ministries in a poor neighborhood of Washington, DC.

A few years later, in early 1989, when the country was still very ignorant and fearful of AIDS, Lou got a call from the White House. First Lady Barbara Bush was planning to visit Grandma's House, a home for infants with AIDS. It was one of the very first outings in her tenure as First Lady, and Lou was asked to join a team of people to brief her privately before the event.

During the briefing, as Lou told me later, he said: "Mrs. Bush, it is a fantastic thing that you are holding these babies with AIDS. But the country sees them as innocent and the rest of us with AIDS as guilty. The whole suffering AIDS community needs a collective embrace from you today, not just the infants."

Mrs. Bush stood up, walked over to Lou, and gave him a big hug.

After the briefing, Mrs. Bush took a tour of the facility as she talked to the press. She hugged, kissed, and played with three little girls, and then nailed the message, which meant so much coming from the First Lady: "You can hug and pick up babies and people who have the HIV virus. There is a need for compassion."

At the press conference afterward, Lou stood by his point on Mrs. Bush's visit: "I'm afraid that it may send a message that babies are innocent," he said, "but that the rest of us aren't." He added, "I told her it would certainly help to get a collective hug from the First Lady."

Then again, this time in front of the cameras, Mrs. Bush wrapped Lou up in a big embrace.

Mrs. Bush wrote of this visit in her memoir. She noted that "even then, people still thought that touching a person with the virus was dangerous." But she didn't give herself any credit for dealing a blow against stigma by embracing a gay man with AIDS in 1989.

Lou had a buzz from that hug that never went away.

In the fall of 1991, near Thanksgiving, I got a call from a friend that Lou had gone into the hospital again. I knew it was for the last time. I remembered Lou saying to me once, "I'm not afraid of dying; I'm afraid of dying alone." I didn't want him to feel alone.

I called the general number of the White House and asked if I could speak to the First Lady's office. I was a nobody press secretary on Capitol Hill. I didn't expect anyone in the White House to talk to me. But I was immediately connected to the First Lady's press secretary, Anna Perez, who had accompanied Mrs. Bush to Grandma's House that day. I began to recount the events of two years before, and she saved me the time: "I remember Mr. Tesconi," she said. I explained Lou's condition and said, "It would be so comforting for him to receive a letter from Mrs. Bush."

Just a few days later, I went to see Lou in the hospital. As soon as he saw me, he reached beside his bed with a slow and shaky hand and pulled out a letter. "Look what I got," he said.

I read it aloud so Lou could hear it again. The letter was unflinching and full of love. Mrs. Bush didn't duck the issue that Lou was dying. She used it as a pivot to say, "Well done." At the bottom, in her own hand, she wrote to Lou that his life mattered, that he had made an impact.

That was a long time ago. But some things you don't forget, and shouldn't. In a time of ignorance, Mrs. Bush's wise touch eased the sting of exclusion for my friend and many others.

It was an act of mercy and justice and grace.

AMAZING GRACE: THE POWER TO TURN US AROUND

Grace is the source of our power to change—not just the power to act with love in a moment but to act in a new way from that moment on. "I once was lost, but now am found." Grace can turn us around.

Grace, as I see it, powers the shift from the first half of life to the second. The first half is about building up our self-image; the second half is about dissolving our self-image. The first half is about soothing ourselves; the second half is about healing ourselves. The first half is guided by our self-image; the second half is guided by grace.

I've always been fascinated by the shift from the first to the second half of life—especially by what defines the shift and what sets the second half in motion.

We know the pattern by now—as we build up in life, we create a story for ourselves. The job of the story is to give us comfort and security and protect us from pain. But reality is not kind to our conceits. At certain points, the mask cracks, and our disowned self oozes out. Most of the time, we scarcely see it. Quite automatically, with a lifetime of practice, we affirm the false self and move on, hoping people won't notice or make a fuss. But for most of us, at some point, a series of events will crack the mask in ways too great to ignore. In those moments, if we double down, magnify the lie, and hope that people play along, we stay stuck in the first half of life. But if, instead, we try something terrifying and new, and we own the disowned parts in ways we never dared to do before, and we start to admit what we used to deny, we have a chance to become whole.

The resistance to this change is one of the great forces at play in human life. We spend a lifetime denying the difference between who we are and who we say we are. And whenever anyone does or says something that makes us dimly aware of the difference, we hit them with a hot blast of abuse. Anger is often a tactic we use to make people back off when they're probing a painful truth.

The ability to bear the embarrassment of a broken self-image is a measure of whether we can give up our story and step into the second half of life, or still cling to our story and stay stuck in the first half.

If we drop the story, we have to feel the pain that we created the story to avoid. If we can handle the pain, we don't need the mask. As Rohr says, "Spirituality is always eventually about what you do with your pain."

Surrendering the soothing comfort of the story is a revolution in the way we find meaning and purpose and happiness in our lives. It goes against everything we've practiced, and most everything we've witnessed in the world. And we can do it only by grace. Grace is the only force that can help us face the pain we created the mask to avoid.

I experienced a foreshadowing of this shift a few years before my breakthrough. I was working with a woman trained in Somatic Experiencing, a practice described by Peter Levine in his book *Waking the Tiger*.

I was lying on my back and was asked to let my mind wander and to report any images. As I followed the instructions, the practitioner began to ask questions. I told her that I was in my house, not *my* house, but a house that was mine, that I identified with, and there was a snake under the house, engulfed in sand, and it was slithering up toward the house. I saw the snake coming, and I told him aggressively: "Stop. You can't come in. This is *my* house!" The snake stopped and became still. After a few minutes, I began to feel remorse, and I said, sadly, "The snake is lonely." A few minutes later, I said, "The snake has no friends." Then I started to cry, and a few minutes later, I said, "I will be his friend." A few minutes after that, I said, "He is me."

For me, then, the snake, the serpent, became the symbol and image for all the thoughts that I hide and deny and ridicule and disown. The serpent is the shadow—a symbol of all we embrace when we surrender the self-image and enter the second half.

This, for me, is the theme and the story underneath one of my favorite Gospel passages.

Jesus was in the temple

> and beheld how the people cast money into the treasury: and many that were rich cast in much. And there came a certain poor widow, and she threw in two mites, which make a farthing. And he called *unto him* his disciples, and saith unto them, Verily I say unto you, That this poor widow hath cast more in, than all they which have cast into the treasury: For all *they* did cast in of their abundance; but she of her want did cast in all that she had, *even* all her living.

She gave away what she had to live on—with faith that a force more powerful than money would protect her. When we're surrendering our story and our self-image, we're giving away all our security, everything we have to live on, with the faith that somehow all will be well. Only grace can inspire that faith. Grace prompts us to let go, and then takes over when we do.

There is, for me, an especially moving example of surrender in Glennon Doyle's memoir *Untamed*, in the entry titled "Braids."

Doyle's ex-husband, Craig, has a girlfriend, she explains, and when Doyle's daughters go to their father's house, the girlfriend is there with them, and "she braids my daughters' hair skillfully."

Then Doyle confesses, "I have never known how to braid my daughters' hair. I've tried, but it ends up looking lumpy and pathetic, so we stick to ponytails. Whenever I see a little girl wearing complicated braids, I think: 'She looks well loved. She looks well mothered.'"

With hints and feints and miniconfessions, Doyle paints a picture of her envy and anxiety as Craig's girlfriend deepens her presence in the lives of Doyle's daughters. And Doyle tells one story after another of her battle against the girlfriend and of the hopeless loneliness of the ego's isolating wins and losses.

She calls Craig and takes a stand: "She tells Tish that she loves her. Don't you think that's a little much? She is your girlfriend, not their mother. We all need some boundaries. You need to help her set them. What if she leaves and hurts our kids?"

Then Doyle confesses: "I am much more afraid that she will stay and love our kids."

Doyle tells a few more stories of resisting the girlfriend's influence in the lives of her daughters, then she surrenders: "Someday," she writes, "I'll ask her how to braid my daughters' hair."

She admits what she would like to deny. She tells us what she'd rather we didn't know. She commits herself in public to a path of pain and growth.

This is a human being at the peak of beauty.

This is grace.

GRACE TAKING OVER

In the right moments, grace gives us the power to begin turning our lives around. But turning us around is just the start. Grace can also take us over. I saw this up close with my mom, at her death.

My four brothers and I loved my mom madly. But we didn't make it easy on her or think that we should. We were kids, perhaps for too long. And parents are indestructible, especially moms. So, I didn't think of how it affected her when I was a little kid playing with matches and burned down the neighbor's garage, with her Cadillac inside, which was the last gift given to the widow by her dying husband. We didn't think it hurt Mom's feelings when she once spilled milk at the breakfast table and we all leaped from our chairs, screamed in happiness, and held an impromptu parade of joy at the equalizing, democratizing effect of Mom's spilled milk.

We should have known it would have hurt her feelings years later, in our late teens, when Mom told us of an NFL player with a colostomy bag. She feared that her colitis might one day lead her to that surgery, so she heard this as heartening news. "He's doing really well," my mom said. "That's because no one will tackle him," Dave responded. When we blew up in laughter, my mom grabbed the glass butter dish and slammed it repeatedly into the tabletop, showering glass shards on all of us.

She was a loving and patient mom, except for once every few months, when she would blow up—usually in the morning before school. In those moments, anything and everything would set her off. We were both scared and amused, and we did our best not to be noticed until the storm passed. The number one rule of survival was "Do not, *do not*, DO NOT . . . laugh."

One morning, she stormed into the room I shared with Matt, saw some clothes on the floor (or maybe a speck of dust on the dresser), and starting screaming at Matt, who was standing in the middle of the room trying to get dressed. Mom couldn't see me—I was deep inside the walk-in closet on the same side of the room as she was. But Matt could see me. So, I mooned him, which left him looking at a split screen: on the right, a woman raging at him; on the left, nothing but butt. He smirked, which escalated the crisis. But he didn't give me away. (What a brother!)

Mom occasionally flashed an "I know best" side, which could make even her best friends bristle. And she bragged on her kids in embarrassing ways. After I published my first piece of writing—a short op-ed in a tiny newspaper—she showed it to a *New York Times* foreign correspondent in East Africa. She told me he was impressed. Mom, what's he supposed to say?

So, like many great moms, she was slightly nuts—made a little nuttier by the act of raising rowdy kids. But the enduring theme of her life was a commitment to faith. Twelve years or so after my mom died, I was talking to my dad over Zoom.

"Dad, John says you've been talking a lot about Mom lately."

"Yeah," he said. "I really fell for her."

"That's sweet to hear," I said. "What did you find most attractive in her when you met her?"

"She prayed the rosary constantly."

I chuckled at the image.

"What was appealing about that?" I asked.

"I thought she would save me," he replied.

"How did that work out?"

"We don't know yet."

Mom kept nourishing her spiritual side. It was her life's work. She majored in theology at Saint Mary's College in the 1950s, began practicing yoga in the 1960s, took courses in Islam in the 1970s, and did Buddhist meditation retreats in the 1980s. One of her best friends was a Catholic nun we called Sister Alice who'd been in a cloister for twenty-eight years and then emerged, still a nun, but living in society. Mom took a lot of spiritual instruction from her. In fact, one of my cherished gifts from my mom is the book *The Way of the Heart: Desert Spirituality and Contemporary Ministry* by Henri Nouwen. It was a birthday gift to my mom from Sister Alice, and years later, Mom gave it to me with a sticky note on the cover that I've kept there ever since: "Tom, this is a treasure in and of itself, but more so because Alice gave it to me. I've read it so many times. Don't lose it. I might ask for it back if I live longer than I expect to. Love, Mom."

A spiritual presence seemed always to be operating somewhere inside my mother—and it rose up when death came.

In early December 2008, when my mom was seventy-five, I was in my office late in the day in Washington, DC, and got a call from my dad. He explained that they had been going to doctors, trying to find out what was wrong with Mom. (She had said nothing of this to me.) And they had just heard the results of Mom's PET scan from a lung specialist who told them she had cancer: "I'm so sorry," the doctor said. "This is the worst scan I've ever seen."

Dad said the cancer was advanced and very aggressive. Then Mom took the phone. She was very peaceful, very comforting. She explained a bit more of the medical results and then she said in an upbeat voice: "We're enrolling in hospice. We have a terrific hospice here in Austin."

When the hospice nurse was set to arrive for her first visit a few days later, I was sitting with Mom at the breakfast table.

"Alana," Dad said. "The hospice people are coming in five minutes, hurry up and finish your breakfast." Mom answered back in an unhurried voice, "Jack, you know I don't rush well, and I'm sure the hospice people are used to all manner of eccentricities."

After the nurse arrived and we all had exchanged pleasantries, she asked Mom if the pain medication was making her drowsy. Mom said, "I'm not sure," as Dad answered, "Yes!" I stepped in with a third opinion: "If you put both my mom and my dad in a comfy chair at the same time, my dad will fall asleep first." Then Dad said, "But you don't know what *I'm* taking!"

I was surprised by how much fun it was to be with my mom when she was dying.

She told me with a rebellious grin: "I just tore up my dentist's notice. There are positive aspects to everything!"

She told her brother: "I'm ready to return my library book."

She had completely lost her interest in controlling or deciding anything.

Dad said: "Alana, I've given you three important medical cards. Where are they?" Mom said, "Good luck." (As we searched for the cards, we found the TV remote in Mom's purse.)

I talked to her about a career decision I had to make. I laid out all the details and the options, the costs and benefits, and then asked for her advice. She said, "Boy, I'm sure glad I don't have to make that decision."

One morning when I was visiting, we took Mom to an eye appointment. When the doctor studied her eye, he looked startled and said, "You have four tumor metastases under the retina." He wanted to get Mom to another eye specialist that afternoon, but Mom said, "I don't think so. I really don't want to see another doctor." On the way out, the receptionist, who knew my mom well and had overheard the conversation, gave Mom a kiss and whispered, "See you on the other side."

The cancer had entered Mom's back and shoulders, which made it painful to put on certain types of clothes. I suggested we rearrange her closet so she could reach the clothes that are easier to put on.

She sat on the bed, and I took one item at a time out of the closet and showed it to her. Each outfit brought a different reaction.

I held up one outfit, and she said brightly: "Oh, that's one of my favorites for dress-up . . . but I'm not dressing up anymore." When I showed her a light blue skirt and jacket combination, she said, "You can dress me in that for the casket." Then I showed her another dressy outfit, and she said, "Oh, I love this one," and she pulled it into her lap, sort of clutching it. Then she paused a moment, said softly to herself, "*Move on,*" and handed it back to me so I could put it away.

The last day I was there, we sat together in the den. We talked about her headstone. She asked if I thought it should match Matthew's since they'll be next to each other. I said, "Yes, it marks you as family." Then we talked about the funeral—what she would want. She had a funeral file with readings and musical selections, and she said: "Oh, Tom. At one point, I had all these intricate plans. They don't matter now. If Dad or you boys have different feelings, let them override mine."

I asked if she still wanted "Ode to Joy" to be sung, and she laughed at an old memory. "Your dad once said to me, 'If you want 'Ode to Joy' at your funeral, I want a signed statement from you that it was *your* request.'"

I asked if she were afraid. She said: "I really have no fear of death. I'm feeling very tired, and very, very grateful. I'm pleased with my life and comfortable with death. Now I just need to make it through the pain without being a horrible embarrassment to everyone."

I asked, "Is there anything you want to do while you still can?" And she said, "I just want to thank all my friends for being my friend." I said, "Mom, I think all your best qualities are peaking right now." And she said, "We Irish are late bloomers."

I left Mom after a five-day visit in December and told her I would see her at the end of the month at the reunion. She had been planning a family reunion since before she was diagnosed. We met at a dude ranch in Texas—Mom and Dad and the kids, wives, and grandkids.

Mom showed up for every meal. She watched us dance. She went down to the corral to see her grandkids get up on horseback. My favorite photo of Mom and me was taken during the reunion by my brother Dave. Mom and I were seated next to each other at dinner, and we had put our heads close together—the photo shows me talking and my mom straining to hear and understand. She was the best listener I ever knew, right to the end.

On our last day at the reunion, as I packed up, I told Dad to call me when Mom was close. I wanted to be there at the end. But I also knew that even if I made it to her bedside, this farewell would be the last time I'd have a chance to talk with her. Half an hour before we left, I found Mom alone in her room. I pulled up a chair, took a seat beside her, and reached for her hand. I asked if she wanted to say a Hail Mary. She nodded, and I led: "Hail Mary, full of grace . . . now and at the hour of our death. Amen." We sat in silence for a minute. Mom was looking out the window, at nothing in particular, and then said slowly, with energy, emphasizing each word, "I just don't know why I'm so *lucky*."

She wasn't saying, "I've been so lucky" or "I've had a good life" or "I should be grateful." She was saying, here and now, in this wheelchair, breathing with an oxygen tank, my body filled with cancer, a few weeks from death, "I just don't know why I'm so lucky."

She had crossed over.

Two weeks later, Dad called and said, "Come now." That evening, my nephew Will picked me up at the Austin airport and drove me home. I entered the house and walked to the edge of the bed and said, "Mom, it's Tom. I came down from Washington for a visit."

"Tom!" she said, and reached her arms up to me. I leaned down to hug her, then I stood up, still holding both her hands, and she said, "How long can you stay?"

"I'm going to be staying for a while, Mom."

"Oh, Joy. Joy. Joy. Joy."

That was the last thing she said to me.

THE DARK SIDE OF GRACE

The lyrics of the hymn "Amazing Grace," written by John Newton, the converted former captain of a slave ship, include the verse:

'Twas grace that taught my heart to fear,
And grace my fears relieved.

Before we find relief, we face fear. Before grace breaks through, grace breaks us down. It's the unloved, unadvertised role of grace. It's grace's *shadow*. Before it lifts us to heaven, it takes us to hell, humbling and crumbling our conceits. The path of grace is so brutal that we won't take it. It's not that we won't accept grace, but we don't recognize it. "This can't be right. I've taken a wrong turn. This has gone horribly wrong." But the truth *has* to feel horribly wrong—because nothing in the relative truth of the first half of life can prepare us for the radical truth of the second half, where we see that our most cherished beliefs are not only false but the cause of our suffering.

That's why holding on to our beliefs in defiance of reality leads us to anxiety, depression, addiction, illness, and crisis—before we let ourselves surrender into grace.

In one of the most remembered speeches in American politics, given on one of the most tragic days in American life, Senator Robert F. Kennedy stood on a flatbed truck in a parking lot in Indianapolis and told the crowd of African Americans gathered to hear a presidential campaign speech that Martin Luther King Jr. had been shot and killed that day in Memphis.

In the middle of his short extemporaneous talk, Kennedy said: "My favorite poet was Aeschylus. He wrote: 'In our sleep, pain which cannot forget falls drop by drop upon the heart until, in our own despair, against our will, comes wisdom through the awful grace of God.'"

The awful grace of God. The words in *Agamemnon* that precede the verses quoted by Kennedy read, "God, whose law it is that he who learns must suffer."

What is suffering but resisting the difference between what we want and what we have?

And what we want and what we have are both inventions of thought.

Perhaps there are only two elements in the universe—grace and thought. The first is infinite; the second, ephemeral. The first is peace; the second obscures peace. So, in a merciful universe, grace breaks down our thoughts until only peace is left.

Whether in Greek myths, American tragedies, or the mean stuff of our lives, the lessons and truths are the same.

The end of my long, slow breakdown—and the pivot to breakthrough—came when I was forced to give up the idea that I could think my way out of my crisis. The surrender wasn't anything I engineered. I fought against it with all my might. But at a certain point, I couldn't deny it. My search for peace, happiness, energy, health, and youth was over. I had failed. I didn't know where to go. I had no path.

Grace had broken me down—and was about to start filling me up.

CHAPTER NINE

Breakthrough

One early morning in the spring of 2019, I woke up, looked around, and remembered I was in a hotel in Texas attending a workshop to change my brain. I rolled to my left, saw an empty bag of Fritos corn chips on the floor, and burst out laughing.

What was so funny?

I felt like a college boy waking to the messy evidence of a party the night before and smiling in satisfaction over the indulgent life he pays no price for living.

For me, at age fifty-nine, the scene of the drunken bash had been reduced to the sight of a bag of Fritos, but it was just as delicious.

I was in recovery—making my way back from the punishing game of the "perfect diet," and if I had seen the bag of Fritos by my bedside a few months before, my response would have been different: "You *idiot*! How could you be so weak and stupid? You fell for the salt and fat and mouthfeel of the Frito-Lay food scientists. Now you're going to pay! You'll have to eat a perfect diet for a week until you can feel good again. You sluggish, weak, lethargic fool!"

I wouldn't have actually spelled all this out. All I had to say was "You *idiot*!" I knew the rest by heart. But that morning, I laughed with joy because I was no longer in the grip of those thoughts. There is a big difference between what's true and what we keep telling ourselves, and getting free from those food commandments was a big deal for me. I was excited to tell the group.

The group was thirty colleagues and cosufferers attending a five-day workshop Annie Hopper had created and named "The Dynamic Neural Retraining System." I had spent the prior three months doing the exercises guided by the DVDs, but I wanted to attend an in-person training too.

All of us had come to the workshop after years of failed efforts to heal from health issues that had forced us out of our lives—illnesses including chronic fatigue syndrome, chronic pain, Lyme disease, fibromyalgia, food sensitivities, irritable bowel syndrome, postural orthostatic tachycardia syndrome, mold illness, multiple chemical sensitivities, heavy-metal exposure—and no matter how many of these illnesses we were battling, we all suffered from anxiety and depression and some form of isolation. We were united in the hope that with Annie's approach, grounded in self-directed neuroplasticity, we could rewire our thoughts, switch off the fight-or-flight mode, and begin to heal. (I attended the workshop a year before COVID hit, but since 2021, Annie has been using her approach to also help patients with long COVID.)

MIND-BODY HEALING—JOINING A MOVEMENT

I wasn't aware of it at the time, but I was not just going to a workshop; I was joining a movement. Annie's healing model was one of many emerging at the time, conceived by different healers but unified by the life-changing outcomes that occur when insights of neuroscience are applied to heal illness and chronic pain. Annie's approach tends to specialize in mysterious illnesses; the back-pain study I cited in chapter 1 focused on chronic pain. But both models, and others created by innovative doctors and psychologists and health practitioners, are grounded in the discovery that neural circuits in the brain can generate pain and illness in the body, and the "plasticity" of the brain—its ability to learn and change according to its environment—means it can be trained to end the pain and heal the illness.

Dr. John Sarno, a pioneer in this movement who made breakthrough discoveries for healing chronic pain, was largely ignored by the medical establishment in his lifetime—in part, he said, because of "the enduring weakness of bias." The bias of conventional medicine, he wrote, is that "emotions do not induce physiologic change." And yet, Sarno said, "to leave the emotional dimension out of the study of health and illness is poor medicine and poor science."

The role of fear is especially relevant in neuroplastic healing. If the brain comes to believe that something harmless is dangerous, that belief causes fear that can create or contribute to pain and illness. The healing insight of neuroplasticity is that this association can be reversed: the false sense of danger that causes the fear—and the baseless fear that causes the pain—can be unlearned, and the pain can ease and the body can heal.

I began to learn that many of my health approaches actually made me worse because the treatment amplified the fear that made me ill. That helps explain why one of the first rules of the Annie Hopper workshop was "No talking about your symptoms!" And no talking about the tricks and tactics you're using to *fix* the symptoms. Why? Because that conversation itself activates our fight-or-flight response that's making us sick. When we talk about our symptoms, we *stir up* our symptoms. So, we agreed not to ask "How are you?" because this could be an invitation to a conversation that never ends. ("Do you want the ninety-minute version or the long version?")

Instead, we would ask, "What's going well for you?"

What was going well for me that morning, I told the group, was that I ate a bag of Fritos and laughed. People loved it. Many of us had adopted superlimited diets as we began to react to more and more foods. Every new burst of symptoms gave us a new food to avoid, and part of our training was to rewire our response and add some foods back. The day before, one woman said, "I ate half a bagel," and we almost had a parade.

This was not intended to encourage people who are allergic to peanuts to eat peanuts, or to encourage diabetics to eat sugar, or to invite people with celiac disease to eat gluten; the point was to return to diets we used to eat before we began reacting to foods we loved.

After I told the group about the Fritos, I explained my victory. For years, I had carried a scorecard in my head for what I had to eat to feel good. I had to eat good foods to feel good, and if I ate bad foods, I felt bad. And I could never feel better than the scorecard said I should. But the night before, I had eaten something the scorecard said would make me feel bad, and I felt great. So, something other than the food was affecting my mood, and that led me to embrace a new dietary principle: good food eaten in fear is not that good, and bad food eaten in joy is not that bad.

MYSTERIOUS ILLNESS

Long before she became ill and figured out how to get well, Annie Hopper was known in her hometown as an expert in emotional wellness. She wrote a weekly column called "Emotional Rescue" for the local paper in Kelowna, British Columbia, about three hours by car east of Vancouver. She was running workshops. She was a frequent radio guest and seen by her clients as a "core-belief counselor"— working with people to change their belief systems that might block them from joy, love, or success.

She was happy and successful, then she got sick. It started with headaches and spread to pain that would begin in the neck and go to her shoulders and her lower back. Then she started to become sensitive to certain chemicals. She became acutely conscious of smells and began to wear a mask when she left her house. Then one day she walked by a scented-candle display in a bookstore, and her brain started to hurt so much that she thought she was having a hemorrhage. Her partner, James, took her home, and she said when she went to sleep, she was 5 of 10 on a chemical-sensitivity scale; when she woke, she was 15 of 10.

She gave up her work because she would react in her office. She lost friends because people had to avoid contact with chemicals to see her. And her symptoms got worse. When she became sensitive to electricity and electromagnetic fields, she called a friend, borrowed a tent, and went camping with James and her dog. From there, she decided it would be better to be by the ocean, so she took her dog and went to live on a houseboat docked on Vancouver Island.

All along, she was reading medical research about the brain. Why could other people walk down the detergent aisle and have no reaction, and the same smells would put her into seizures? She began to see in her research a correlation in brain function among people who had multiple chemical sensitivities, chronic fatigue syndrome, fibromyalgia, depression, anxiety, and post-traumatic stress disorder. She became convinced that the problem was not in the substance but in the response.

Annie had a head start in finding a cure for her chemical sensitivities, and it came from work she had done with her clients on "core beliefs." Core beliefs, Annie says, are a collection of thoughts, feelings, experiences, and attitudes that shape how we interpret and experience life. Our core beliefs drive our lives because we are constantly searching for evidence that our beliefs are true, even when they don't serve us. In Annie's research, she learned that our core beliefs also shape our brains. In her book *Wired for Healing,* she writes:

> Through my own experience and reading publications from leading researchers like Dr. Norman Doidge, Dr. Jeffrey Schwartz, Dr. Bruce Lipton, Dr. Joe Dispenza, Dr. Jill Bolte Taylor and Dr. Candace Pert, I became familiar with the idea of neuroplasticity. . . . The term refers to the brain's ability to change. It is an innate quality of the human brain and is neither positive nor negative; rather, it is reflective of our life experiences. . . .

It is this body of research, combined with my own experience and my research, that led me to the conclusion that I had most likely suffered from a toxic brain injury that affected the limbic system. . . . During the initial trauma, my brain had created the association between chemicals and trauma, and subsequently, anything that was remotely similar to the initial injury triggered a severe toxic threat response. It had somehow wired any perception of chemicals with profound trauma, which triggered the "get the heck out of here before you die" pathway.

The pattern is similar from patient to patient—perception of danger causes fear in the brain, fear in the brain causes havoc in the body. In Annie's case, the havoc presented as chemical sensitivities, but it can come in many forms. Nicole Sachs, a psychotherapist who focuses on healing chronic pain has said, "One man's migraines is another woman's back pain is another man's irritable bowel syndrome is another woman's pelvic pain."

"The idea that my brain could be sending my body false messages was mind-blowing," Annie wrote. Avoidance of the trigger gave short-term relief but made the illness worse. "Every time a specific encounter is avoided out of fear, the threat response to that stimulus is heightened," Annie wrote.

Recovery, Annie says in her workshop manual, "requires that we don't believe everything we think, every emotion we experience, or every sensation our body is relaying to us." In fact, in an insight that holds true across approaches to physical health, emotional health, and spiritual health, she writes, "In order to stop limiting core beliefs and behaviors from sabotaging your success, you must bring them to the forefront of your mind so that you can expose them and change them."

This insight led Annie to the practice of incremental exposure. She began to shift from avoidance to exposure and used the exposures as a chance to rewire her response and change her brain. She said it required a "leap of faith," because her brain said these exposures were life-threatening. But the change worked.

"Incremental exposure" became a core feature of Annie's Dynamic Neural Retraining System—exposing yourself to a small dose of the triggering substance and meeting the stimulus with a different response—not fear and avoidance, but lightheartedness, even laughter.

> Ultimately, what I came to understand is that changing my emotional state was a major component in changing the wiring of my limbic system and thereby healing my body. . . . When feelings of anxiety or fear would come up from symptoms of illness, or when I was around stimuli that would 'normally' trigger a reaction, I would consciously reframe the experience while anchoring myself in a positive emotional state. When . . . I could feel what I call the 'warm and fuzzies' and a kind of tingling sensation through my head and body . . . I knew that I was on the right track.

REVERSING AVOIDANCE—MY WAY BACK TO HEALTH

As I read Annie's books, did the practices, and attended the workshop, I came away with a transforming insight: my strategy of avoidance was making me sick. I had been searching for a place, a diet, a regime, a lifestyle that avoided all triggers and would calm me down, but my avoidance was *driven* by anxiety, so it could never *calm* my anxiety. Instead, my avoidance made my anxiety worse.

The new approach was for me to expose myself to a small dose of something that triggered me, challenge the false message of danger, resist the rush to avoidance, and respond to the fear by elevating my emotional state. So, I began taking small steps to reverse the avoidance that shaped my life.

As I exposed myself to the things I used to respond to with fear and anxiety, I put myself emotionally, vividly, and experientially into memories of joy, activating all five senses, and bathing in that experience. I was thrilled to find it easy, after a bit of practice, to bring up tears of joy while reliving old memories I hadn't thought of in years. Armed with this skill, which all of us have, I began exposing myself to things I was afraid of—starting in my apartment.

In my first days after moving in, I had begun reacting to my newly purchased, super-hypoallergenic mattress, so I got rid of it and slept on the carpet. Then I started reacting to the carpet, so I vacated the bedroom and began sleeping on blankets laid out on the kitchen floor. Within a week of starting Annie's program, I moved back into the bedroom, began sleeping on the carpet, and started working from a table in the same room.

I also began to lose the habit of tracking down the triggers. In the past, if I had had a burst of anxiety or dizziness, I would think: "What did I eat? What was I exposed to?" I would try to hunt down the trigger so I could identify it and eliminate it. That habit just created more anxiety, gave the trigger more power, and made my system more sensitive. I saw that pattern and began to reverse it.

I began to eat more things that I had been avoiding—dairy, gluten, sugar, chocolate, caffeine. The point of my diet had been to keep my system from reacting. And all those foods had provoked reactions ranging from anxiety and depression to dizziness, confusion, and panic. So, I would eat nothing but vegetables and animal protein. Any variation—especially eating gluten, grains, dairy, or sweets—was "poison." I was obsessive: "Is there any of this in that? Is there any of that in this?" I would avoid everything.

But now it was my duty to live out a rebellious dream where a trusted health practitioner comes to me and says: "Tom, if you want to heal yourself, you must eat this blueberry muffin, then have a cup of coffee with a toasted cinnamon-raisin bagel with cream cheese. And when you start to panic, eat this cookie."

It seems irresponsible, even reckless—at least it did at first to me. But before I was able to settle into a healthy diet, I had to get over my fear of normal foods. Even the best diet can't cure fear, and fear was the problem. At the peak of my symptoms, I was convinced that if I slipped on the diet, I would feel awful, and it had been true enough times to sustain my fears. But now, I "slipped" intentionally, and I felt good, so the regime began to lose its authority.

I started to separate from the regime in other ways. I stopped the saunas I had been doing for detox. I stopped the supplements. I stopped taking "binders," which I was told would bind the toxins and move them out of my body. I stopped taking "chelating agents," which would remove the heavy metals from my body. And I spent more time back home in my house. In fact, there was a two-week period after my Annie workshop when every member of my family was out of town, and I went back to live at home and test it out. I made a point of practicing incremental exposure, spending time in the areas and spaces of the house where I used to react.

Of course, I couldn't have handled the exposures without a different response, so I met the initial reactions with positive emotions, not with fear. That was the part of the program that demanded the greatest and most continuous effort from me: "generate a positive emotional response." I found it especially difficult to generate positive emotion in the face of depression.

Depression makes me want to quit. That's its power. It comes with thoughts and feelings that send the message: there is no hope. When I was depressed, I sought comfort by sinking deeper into depression. "There is no hope, so no one can blame me for just sitting here." But despair is just a story we tell ourselves when we want to give up. And I didn't want to give up.

Countless times in those early months, I remember feeling depressed and exhausted and thinking, "But I don't *want* to create a positive emotion." I tried anyway, and the effort was like a street fight, getting knocked to the pavement and getting back up and charging the person who knocked me down. I used every trick I could think of—generating positive feelings, challenging the thoughts, contradicting the thoughts, mocking the thoughts, adding positive thoughts, entering the scenes of happy memories, dancing, skipping, clapping, thinking of jokes, making myself laugh. Every bit of this was crucial in defusing the thoughts that fed the feelings that ran the system that kept me trapped.

When I realized that this approach was working, I was awash in humility and gratitude. I never would have been able to figure this out by myself, and certainly I wouldn't have had the courage to try it out on my own without the evidence and guidance of people who had gone before me. I needed someone who could say to me: "I had what you have. Here's how I got better." And it's one of the greatest blessings of my life that I found one.

In the months after the workshop, I saw that I was getting better in ways I hadn't expected. I started to lose poisonous thoughts like "I can't eat that food or I will be depressed for three days." But other beliefs started to fall away that I hadn't even focused on: "I need my kids to do what I tell them." "My dad should treat me better." For some reason, the exercises I was doing to challenge false beliefs about my health took down other false beliefs with them. I didn't notice this at first. I just noticed that I was feeling a lot better. I was feeling more joy than I'd ever felt. I was laughing more than I'd ever laughed. And I was becoming convinced that self-directed neuro-plasticity was spiritual practice.

NEUROSCIENCE AND SPIRITUALITY

When people from different backgrounds and disciplines converge on the same insights, it raises my hope that they're putting forward universal truths. I was thrilled when I saw that Annie's reading list included *Hardwiring Happiness* by Rick Hanson—because I knew Hanson's research had been included in Richard Rohr's book *The Universal Christ*.

Early in the book, Richard writes:

> Studies like the ones done by the neuroscientist Rick Hanson show that we must consciously hold on to a positive thought or feeling for a minimum of fifteen seconds before it leaves any imprint in the neurons. The whole dynamic, in fact, is called the Velcro/Teflon theory of the mind. We are more attracted to the problem than to the solution, you might say. . . .

True freedom from this tendency is exceedingly rare, since we are ruled by automatic responses most of the time. The only way, then, to increase authentic spirituality is to deliberately practice actually enjoying a positive response and a grateful heart. And the benefits are very real. By following through on conscious choices, we can rewire our responses toward love, trust, and patience. Neuroscience calls this "neuroplasticity." This is how we increase our bandwidth of freedom, and it is surely the heartbeat of any authentic spirituality.

Encouraged by Rohr and Harper, I dove into Hanson's book. Hanson would certainly agree with Rohr on the link between neuroscience and spirituality. He refers to his approach as "the historically unprecedented intersection of psychology, neurology, and contemplative practice."

Hanson explains neuroplasticity at the start of *Hardwiring Happiness*: "The brain is the organ that learns, so it is designed to be changed by your experiences. . . . Whatever we repeatedly sense and feel and want and think is slowly but surely sculpting neural structure.

"Simply observing your mind is extremely useful," he says, "but you also need to decrease what's negative and increase what's positive. My focus is on increasing the positive."

So, I started one of the practices Hanson recommended, one named by the acronym HEAL. *H* stands for "Have a good experience." We are always having good experiences, he says. They might be buried under a mountain of bad experiences, but we're having them. *E* stands for "Enrich it." Spend time with the experience, feeling it and extending it. *A* stands for "Absorb it." Let the experience sink into you and become a part of you that you can take wherever you go. *L* stands for "Link positive and negative material." When you're having, enriching, and absorbing the positive experience, link it to a negative experience. The positive experience must stay in the foreground and be stronger; the negative experience must remain in the background. This fourth step can reduce and even uproot negative material.

I did this practice myself, and it was powerful. But I was eager to try it in a "live-fire exercise," and I had the perfect chance in a frank talk with my friend Brooke Anderson. Brooke and I met in Cape Town in 1999, when we were staffing a meeting of the US-South Africa Binational Commission, and we have worked closely together in different roles and stressful jobs ever since. She has probably reviewed half of all the speeches I've ever written. She knows my flaws as well as anyone in my family, and—somewhat like a big sister—is happy to point them out to me. At that time, I was talking to her about an experience where I had been momentarily "demoted" by a client. I had been given some special access and, unsurprisingly for me, I overdid it. After I ignored a number of signals, I was bluntly told, "Tom, *stop!*" I was surprised when Brooke suggested she knew details of that event, so I was pestering her for information: "What did you hear? C'mon. Tell me what you heard!"

As she started sharing what she knew, I secretly started doing the HEAL practice, having my positive experience, enriching it, and absorbing it—confident that I would soon be able to link it to the negative feelings that would come from the details Brooke was about to share. Then she finished telling me what she'd heard and concluded, "You took it too far."

I paused, nodded, and said, "Yeah. I couldn't help myself."

That set her into a peal of laughter. When she recovered, she said, "That's the most endearing thing you've ever said." She had heard me get defensive so many times that I think my defenseless surrender caught her by surprise. It's better to be endearing than defensive; that's what I always say. (I've never said that.) My surprising response was purely a result of the neuroplastic practice.

So, accepting Rick Hanson's simple guide, "What flows through your mind changes your brain," and Richard's advice to practice a positive response and a grateful heart, I began a new spiritual practice that I called the "spirituality of silliness."

THE SPIRITUALITY OF SILLINESS

I had discovered that, for me, the most effective approach for switching off the negative and turning on the positive was laughter, so I began looking for ways to make myself laugh. I would find myself hating a situation and whisper, "I am *loving* this!" That statement alone would make me laugh. Sometimes I'd be in a dark mood and say to myself, "Ha! Ha! Ha!" That worked too. Other times I would clap. A friend of mine said, "Clap?!" "Yes," I said, "clap my hands together like a small child." Her response told me that I had crossed the border into silly.

A few days later, I wrote to a friend: "I think one of the secrets is laughter, and a good way to get to laughter is being silly. Being silly is hard for people who are attached to a dignified self-image. Like me. But, wow, is it helpful."

She wrote back: "Yes! The danger of evil is that it consumes us, and makes us think that laughter, silliness, and love are irresponsible. Let's turn that thinking on its head!"

That's when I began to believe in the spiritual power of silliness. The good news is that we were born to be silly, and there are little pockets of our lives where it's safe to be silly. When our dog Walter died, we didn't just miss *him*, we missed the way we were when we were with him. So, after a pause, we adopted Chester and restored silliness to our home!

Little kids, too, give us permission to be silly. When I was a dad taking care of little boys, I was allowed to act like a little boy. (*Yippee!*) Some years ago, I was wedged in a crowded elevator when a three-year-old girl gave an inspiring performance of "Itsy Bitsy Spider." My mood shot up like a rocket, and I got off the elevator thinking, "Oh my God, I should have sung it with her!" Later in the day, when I was doing my practice alone in my basement, I sang "Itsy Bitsy Spider" all by myself, including with the cute hand gestures.

Which brings me to the biggest barrier to silliness—*embarrassment.* I try to find the border where embarrassment begins, then cross it. I look for ways to embarrass myself, but usually only in front of myself. If there's a theme in my practice, it's imitating children or myself as a child or just doing make-believe. I have jumped up and down, clapped my hands, and shouted: "Cookies! Cookies! Hooray for cookies!!" I have paraded around my basement to John Philip Sousa marches. I have raised my right hand, placed my left hand on the Bible, and recited the oath of office of the president of the United States. (I've memorized it. It's wise to be ready. These are unpredictable times.)

My antics taught me something startling. When I do a new silly thing, I feel a wave of shame, but if I stick with the silliness, the shame passes, and I laugh out loud. I was surprised that I could feel shame when no one was watching. But then I thought, *"Of course I feel shame when I let the shadow in; it's fear of shame that made me cast the shadow out."*

In Brené Brown's book *Rising Strong*, an editor quotes Nietzsche to her: "What is the seal of liberation? To no longer be ashamed in front of oneself."

Silliness draws out shame in order to defeat it. Silliness is rebellion. Silliness is being daring. Being defenseless. Being vulnerable. Silliness is dropping the mask. It's an act of faith, a mark of trust—even when it's only with yourself. But when silliness is shared, it's intimacy. It's celebration.

Of course, the tyrant-scold in me says, "How can you be silly when people are suffering?" But that's easy. Love is the only force that can heal the world, laughter is a gateway to love, and silliness is a shortcut to laughter. Life is too serious for us not to be silly.

Now all of you repeat after me: "The itsy bitsy spider crawled up the water spout . . ."

NEUROSCIENCE, SPIRITUALITY, AND MAINSTREAM MEDICINE

When these neuroplastic approaches started to change my life, I began thinking like a missionary: "That guy really needs to try this!" "Medical schools need to teach this." "Health writers need to cover this!" But knowledge doesn't change quickly. The self-image ties things up and slows things down.

It's one of the hardest things in the world to say "I was wrong"—especially for brilliant and ambitious people at the top of the medical profession who want to make discoveries, cure diseases, and end suffering. They certainly don't want to be shown up by health practitioners who heal patients with new approaches. So, the field has been slow to take up health advances from mind-body medicine, even when those advances are pioneered by professionals inside the system. ("Mind-body medicine" is a term that covers approaches that Annie Hopper calls "self-directed neuroplasticity.")

Howard Schubiner, a clinical professor of internal medicine at Michigan State University and one of the leading voices in mind-body medicine, came to the field in the middle of his medical career, in 2002, when he began to read Sarno's work. Schubiner later worked personally with Sarno, then developed a new line of practice and research—becoming founder and director of the Mind-Body Medicine Center at Ascension Providence Hospital in Southfield, Michigan.

Schubiner is a coauthor of the University of Colorado at Boulder back-pain study that I cited in chapter 1. He is a cofounder of the Psychophysiologic Disorders Association, a health nonprofit that promotes mind-body medicine and helped fund the Colorado study. He is the author of more than one hundred articles and three books, including *Unlearn Your Pain* and *Unlearn Your Anxiety and Depression,* and teaches a course on the Coursera platform called The Reign of Pain. His work captures the state of mind-body medicine in the country today, which he is trying to bring into the mainstream of medical practice.

THE THEORY OF PREDICTIVE PROCESSING— HOW PHYSICAL PAIN STARTS IN THE BRAIN

The core neuroscience insight that gives rise to mind-body work, Schubiner told me in a phone call, is the theory of "predictive processing." The brain does not perceive the outside world as it is, he explained. The brain doesn't see or hear or feel its surroundings. Instead, the brain interprets stimuli to help us navigate our lives. It's as if the brain were in a black box, estimating and predicting what's going on outside as it tries to respond and keep us safe. In other words, he says, our brain actually generates what we experience.

The core point—and what makes predictive processing so relevant for the work of healing chronic pain and illness—is that the brain doesn't actually "know" what is "out there" or even what is inside of us. The brain only guesses at what's happening, based on inputs and concepts, which can lead it to make some bad guesses about the danger of our surroundings and what's happening in our bodies.

"Fear," Schubiner writes, "is the basis of Mind Body symptoms and the driving force in activating and perpetuating pain."

We know that a sense of danger in the brain can lead to insomnia or anxiety, he says. But it's less known that an activated danger signal in the brain can also create back pain, fatigue, diarrhea, stomach pain, urinary frequency, migraine, pelvic pain, and the inability to concentrate or think clearly. That's why a mind-body approach that reduces the sense of danger can treat all these ailments.

The people who are most susceptible to these mind-body symptoms, says Schubiner, tend to be those who try hard, care what others think, want to be good, and want to be liked. They tend to not stand up for themselves, and they tend to suppress their anger. The tension between what they need to do to protect themselves and what they need to do for others can create internal conflict. It is this conflict that eventually results in mind-body symptoms.

REDUCING THE DANGER SIGNAL

Schubiner and his colleagues have developed two neuroplastic approaches to reducing the danger signals that contribute to chronic illness. The first is Pain Reprocessing Therapy, which is the method used in the Colorado back-pain study. PRT is a basic reprogramming technique. Once it's been determined that the patient has a mind-body condition (for example, it's shown that the back pain is not due to tissue injury), patients are taught to interpret the pain as a neutral sensation and not something that signals danger. The principal healing mechanism of PRT is its ability to convince patients that they are not in danger, which leads to a reduction of fear, which leads to a reduction of pain.

Schubiner teaches several exercises for reversing fear and reducing pain. He writes: "Since your brain is sending you messages almost constantly that you're damaged or broken, that you're not worthy, and that you are in danger, you will need to counteract these messages. Take time each day to stop and remind yourself that you are well, you are healthy, you are strong, you are not damaged, that you are safe. . . . This may take some time, but you will succeed as you allow yourself to let go of the false messages that your brain has been sending."

It is an axiom that "neurons that fire together, wire together," so the point of the exercise is to pair the message of safety with activities that formerly triggered the pain, so that the brain "unlearns" the link between the activity and the symptom, and begins to turn down the danger signal.

The Colorado back-pain study proved the value of PRT in treating chronic back pain. At approximately the same time, Michael Donnino, a professor of emergency medicine at Harvard Medical School, authored with colleagues a back-pain study that used a form of PRT (which Donnino calls Psychophysiologic Symptom Relief Therapy, or PSRT) and showed results comparable to those of the Colorado study. In another study, Donnino and colleagues showed that PSRT can decrease symptoms in patients suffering from long COVID.

A second approach that heals mind-body symptoms is called Emotional Awareness and Expression Therapy (EAET). EAET, which was developed jointly by Mark Lumley, a professor of psychology at Wayne State University, and Dr. Schubiner, is derived from Intensive Short-Term Dynamic Psychotherapy (ISTDP), which was created by Habib Davanloo, a professor of psychiatry at McGill University in Montreal.

ISTDP has been extensively studied, most notably by Allan Abbass, a professor of psychiatry at Dalhousie University in Halifax, Nova Scotia, who documented the effectiveness of ISTDP for pain and unexplained medical symptoms. The ISTDP model has also been documented in detail by psychologist Dr. Patricia Coughlin Della Selva, who trained with Davanloo and has written landmark books and articles in the field.

The healing power of EAET and ISTDP comes from helping

patients experience feelings they have avoided. As Coughlin summarizes in her book *Lives Transformed,* "Full and direct experience of previously avoided feelings is the key to healing."

ISTDP and EAET are both premised on the understanding that all of us, from infancy, have a full range of impulses and feelings inside, some of which we learn are dangerous to express because they can threaten our most important bonds. So, we come to fear these feelings and we learn to hold them in.

This is not just when we're children. Even as adults, we're afraid that if we let ourselves feel all these feelings, we might act out, lose our family and friends, and get kicked out of the clan. And the danger of getting kicked out of the clan—in whatever form that takes at this stage of evolution—sounds alarms in the brain. So, we hold in the feelings and are on constant guard against the danger, and those maladaptive responses create a continuous stream of fear going from our brain to the body.

So, what do we do? Acting out powerful feelings will destroy our reputation and our relationships. Holding in powerful feelings eats away at us from the inside. What's the middle path? Coughlin writes, "Use of visualization and imagery seems to provide an intermediate stage between suppressing emotion and discharging it via action."

Schubiner has also found that when his patients experience and express these emotions in a safe, private, and therapeutic way, the effect on physical and emotional health can be quick and dramatic.

As Schubiner guides his patients in this approach, he suggests that they identify a traumatic or stressful event from the past and enter that scene, trying to feel the feelings that arose at the time. Then, he instructs, "speak the words that you would have said at the time if you were powerful enough to say anything that should have been said. Be powerful and say whatever comes to your mind to express your anger to the offender. Be strong and honest. Speak out loud. Don't hold anything back."

Note that the person is not actually reliving the hurtful experience, which can be retraumatizing, but changing it by expressing emotions that could not have been expressed and acting out a different ending.

This process—which includes naming the emotion, feeling its sensations in the body, and visualizing your words and actions—can be transformative. Not only does it release the long-held emotion but it reduces the symptoms we create by holding the emotion in, and it exposes the lie that the feelings are dangerous.

Coughlin, who calls this process "dreaming while awake," says it allows patients to experience and express their most heavily defended feelings and impulses in a safe way.

"Following the full and direct experience of the previously avoided feelings of rage, guilt, and grief, patients often experience strong feelings of relief, along with surges of love, joy, tenderness, and happiness." She calls it the "liberation of positive emotion."

The positive emotions are trapped underneath the negative emotions. When we experience and express the negative emotions, the positive ones have a chance to come out.

"A nun I was treating," Coughlin writes, "who had always considered anger to be a sin, experienced an outpouring of love, compassion, and openness each time she acknowledged and faced her anger directly. Accompanying these emotions was a deep sense of acceptance of herself and others, which had previously eluded her. She noted that this was one of the great surprises of our work together."

In his book *Unlearn Your Pain*, Schubiner includes a story told by a patient named Vicky.

> Lucky. That's how at 18 years old, I described being raped at knifepoint by an intruder in my very first apartment. Lucky. A lot of women get raped and murdered, I told myself. I'm still alive, so I have no right to feel sorry for myself, to be angry. Thirty years later, debilitating migraine headaches led me to read *Unlearn Your Pain*. I got angry at my rapist for the very first time. I screamed, "You have no right to touch me!" over and over until decades of pain erupted like an exploding volcano. I imagined my neighbor and I kicking his crumbling ass to the ground in the narrow courtyard of the apartment building. I finished the story with the police arresting him. I began to heal a wound I never even knew I had.
>
> I don't remember ever thinking I deserved to feel compassion for myself, no matter how bad the situation. There was always someone who had it worse than I did. This caused me to take care of everyone else and put everyone's needs before mine. . . .
>
> Just deal with it and keep smiling. Throughout my life, this trait earned me all kinds of praise, "She's so strong. . . . She's so nice. . . . She can handle ANYTHING." No one ever saw me upset, or angry, or grumpy, or rude. I did everything I could to ignore my body and brain's attempts to get my attention. It wasn't just chronic migraines. My back went into spasms during a bad marriage. I doubled over in abdominal pain for 9 months under the subordination of a terrible boss. . . .
>
> To heal, I needed to allow myself to feel; to feel the grief as it welled up and flowed out of me, and to feel the anger. . . . This anger came quickly, boiled up unexpectedly, and gave me

an instant feeling of healing from physical symptoms in my chest and head. My migraines have all but subsided.

Learning how to safely experience and express feelings that we hold inside has a powerful effect on the thoughts and emotions that contribute to pain and illness.

Schubiner uses EAET to treat a range of mind-body symptoms. He and Mark Lumley studied a group of fifty-nine adults with chronic musculoskeletal pain, with an average pain duration of nearly nine years. Six months after going through the mind-body program, more than half showed a reduction of pain scores by at least 50 percent.

In a larger study funded by the National Institutes of Health, Lumley and Schubiner found in a randomized controlled trial of people with fibromyalgia that 22 percent of those treated with EAET had more than 50 percent pain reduction at a six-month follow-up in comparison to 8 percent who achieved this pain reduction using cognitive behavioral therapy. This was the first large-scale study to show that one psychological therapy for chronic pain was superior to another.

Dr. Brandon Yarns at the UCLA School of Medicine employed EAET in a trial with military veterans suffering from chronic musculoskeletal pain and showed that 31 percent had greater than 50 percent pain reduction, compared with none achieving that result in a cognitive behavioral therapy group.

As I was talking to Schubiner about these studies, I told him I had gone to the websites of some of the nation's top hospitals to search for their advice for patients with fibromyalgia, and I saw that they didn't cite this approach.

"That's interesting," Schubiner said. "I've talked to those people. I've presented my data there." Then he listed the names of top hospitals he's visited, chuckled, and said, "Well, things change slowly. We have more studies on the way."

THE NEXT STUDY

I didn't realize how soon the next study would come, but I found out in December 2023 after I sent Schubiner a video clip from the Netflix series *The Crown*. In the scene I sent, Prince Philip was talking to Prince William, who was devastated over the loss of his mother and was furious with his father. Prince Philip's message suggested that the writers for *The Crown* were more aware of mind-body medicine than are some doctors in US hospitals.

> Before we talk about you and your father, I'm assuming it's your father, I want to talk to you about something else—back pain. I get it from time to time, and when I do I find it easier to label it just that, back pain or neck pain or shoulder pain, rather than what's actually causing it—unresolved anger, feelings of guilt or resentment. . . .
>
> Maybe you're angry with your father because it's more acceptable than admitting who you're really angry with . . . Is it possible you're angry with her because, well, because of her leaving you? . . . Except what son can ever be angry with his mother, especially when he's grieving for her and missing her so terribly? So, you take it out on someone else and blame him for the fact that she's gone.

Schubiner sent an email back saying, "Yes, others have also sent out this clip!" Then he told me of a study he was publishing in March 2024 in *The Journal of Pain*. The study, done at the Center for Orthopedics in Lake Charles, Louisiana, evaluated 222 people with chronic neck or back pain and found that 88 percent suffered pain caused by brain circuits alone, while only 12 percent suffered pain caused by tissue damage.

The study is significant for demonstrating a clinic-ready method for determining the cause of chronic pain, and an article in the *Los Angeles Times*, by science writer Nathaniel Frank, says the study also "offers robust evidence that the overwhelming majority of chronic neck and back pain cases . . . come from the mind, despite the fact that most diagnoses cite a physical cause."

Frank notes that between fifty million and one hundred million Americans suffer chronic pain, and "for the most part, these patients are spending billions of dollars pursuing physical treatments. If the cause is nonphysical, the money is wasted and . . . not only are we failing to alleviate the pain, we are creating dangerous side effects that include the opioid crisis as well as surgeries that may be unnecessary and leave patients worse off. . . .

"The existing medical paradigm assumes a physical cause for most chronic pain," Frank writes. "The findings in the Louisiana study suggest that's often wrong."

This shows not only that we can heal much of our chronic pain by addressing our thoughts and feelings but that we can't heal our pain *unless* we address our thoughts and feelings. When pain starts in the brain and is sustained by stress, we're the *only* ones who can heal the pain because we're the only ones with direct access to the thoughts and feelings that *cause* the pain. When we learn to respond differently to our thoughts and feelings, we can ease the fear and end the pain. No outside force can do this for us.

In an exchange with Frank, who is now authoring a book on mind-body pain for the Mayo Clinic Press, I asked him why—with all the studies and data now available—the mind-body movement is still in slow motion. He told me: "A lot of the people with the power to advance these ideas—science editors, medical doctors, and the like—dwell in highly educated, hyperrational circles, where suspicion of mind-body medicine rules the day. While skepticism is healthy, the lengths to which some of these folks will go to avoid mind-body explanations for things they can't otherwise understand is astounding."

NEUROSCIENCE AND SPIRITUALITY— PENETRATING THE DARKNESS

We've looked at two broad approaches to shaping the thoughts, beliefs, and feelings that sculpt our brains and guide our lives. The first approach is to accentuate the positive, reprogramming dark thoughts with lighter thoughts. The second is to bring up the negative—*as a way to clear the way for the positive*. Just as Richard Rohr says that cultivating a positive response is the heartbeat of any authentic spirituality, he also teaches that profound spiritual practice requires going deep into our unconscious minds.

In *Dancing Standing Still*, Rohr writes: "Contemplation is trying to address the root, the underlying place, where illusion and ego are generated. It touches the unconscious, where most of our wounds and need for healing lie."

"If your prayer goes deep," Rohr writes, "your whole view of the world will change from fear to connection. It is absolutely essential that we find a spirituality that reaches to that hidden level," he says. "If not, nothing really changes."

The Dynamic Neural Retraining work of Annie Hopper, the mind-body work of Howard Schubiner, the neuroplastic approaches of Rick Hanson, the psychological techniques that bring up the feelings we shove down—and the convergence of all of it with the wisdom of Richard Rohr and other spiritual teachers—support the view that a common and defining feature of these healing approaches is to reduce your fear by challenging the belief that you're in danger. And that suggests to me that the brain-centered treatments to cure chronic illness—in their fullest application—unify the scientific and spiritual approaches to easing pain and suffering.

The core breakthrough for me was finding practices that began to expose and dissolve my false beliefs—first about my health and ultimately about my "self." Loosening and then losing false thoughts that formed my self-image did not just mean surrendering flattering views of myself; it meant getting free of false beliefs about what would make me happy, what would put me at risk, what would make me safe, and what would bring me peace.

Remember Thomas Keating's definition of repentance: "changing the direction in which you're searching for happiness." For me, this required changing my response to fear. I noticed that my plan for health was based on avoidance—and that avoidance reinforces the fear. So, my breakthrough was the move from avoidance to exposure—which meant a shift toward courage.

It wasn't a wholesale change; it was a change in direction, a shift in emphasis. It meant slowly defying old beliefs and thus dethroning the fear that kept them in place. So, I began to do things I had not done before, which led to a larger picture of who I was. These weren't features I intentionally added to my sense of self; they were parts of myself that rejoined me once my fear stopped forcing them out.

This sense of joy—the fountain of good feelings that rises up in me without reference to anything in the material world—comes from being welcomed by the spiritual world. I found the spiritual power of neuroscience in practices that help us find peace on the other side of our false beliefs.

And the innermost breakthrough was a well-guided shift in my response to fear. That shift set all the other changes in motion—from avoidance to exposure, from believing false messages to challenging them, from obeying them to defying them, from fearing emotions to feeling them. That shift is the epicenter of breakthrough—the original step on a journey toward joy that goes on and on and on.

CHAPTER TEN

Breakthrough after Breakthrough

One breakthrough makes another breakthrough more likely—whether we want it or not.

In early 2020, during a brief moment on a busy morning, I glanced at my emails and saw a message from Annie Robinson, a woman I'd met in 2013, when she was facilitating a workshop I attended at Georgetown University. Annie later became head of the Well-Being Program for resident physicians at NYU School of Medicine, and she's shown a gift for sending me what I need to read.

Early on, she introduced me to the writings of John O'Donohue, the stunning Irish mystic I had never heard of. A few years later, she sent me the first TED Talks of Brené Brown, a social-science researcher I had never heard of. That morning, she was sending me a link to something called The Work, by Byron Katie, whom I had never heard of. "My friends and I think she's amazing," Annie wrote. "You should know about her."

"No!" I thought, searching for a reason to denigrate this new call to growth. "*The Work*, by *Byron Katie*?" I sneered. "People will do *anything* these days to slap their name on something! Imagine: *The Noble Eightfold Path*, brought to you by *The Buddha!*"

I gave it a sarcastic glance, started reading it to find a reason to dismiss it—and then postponed my deadlines and changed my day so I could learn all about it.

Katie's story was irresistible, especially for someone like me who fantasizes about overnight enlightenment. After more than a decade of suicidal despair, she had entered a treatment center, where she slept on the floor because she didn't believe she deserved a bed. The other residents had barricaded her into an upper floor because they were terrified she was going to descend in a rage in the middle of the night and kill them all. Then, one morning, she opened her eyes, and her depression was gone. Her rage was gone. The thoughts that were tormenting her were gone. And she was intoxicated with joy.

It took Katie some time to figure out what had happened, and more time to figure out how to teach it. But as she found her voice, she explained that she had seen the cause of all suffering—that her depression had nothing to do with the world around her. It was caused by what she believed about the world. When she believed her thoughts, she suffered. When she didn't believe her thoughts, she didn't suffer—and this is true for every human being.

There are powerful similarities between The Work and the practices of Annie Hopper and Howard Schubiner, which I described in the previous chapter. They all derive their teaching power from the reality of neuroplasticity, that we can use our mind to change our brain. They all teach that we suffer from false beliefs, and they all offer techniques for bringing forward our false beliefs and dissolving them. They all move our attention from the outside world to the inner world, showing us that suffering doesn't come from the stimulus but from our response.

Schubiner cites the experience of both Byron Katie and Eckhart Tolle in his book *Unlearn Your Pain*. "They both realized that they were telling themselves a false story, believing self-defeating thoughts as if these thoughts were true," Schubiner writes. "When they challenged them, they recovered." In fact, Schubiner directs his readers to Katie's website, saying, "Those materials have been invaluable for many of my patients."

Katie's method takes a precise and distinctive approach to our thinking.

We can't let go of our thoughts, she says. But if we question them, they let go of us. That is the core of Katie's simple and penetrating spiritual practice, which she calls both The Work and Inquiry. The centerpiece of the practice is the "Judge-Your-Neighbor Worksheet," which Katie summarizes with a little rhyme: "Judge your neighbor / Write it down / Ask four questions / And turn it around."

We write down our stressful thoughts on the Worksheet. We question the thoughts. Then we turn the thoughts around and test whether the opposite thought is just as true as or perhaps even more true than our original thought.

The practice shows us the role of thought in our stressful feelings; that if we didn't believe the thought, we wouldn't have the feelings; and that either the thought is untrue or the opposite of the thought is just as true. That shows us that we're suffering for nothing. It shakes the foundation of the thought, and it begins to lose its power over us.

My first experience of the humbling and liberating power of The

Work came a week or so after I first learned about Katie. I was invited to lead a regular Monday-morning meditation meeting, and I decided I would invite everyone to do a Judge-Your-Neighbor Worksheet.

We all wrote down a stressful thought. And then we asked Katie's four questions:

1. Is it true?
2. Can you absolutely know that it's true?
3. How do you react, what happens, when you believe that thought?
4. Who would you be without the thought?

Some volunteers shared their answers, then it was time to turn around the stressful thought and articulate its opposite. I went first. The "neighbor" I was judging was someone I'd known for years who had committed the unforgivable Washington, DC, sin of making me feel unimportant. I had just read a newspaper article describing his rise to new levels of power. This appalled me. As I read the article, I began reviewing all his flaws in my head. Then I began plotting my rise to a position of power from which I would snub him vigorously, making him repent of his past cruelty.

In our session that Monday morning, I had written down the stressful thought: "He's shallow. He's narrow. He bounces like a pinball back and forth between power and money, always seeking the higher position, circling until he gets it, never motivated by a cause or a good deed, but only seeking the highest place of power and wealth and prestige for himself."

As I read it aloud, everyone in the room laughed at the intensity of it. Then I got to my turnaround: "I'm shallow. I'm narrow. I bounce like a pinball back and forth between power and money . . . never motivated by a good cause, but only seeking the highest place . . ."

The group laughed even louder. And so did I.

Then I had to explore: How is my statement "*I'm* shallow, etc." just as true as or perhaps more true than the original statement "*He's* shallow"?

Here's how: The guy who inflames me is engaged in public service, trying to advance causes that can improve the lives of hundreds of millions or more, while I—nursing a childish grievance from years before—am listing all his imagined flaws with a keen sense of moral righteousness. What could be shallower than *that*?! As for circling and seeking a better position, in exactly what way am I different from him—apart from him being more successful?

Welcome to The Work, Tom.

BREAKTHROUGH AFTER BREAKTHROUGH

A breakthrough, as we've been discussing it, involves changing your behavior, your brain, your life by feeling avoided feelings and shedding false beliefs. A breakthrough *after* a breakthrough is likely to involve exposing *more* false beliefs, finding a new approach to exposing false beliefs, or exposing false beliefs that are closer and closer to the core of who you think you are. For me, The Work delivered all three, and especially number three.

To explain, let me cite Katie's book *Loving What Is*, and the introduction written by her husband, Stephen Mitchell. Mitchell is a veteran of intensive Zen practice and also a translator of ancient literary and spiritual masterpieces, including the *Bhagavad Gita, Gilgamesh, The Book of Job,* the *Tao Te Ching, The Iliad,* and *The Odyssey.* Drawing on his own spiritual practice, and his intimate knowledge of the world's spiritual masterpieces, Mitchell has in some ways taken on the task of translating and interpreting Katie to the world, sometimes using the language of classic spiritual texts and at other times using the language of science.

In his introduction, Mitchell writes:

> It's worth noting that inquiry fits precisely with current research into the biology of mind. Contemporary neuroscience identifies a particular part of the brain, sometimes called "the interpreter," as the source of the familiar internal narrative that gives us our sense of self. Two prominent neuroscientists have recently characterized the quirky, undependable quality of the tale told by the interpreter.

Antonio Damasio describes it this way:

> Perhaps the most important revelation is precisely this: that the left cerebral hemisphere of humans is prone to fabricating verbal narratives that do not necessarily accord with the truth.

And Michael Gazzaniga writes:

> The left brain weaves its story in order to convince itself and you that it is in full control. . . . What is so adaptive about having what amounts to a spin doctor in the left brain? The interpreter . . . is really trying to keep our personal story together. To do that, we have to learn to lie to ourselves.

These findings of brain-science research are hugely significant. They do more than expose the false and deceptive brain messages that say chemical smells are life-threatening or that our back pain is a sign of danger. This is scientific evidence that the brain is falsifying our understanding of who we are. Our self-image, our personal identity, our thoughts that make up our personal story—all these are soothing, reassuring, cherished lies.

This is a reality far outside most cultural narratives about the meaning and purpose of our lives. But one narrative that has reached enough readers to become a cultural reference point is the story Eckhart Tolle tells of his own awakening.

In *The Power of Now*, he describes waking at night with "absolute dread" and thinking, "I cannot live with myself any longer."

Then he asked himself, "Am I one or two? If I cannot live with myself, there must be two of me: the 'I' and the 'self' that 'I' cannot live with," "Maybe . . . only one of them is real."

At this point, he said, he was fully conscious, but there were no more thoughts. He woke the next day to the chirping of a bird, feeling as if he had just been born. He enjoyed a state of bliss in the coming months and came to realize that "nothing I ever did could possibly add anything to what I already had."

The findings of the neuroscientists combined with Eckhart's and Katie's stories of their awakenings suggest two things: first, that we need to question the deepest possible thoughts we have about ourselves—because these accounts imply that our most sacred and personal beliefs are not only false but are the cause of our suffering. Second, we're being lied to by our own brains, which is tragic, but actually a bit funny if you think about it. (Like, who can you trust anymore?)

Perhaps it's seeing the lie of the false self that explains why some spiritual teachers are so lighthearted and laugh so much—because they're in on the joke, and they don't have to pretend anymore. At the moment of her awakening, Katie says, "Laughter welled up from the depths and just poured out."

Remember the old line that says the truth will set you free, but first it will piss you off? Maybe it's the opposite. It's the false stuff that pisses you off. The truth makes you laugh.

That's why The Work is filled with humor and laughter—and much of the humor plays at the border between who we are and who we're pretending to be. For me, the laughter can come in a variety of ways—but they're all a bit like the humor of finding an adorably fat toddler stealing a cookie and thinking he can't be seen. It comes when I catch myself blaming others when I'm obviously at fault, accusing people of doing stuff that *I'm* doing, posing as virtuous when I'm being selfish, or pretending to be kind when I'm feeling competitive—that's comic material if I can see it and share it with someone who understands and smiles.

There's something funny about exposing the trickery. But it's only funny if we know we're a bit of a fraud, and we know it's all still okay. If there's forgiveness, it's funny; if not, it's scary.

That's one reason why angry, negative people have such a hard time smiling and laughing. They are trying to get their sense of meaning and purpose and importance from declaring that everything is terrible. They've been cheated and robbed by bad people. They need that story, so they *have* to be grim. They can't be lighthearted. Ever. If they break character, they betray the knowledge that it's all a performance.

In 2022, toward the end of COVID, I went on retreat with friends at the Abbey of Gethsemani, the Trappist monastery where Thomas

Merton lived and is buried. We met an exuberantly cheerful monk there named Brother Luke Armour, who was seventy years old and looked forty. Brother Luke was music director at the abbey. (He told us that Bach would write *"Jesus, juve!"*—Jesus, help!—on his music sheets before he began composing.) Luke said that years before, one of the monks at Gethsemani saw another monk running up the stairs and brought him before the abbot on a charge of "lack of monastic gravity." The abbot considered the charge and said, "I don't know what 'monastic gravity' is, but it sounds like something we all should lack."

MY TOP TEN LIST

As I deepened my practice in The Work, I found it helpful to see the humor in it. So, I decided to make a list of the stressful thoughts that were funny. Of course, when the thoughts first come, they're not funny; they're grim and serious. But when I write them down and question them, they make me laugh. Here are my top ten, each spoken with a deep sense of grievance, in the tone of a child crying, "It's just not FAIR!":

10. They're just mean people trying to hurt me!
 9. They're ruining my dreams!
 8. I can't take *one more thing*!
 7. Everyone should do as I say!
 6. I'm *never* going to get better.
 5. My days are numbered!
 4. I'm dying.

3. These jerks don't love me enough.

2. I should have been a monk.

1. I will never be happy until these people understand how very special I am.

Some of these statements have killer turnarounds, especially number one: "I will never be happy until I understand how very special these people are." Another turnaround I love, for different reasons, is a response to my constant subconscious thought "I need to keep getting better." So, I sometimes say, "I need to keep getting worse." Or even "O Lord, please give me the grace to become the worst person I can be in the time I have left." It strikes a defiant blow for freedom against the tyrannical inner scold, and that makes me laugh.

If we really do believe our dark thoughts, then we can't laugh. But when cracks begin to appear in their austere majesty, we start snickering, even in the face of the most serious matters.

In *Loving What Is*, Katie visits a woman with cancer:

> I have sat with many people on their deathbeds, and after we do The Work, they always tell me that they're fine. I remember one very frightened woman who was dying of cancer. She had requested that I sit with her, so I came. I sat down beside her and said, "I don't see a problem." She said, "No? Well, I'll show you a problem!" and she pulled off the sheet. One of her legs was so swollen that it was at least twice the size of the normal leg. I looked and I looked, and I still couldn't find a problem. She said, "You must be blind! Look at this leg. Now look at the other one." And I said, "Oh, now I see the problem. You're suffering from the belief that that leg should look like this one. Who would you be without that thought?" And she

got it. She began to laugh, and the fear just poured out through her laughter. She said that this was the happiest she had ever been in her entire life.

BEFORE IT GETS FUNNY

When someone can laugh in the face of death, I bow my head to them. When I'm digging into my deepest, darkest beliefs, I'm not laughing. I'm grim. At least at the start.

When I was a few months away from delivering the first draft of this book, I had to put everything aside to prepare a presentation for an event that was very important to me. It was a high-stakes moment. It wasn't about cancer or violent crime or the threat of war. It was about my self-image.

If I'm taking a walk, there's no self-image involved. If I'm giving a talk, there is. If I'm giving a talk on a topic I've spent my life on, it's a big self-image moment, and I'm scared.

I was getting up early in the morning and working till midnight to get that presentation right. And even though I was fully aware that my self-image was driving the perfectionism, I was still ensnared by it. My conscious mind knows the game, but my subconscious has a lot of addictive habits, and they take a long time to drain out.

So, one morning I got up grim again, ready to start work at 5:00 a.m.—that's my best and highest energy of the day—and instead of jumping out of the gate in a sprint, I took out a Judge-Your-Neighbor Worksheet. I sat quietly and asked myself: "What is the thought that's driving me to work so hard? What is the belief I need to question?"

I had to filter through a lot of thoughts that swam on the surface: "Those people are expecting too much. They're making me work too hard! They should back off and give me a break. They shouldn't expect me to get all this done. They need to tell me to slow down. They're stealing the joy out of doing what I love."

That was the content of the first few worksheets, and when I started questioning those statements and turning them around, it became clear that a big mischief-maker was a thought underneath all those other thoughts: "I need to *amaze* people."

That thought is the source of so much of my suffering.

I get it. My need to amaze people is driving this stress, and it's my own doing. But why do I need to amaze people? What's in it for me? What do I stand to gain when I "amaze" people. And what do I stand to lose if I fail?

"If I amaze people, I'll get belonging."

Okay, but what am I calling belonging? Belonging is not a fact. It's a feeling. It's a buzz I equate with the belief "People love me. I'm safe. I'm secure." That buzz is what I'm after. I have arranged my life to provide the events that create the thoughts that lead to the feelings that give me the buzz I crave.

So, when I get stressful and overprepare and get perfectionistic and get angry with all the obstacles, it's all for the sake of trying to achieve a postevent buzz that lets me feel peaceful for an hour or two, until the cycle starts again.

That's the path of breakdown. If I'm going to get a breakthrough, it won't come from fulfilling the story I'm longing for. It will come from losing the story. So, I questioned the underlying beliefs. What are the beliefs that have made "I need to amaze people" a nonnegotiable condition of my life?

"If I don't amaze people, no one will love me, and I'll be sad and die alone."

"If I *do* amaze people, everyone will love me, and I will live a life of meaning and purpose."

Lies.

But I can't push back on the lies, or I'll strengthen them. All I can do is inquire and question and keep going deeper. Because when an underlying belief is shaken, everything above it falls with it.

"If I amaze people, everyone will love me; if I don't amaze people, no one will love me."

Is it true?

The questioning unpacks a stack of lies: "I need to amaze people because I need to prove my value and earn my place, or I won't be loved. But I must do more than earn my place. Merely belonging won't get me the love I need. It won't protect me from getting kicked out. I must be the MVP. I must be the hero. I must be indispensable, or I will be expendable. I could be humiliated. The only way to prevent humiliation is to be amazing—continuously amazing."

I did worksheets to question these thoughts, and I did a lot of turnarounds of the thought "I need to amaze people," and the turnaround that moved me most was: "I need to be amazed by people."

When I turned the thought from "I need to amaze people" to "I need to be amazed by people" I replaced the goal of creating a buzz in someone else's mind with the goal of opening to a sense of awe in my own mind. Still a goal, but one more aligned with the movement of grace.

What good did this do me? The internal engine throttled back a bit. I laughed at some of the insights. And at the workshop, without scripting it or intending it, I found I had more appreciation than usual for the gifts of everyone who came—and after my talk was done, I spent surprisingly little time thinking about how it had gone.

THE WORK AS SHADOW WORK—
FROM PERFECTION TO WHOLENESS

In the spring of 2023, I joined three hundred people at a nine-day "The School for The Work" offered by Katie in Los Angeles. In one exchange with a student who was finding it hard to acknowledge some truths about himself, Katie encouraged him by saying, "We prize meeting just one authentic, transparent human being in our lives. When we hold it in, we separate ourselves from the whole human race."

That's inspiring. But when we *don't* hold it in, we separate ourselves from the whole human race too. If we say whatever's on our mind, people will take us down or kick us out.

So, at the close of a long day toward the end of the retreat, I saw Katie making her way out of the hall, and I went over to talk to her. There were a couple students ahead of me, and when my turn came, I said, "But I *have* to hold it in—or all my relationships are going to blow up!" She said, "Don't hold it in. Draw it out, write it down, and then question it."

Then I asked a follow-up:

"Can I have a hug?"

"Oh, sweetie!" she said, and gave me a big mama-bear hug.

When we released, I said, "I will never feel satisfied that I have thanked you enough."

She reached up, took my face in her hand, and said:

"I would question that thought."

A few days after the Katie retreat, I was back home sitting on my porch when I was hit with an insight and started to cry. I reached for my phone and called a friend. I had just had a glimpse of what Katie was up to.

But before I tell you that, some background . . .

Toward the end of his life, Carl Jung was spending a lot of time thinking about the evolution of humanity, the movement from an all-masculine concept of reality to a view that included the feminine. The movement of evolution, as Robert A. Johnson writes, is to replace an image of perfection with the concept of wholeness.

"Perfection suggests something all pure," Johnson says, "with no blemishes, dark spots or questionable areas. Wholeness includes the darkness but combines it with the light elements into a totality more real and whole than any ideal."

In Jungian terms, becoming whole means bringing in what we've been shoving out, revealing what we've been hiding, admitting what we've been denying. It means acknowledging and integrating the shadow—all the parts of ourselves we've denied and pushed aside.

Johnson writes in *Owning Your Own Shadow,* "To honor and accept one's shadow is a profound spiritual discipline. It is whole-making and thus holy and the most important experience of a life-time."

It's tricky work. Our challenge is to avoid suppressing the shadow so aggressively that it blows up on us and avoid expressing it so freely that it destroys our reputation and relationships. The answer, in Johnson's words, is "to pay out that shadow in an intelligent way."

What does that mean? Johnson talks about various ceremonies and rituals that have been society's ways of paying out the collective shadow. "Culture can only function if we live out the unwanted elements symbolically," he says. "All healthy societies have a rich ceremonial life. Less healthy ones rely on unconscious expressions: war, violence, psychosomatic illness, neurotic suffering, and accidents are very low-grade ways of living out the shadow."

Of course, we also need to pay out the shadow wisely as individuals, and we suffer consequences when we don't. Johnson says that after we've suppressed our darker impulses to endure a painful social situation in a courteous way, we need to do some creative work to "pay the dark price" so our anger doesn't blow up unexpectedly. He suggests, for example, that when he needs to pay out the shadow, he might "write some blood-and-thunder low-grade short story."

I know what he's talking about. I remember getting a friendly email from a colleague, at the end of a stressful project, telling me I was a "delight" to work with, and I thought, "You have no idea how much I had to suppress to achieve that effect." At one point, I had received an angry email from a different colleague, and I was three keystrokes away from sending back this message: "Here you are, coming to the end of your life, and you still haven't learned how to meet stress with grace." But I realized that if I sent that message, it would have been equally true of me, so I suppressed that too.

I had read Johnson's book in 2018, marked it up obsessively, and continued to hold these ideas in my head. It was only upon sitting in the sun on the day of my return that I made the connection between

Jung and Katie, and I called my friend Rose Shriver, a Jungian therapist who knows and loves The Work.

More than a year before, I had sent her my book proposal and asked her to be my guide in these areas that she knows much better than I do. That day, I left her a long message. "Rosie, I think the Worksheets are drawing out the shadow. As we write them out, we're paying out the shadow. As we question our thoughts, we're reducing our shadow. That's what's going on. We're solving the riddle of the mask and the shadow."

This felt *enormous* to me. Projecting the shadow, scapegoating, seeing our sins in others—this is foundational to human society. This is original sin. This is *the* tragic flaw in humanity, and it will destroy us unless we solve it.

After I left the message, I began cycling through memories of Katie's comments and then looked over my notes from the nine days. Katie uses the term "ego," but I could see that it aligns with what a Jungian would call the shadow.

Here are some of her quotes:

- "The ego's job is to live in secret, not to get found out."
- "Be very respectful of the ego. If you attack it, you'll make it stronger."
- "When you're in inquiry, the ego will begin to trust that you're not trying to kill it."
- "The ego is fighting for its life. Don't you have compassion?"

Then as I reviewed Katie's instructions for filling out a Judge-Your-Neighbor Worksheet, I saw the same message:

> I invite you to contemplate for a moment a situation where you were angry, hurt, sad, or disappointed with someone. Be as judgmental, childish, and petty as you were in that situation. Don't try to be wiser or kinder than you were. This is a time to be totally honest and uncensored about why you were hurt and how you felt in that situation. Allow your feelings to express themselves as they arise, without any fear of consequences or any threat of punishment.

Clearly, she's telling us to welcome back the feelings we've shoved out. A day or so later, a friend I'd met in The School for The Work sent me an email: "This guidance from Katie just popped up in a facebook group, right in time to send it to you":

> "I suggest that we direct gentleness, understanding, noticing, clear-mindedness, and compassion towards our own unloved thoughts, rather than seeing them as something to let go of or overcome. Thoughts have been excluded, blamed, shamed, cursed, meditated away, medicated away, tricked and denied and dealt with continually as though they were the enemy. I have come to see that thoughts are the beloved. Leave no thought unloved or any belief unrecognized."
>
> —*Byron Katie*

The more I studied my notes and read passages from Katie's books, the more convinced I became that this is shadow work. And I marveled that one of the most beloved and revered Jungians in one of his most widely read books writes about the need for ceremonies and symbolic rituals to pay out these dark forces—while Katie simply invites the shadow in for tea.

Later that day, I got a voice text back from Rosie, who was at the park with her two-year-old.

"Got your message," she said. "Makes so much sense. Love that she is encouraging us to bring it out more. That's The Work. Curious to know more. Have to go. But Worksheets as shadow work: Yes. Yes. Yes. Amen."

If this is right, and a Worksheet is shadow work, then there seems to be alignment between the neuroscientists who say we're lying to ourselves to hold our story together; the Jungians who advise us to integrate the mask and the shadow; the mystics who find the divine on the other side of our thinking; and Katie, who says, "Question your thoughts." They're all offering a solution to the perennial question facing humanity: How do we end the divisions in ourselves so we can mend the divisions in our world?

CHAPTER ELEVEN

What Works?

I n his book *Opening Up by Writing It Down*, Dr. James W. Pennebaker, a pioneer in writing therapy and an expert in the health consequences of secrets, tells the story of Warren—a bright young man who was doing well in college until he developed test anxiety and was forced to withdraw from school.

After two years of failed approaches, Warren was referred to Pennebaker, who asked him to talk about his life while wearing a heart monitor. As Warren talked about his girlfriend, his college courses, and his future—his heart rate stayed in the 70s. When he talked about his parents' divorce, it jumped to 103. As Warren's heart was signaling his distress, his words were telling a lie. "It's no big deal, really," he said. "They are a lot happier now."

Warren had learned about his parents' divorce a week before the test anxiety emerged, and he hadn't talked about it to anyone, hiding it even from his girlfriend, because he thought it was a private matter. Following the heart-rate test, he talked about his anger and despair with Pennebaker and later with his parents and his girl-friend, and while he still had those feelings, the test anxiety disappeared, and he returned to college.

"Keeping secrets is physical work," Pennebaker writes. "When we try to keep a secret, we must actively hold back or inhibit our thoughts, feelings, or behaviors. . . . Over time, the work of keeping secrets serves as a cumulative stressor on the body, increasing the likelihood of illness and other stress-related physical and mental problems."

Secrets can serve as a central concept of spiritual practice, no matter what the method, because secrets are the building blocks of the self-image. The self-image is a continuous act of secret-keeping that goes on all day long, one day after another, every year of our lives.

Putting forward the image that "I'm an honest person" means I must make it a secret that I sometimes lie. Projecting the image that "I'm a happy person" means I must make it a secret when I'm depressed. Putting out the view that "I'm a good person" means there are whole fields of reality that I must deny.

Achieving a self-image means adding and defending secrets. Dissolving the self-image means surrendering our secrets—and this means secret-keeping can give us a tool for assessing a spiritual practice and asking the question, What works?

The answer, to be helpful, should come not in the form of a single technique or approach but in the insights and principles that underlie numerous approaches. A successful practice will help us lose the secrets, including the secrets we keep from ourselves. Some people don't feel comfortable talking about the unconscious. But whether we use the words *unconscious* or *nonconscious*, or *subconscious*, or *semiconscious*—whether we talk about repressing our feelings, or suppressing them, or shoving them down, or holding them in—it doesn't really matter. In any language, in any approach, bringing out the things we're hiding is healing.

WHAT DIDN'T WORK FOR ME

In theologian Henri Nouwen's book *Life of the Beloved*, he offers spiritual guidance to a young friend:

> If you are interested in starting on the journey of the Beloved, I have a lot more to say to you, because the journey of the spiritual life calls not only for determination, but also for a certain knowledge of the terrain to be crossed. I don't want you to have to wander about in the desert for forty years as did our spiritual forebears. I don't even want you to dwell there as long as I did.

I spent forty years trying things that didn't work. Of course, I remember the counsel of my doctor friend who said, "Never devalue the work you do before your breakthrough." I *do* value that work. But I value more highly the principles and practices that began to break me free. It is what I long to share with my boys and others who want the same things in life that I do—and might use my experience to take a more direct path to them than I did.

In the painfully long preamble to my spiritual life, I wasn't bringing out the things I was hiding; I was burying them. I wanted to be a saint. And I had the traditional set of tools—an image of perfection, a longing to be better than others, a deep well of willpower—and guilt. That was my religion: try hard, fail big, feel guilty, and do it again—but *this* time, shove the bad stuff down deeper.

A tragic and hilarious fact about seeking sainthood is that it's a very short step from "I want to be a saint" to "Let's pretend I *am* a saint!" This game of make-believe was the cause of enormous suppression and self-deception for me. It's obvious to me now that it's a disastrous approach, but it has been passed down through the ages as the wisdom of sages, so I had it on good authority that it was the right thing to do. Here is a favorite passage of mine from Thomas à Kempis's *The Imitation of Christ* (first published in 1418): "Bewail and lament thy daily transgressions. And if time allow thee, confess unto God in the secret of thine heart all the wretchedness of thy evil passions. Groan and lament that thou art yet so carnal and worldly."

He goes on (and on). I made it into my official Christian guide to self-hatred, and it gave me my early approach to peace—bewailing and groaning and lamenting. Also shoving down impulses so my friends and family wouldn't see all the wretchedness of my evil passions—because they would prove I wasn't spiritual. Thus, I accumulated secrets, and kept looking for a method that would work spiritual magic. I started practicing Transcendental Meditation in the summer of 1980, when I was twenty. I received some "tourist grade" Zen instruction when I was in Japan a year later. Then in the summer of 1983, I took up what would become my main spiritual practice when I sat my first ten-day course in Vipassana meditation.

The central instruction of this practice was to "just observe"— first the breath, then primarily the subtle sensations on the body. For me, taking up the practice when I was a young man in a hurry, "Just observe" was synonymous with "Just suppress." And the companion instruction "Don't react" compounded the urge to hold things in. So, if I felt anger, I tried hard not to express it and instead "just observe" the sensations that came with it. But that was too subtle an instruction for me at that stage of my life. So, I unconsciously converted the practice into a spiritual contest where victory meant not showing any outward signs of emotion, which meant shoving my reaction down so deep that even *I* couldn't see it.

When I was at the height of my Vipassana practice, I remember telling a friend about a lie a colleague had told about me, and I said, "You know what's *amazing?* I'm not *angry!* You would think that would make me super angry, but I'm just not angry. In the past, that would have made me very angry, but I really don't feel any anger at all—and it's pretty impressive, actually, that I'm not angry."

I was *furious.* I was so transparently angry that the person I was talking to later told me she thought I was joking. Anger was just one of the emotions I buried. Another was guilt. There was such an ethic of work around that technique—"Work. Work. Make the best use of your time!"—that I felt guilty when I wasn't working, so to avoid those feelings of guilt for not working, I worked. All the time. Not just spiritual work. Any work. Work is very effective for burying feelings of guilt for not working.

During long stretches of anxiety and depression, I kept following the technique and observing the sensations on my body, but I couldn't get deep enough. I was practicing awareness, but I was aware of the sensations on my body that were the *result* of my painful stories; I was never able to become aware of the deeper thoughts and feelings that were the *source* of those stories, and so I was stuck in a practice that left me one layer away from true leverage—managing my anxiety and depression, but never ending it.

I had seen this method get positive results for people. But no matter how many others had benefited from the practice, I finally had to accept that no method works for everyone, and this method hadn't worked for me.

Two things brought me to that conclusion. First, even after decades of practice, I was suffering from anxiety and depression and a serious stress-related illness that dominated and disrupted my life. Second, when I switched to another practice, things began to get better immediately, and the features of the new practice—actively intervening in the events of my mind and working to challenge and question my thoughts—were completely outside the method of my old practice.

Only then did I acknowledge the humiliating secret I had been keeping from myself: the spiritual practice that I had worked so hard on and made me feel so special for so long hadn't worked after all, and it had taken me nearly forty years to see it. When I finally faced and confessed that secret, a fat slice of my arrogance fell away.

Why did it take me so long to make the switch? Partly because of the momentary feelings of peace the practice had sometimes given me and partly because the time and effort I had invested in the practice biased me in favor of the technique and allowed me to convince myself that it was working when it wasn't.

In retrospect, if I were advising my younger self, I would suggest not getting so attached to one practice. Attachment creates a bias in favor of "my practice" and against the potential of others. It's hard to say, "My practice isn't working." It's much easier to say, "*This* practice isn't working." And because I was so attached to my practice, it took me a long time and a lot of suffering before I would try anything new. I would have been better off if I had focused on the goals and insights and principles of the spiritual path broadly and then tried a variety of approaches. That would have made me more open to trying something new during my *next* breakdown—which means the next moment in my life when I was suffering because my story and self-image were once again contradicted by the facts.

THE NEXT BREAKDOWN

We will keep having breakdowns until the self-image is empty. And the breakdowns may not get any easier because each new breakdown will be pushing you to give up a part of the self-image that was too painful to give up during your *last* breakdown.

After five years of doing various forms of neuroplastic-related practices and feeling continuously better, in the late summer of 2023, I faced a series of challenges that revived my anxiety and depression.

First, I was approaching the final deadline on this book, and when I pictured myself handing it over to the publisher and speaking on it publicly, I had a relapse of my perfectionistic, anxiety-ridden, get-it-done addictions.

To offer a bit of an explanation for my anxiety, I'll note that my choice of speechwriting as a profession is not an accident. It's not merely that I love writing and enjoy the rhythm of the work, which I do. Speechwriting serves some psychological needs as well. I don't love being on stage. It scares me. I have run away from reporters with TV cameras—*when I was a press secretary*! When I'm asked to give a speech or I have a chance to go on TV, I usually say, "Yuck, no thanks."

So, speechwriting has allowed me to insinuate myself into the lives of people with power, which offers me a vicarious taste of public notice while avoiding the anxiety of the stage and denying any interest in attention for myself. I get to enjoy a bit of the spotlight, but from a safe distance—protecting my self-image from any serious scrutiny while getting private praise from people close to me. The other emotional benefit is convincing myself that "I'm not like those *other* people; I don't really *need* attention." This fable allows me to obey my fear that says, "Stay off the stage, you could get hurt," while telling myself that it's virtue, not fear, that keeps me in the background.

In fact, this whole book thing is threatening to expose and upend an ingenious neurosis of mine that had been serving me well my whole life. When I began to see it, I labeled it my Four Fears. The fears are (1) being on stage; (2) being overwhelmed; (3) being a nobody; and (4) being accused of seeking fame, wealth, or power.

Can you guess the magic remedy for soothing the Four Fears? Stay home and work. So clever. I'm not a nobody, because I write things that people use. I don't have to be on stage, because I hand the words off to others. I don't get overwhelmed, because I'm staying on top of things by always working. And nobody can accuse me of ambition or seeking attention, because I'm always home. All of which proves I'm needless and selfless.

But the whole beautiful system is being threatened by my plan to put out a book with my name on it and my story in it, with the agreement that I will promote it. That prompted me to retreat into my old addictive, perfectionistic work habits and the anxiety and depression that come with them.

That anxiety came in August. Then in September, I was hospitalized for a week with a urinary-tract infection that turned into sepsis. My blood pressure was low enough when I arrived at the emergency room that the staff kept me there for a while, checking my vitals every fifteen minutes. They then gave me a bed on the heart floor. It was the second time I had had an infection of this type, the first was in 2021, so the doctors sent me home with a PICC line so that I could give myself IV antibiotics for five more weeks, along with instructions to then see a urology team to find out if there was a physiologic cause for these infections, so we could prevent the next one.

Then in October, my dad died. I loved him deeply. He was a devoted father. There was no limit to the time and money he had been willing to dedicate to my travel and education. At the same time, he had said more harsh things to me over the course of my life than everyone else combined. So, I had little fantasy he would apologize at the end for the times he had been a jerk. And yet I knew from what I'd learned of his childhood that he had outperformed his upbringing; that I had a much better dad than he did. Those were some of my feelings at the end—gratitude, grief, guilt, admiration, regret. And on the day he died, my perfectionism exploded: "I have to write the best obituary ever. I have to write the best eulogy ever. I have to do Dad *justice!*"

Each of these events compounded my emotional response to the others, and they all came at a time when I was researching and writing the last substantive section of this book—on Howard Schubiner's EAET and Patricia Coughlin's ISTDP. I was confident I could come out of the anxiety by stepping up my practice with Annie Hopper and Byron Katie, but I decided to try these new methods I was reading about.

TWO NEW APPROACHES

I did the twenty-eight-day program that Howard Schubiner laid out in *Unlearn Your Pain* and *Unlearn Your Anxiety and Depression*. I read three books by Patricia Coughlin on Intensive Short-Term Dynamic Psychotherapy. Then I began ISTDP sessions with a highly experienced therapist who was a genius in getting me to face and stay focused on feelings I've organized my life to avoid.

As I wrote in chapter 9, the premise of both approaches is that we all have impulses and feelings that are natural but scary to express because they can endanger our bonds with the important people in our lives. So, we learn to bury those feelings, and the trouble begins.

Both approaches are grounded in the foundational work that opens this chapter—finding and revealing our secrets, which can take the form of buried feelings. It's worth noting that Warren had two secrets: the factual secret about his parents' divorce, which he kept from his girlfriend, and the emotional secret that he was angry about it, which he kept from his parents and himself.

It seems to me that the emotional secrets are the primary secrets, and the factual secrets guard against any probing that will expose the emotional secrets. So, I went hunting for my emotional secrets—hoping to dig up the feelings I had buried in my childhood attempts to be loved and *kept* burying in my adult attempts to appear spiritual.

I did a lot of work imagining myself back in painful situations from my past, feeling all the feelings of those moments, and expressing those feelings in a way I was too weak or scared to do at the time. When I tapped hidden anger, it surged through me with a power that made me think, "Whoa, this is new." It wasn't negative power or dark power; it was just power—a feeling of surprising energy that had just been released. And over time, not right away, as the anger dissipated, it was followed by feelings of grief, guilt, loss, forgiveness, and ultimately love and compassion for the person I was angry with.

Guilt over aggressive feelings toward loved ones is especially important to find and feel—because unconscious guilt can keep us locked in patterns of self-punishment for years. Coughlin cites the meticulous research of Abbass and writes, "The proportion of patients in his practice who did not suffer from guilt and self-punishment over primitive murderous rage toward people close to them lay in the region of 17%."

If I am in the majority of people whose rage leads to guilt and whose guilt leads to self-punishment (and I have no doubt that I am), then it seems reasonable to suppose that a form of my self-punishment is my addiction to work and my self-imposed standard of perfection. It's not hard to imagine my semiconscious dialogue: "I'll do *anything* to avoid those feelings. How hard do I have to work?"

So, I work hard—driven by the semiconscious fear that if I stop working and producing (and stop getting the praise and appreciation that comes with it), I'll be back in the feelings I want to avoid. But I don't really know that this is what's going on—so I naively focus on the workload and the timelines and the deadlines and the task lists, thinking that the only way to feel better is to get it all done, instead of seeing that the way to feel better is to feel the feelings I'm doing all the work to avoid.

When I can directly experience feelings of anger and guilt and grief and loss that I would previously have insisted weren't even there (because I'm a spiritual person)—I no longer have to do heroic things so I don't feel them. In fact, I don't have to be a hero at all. I don't have to work like an addict. One purpose of working like an addict was to keep me from feeling guilt. But if I'm okay with feeling guilt, I don't have to work like an addict. I can say: "I'm feeling guilty about wanting to strangle my father. . . . Now let me see what's on TV."

The practice is to feel those feelings so we can take down the defenses we put up to avoid them. And, vice versa, take down the defenses so we can feel the feelings. My copy of the book *Lives Transformed* is filled with multicolored margin notes and highlighted passages, but there are two lines heavily circled and starred: "When emotions are considered unbearable, then there is trouble" and "Feelings do not cause problems, defences against them do."

If I'm trying to avoid a feeling that "I will do anything not to feel," I'm going to create a lot of suffering for myself. And I do not know—until someone wakes me up—how much easier and wiser it is to feel the feelings I'm avoiding than to do the crazy things I'm doing to avoid those feelings.

How do these practices from Schubiner and Coughlin connect to the other approaches in this book? Remember, the healing power of neuroplasticity lies in the insight that pain and illness can start in the brain, and if we change our thoughts, beliefs, and feelings by *changing how we respond to them*, we can heal pain and illness. If we continue to believe and obey the thoughts and instructions that hide our secrets and suppress our feelings, we will keep suffering.

Schubiner uses EAET to treat chronic pain and other ailments that conventional medicine has no effective response for. And in *Lives Transformed*, in just one example, Coughlin shares a case study called "The Good Girl with Ulcerative Colitis" who by the end of her ISTDP sessions no longer had ulcerative colitis. These pioneers are showing it's possible to heal emotional and physical ailments that come from believing our thoughts and avoiding our feelings.

DID IT WORK?

After my dad died, my therapist asked me about my rivalry with him. I said, "I had no rivalry with my dad, because I won." (Unpack *that!*)

She said, "Oh?"

Soon, under her questioning, I was feeling heavy guilt over my father—feeling that I had been disloyal and ungrateful; that I had been a spoiled, privileged, arrogant brat of a kid for looking down on my dad for not being "deeper." The tears and the feelings that came with them were a new emotional experience for me and validated the idea that I was feeling emotions I hadn't allowed myself to feel before. Similarly, when I allowed myself to feel anger for people in my life that I loved and needed, I felt a surging energy that seemed to lift me on a wave and then drop me on the shore with feelings of remorse, grief, and love. It was stunning how often I found myself in a blast of emotions that started with anger and turned into love for the person I was angry with. And that energy that surged through me when I felt the anger—I don't think it was the energy of anger; it was the energy that had been *holding in* the anger.

The most transformative episode in this work for me came one morning at 4:00 a.m.—the usual hour for such things. I was awake in bed, restless with emotion, and decided to go downstairs and lie on the couch in the family room. I was sensing the rise of feelings I'd long been forcing down. I knew I was entering forbidden territory. As the feelings surged, blasting past old defenses, a panicky voice rang out in my head: "No! NO!!!" But that voice was drowned out in the rush of feeling that exploded like a breaking dam. The feelings broke through, the resistance was breached, and the energy that had forced down the feelings became available for other uses.

A few hours later, working at my kitchen table, I took up a project I had been dreading and delaying for six months. I needed to update a conceptual framework that was the core of a multiyear project of mine, but I was afraid that if I dug into it, the idea wouldn't hold and the project would collapse. Yet that morning, in one hour and with no effort, I wrote the new framework. The ideas flowed like liquid insight.

Soon after that, I noticed I was doing things that were "just not like me"—going for a walk in the woods in the middle of a busy day, seeing a worker in front of the house and inviting him in for coffee, leaving a project undone to go Christmas shopping, scraping the snow off my car and then doing my neighbor's car too. These are all fine things, and I heartily recommend them for others, but I never do them myself because they get in the way of my addictive need to "get things done." So as I saw myself doing these things, I wondered what was going on, and here's what I concluded:

Many of us, often without knowing it, live our lives in narrow corridors, hemmed in by fear. It's as if there were walls of electrified fencing on the right and left of us, and we're wearing a shock collar. If we veer too close to one side, we start feeling the fear, and we move back toward the center, often without noticing it. The challenge of change is not to get better at withstanding electric shocks, but to somehow reduce the voltage or remove the shock collar. It's not about becoming more courageous; it's about becoming more fearless. When the fear subsides, the walls come down, and we can go anywhere.

This is not learning a new coping skill; it's becoming a new person. We do things we've never done before because the fear that hemmed us in is gone, or reduced. The loss of fear is the mark of change, and the proof of change is what's happening when we're not trying.

When I was seated at my father's memorial service waiting to deliver the eulogy, I felt no anxiety at all, just a calm energy and an eagerness to say what I had come to say. That experience was utterly new to me, and it came in a cluster with other changes. I started to find it easier to tell people what I was thinking. I found it easier to ask for what I wanted. But the most striking change of all has been the stillness. I've tried many approaches over the years to quiet my mind—watching my breath, repeating a mantra, observing sensations, reciting a prayer. This approach is different: I quiet my thoughts by facing my feelings. When I began to find a way to bring up the emotions I'd been shoving down and face the avoided feelings directly, the thoughts became quiet. It's as if the chatter were a side effect of shoving down the feeling—or maybe the thinking was a device to keep me from facing the feeling. Either way, it seems that when I can face those feelings directly, my obsessive thoughts lose their purpose and begin to fade, which leaves my mind still.

In stillness, it is *thought* that is still. I hear the sound of my footsteps without listening for them. I hear the sound of my pen on the page. It prompts me to wonder: Where is beauty? Is it in the song of the bird—or in the mind that's quiet enough to hear it?

After church one Sunday years ago, I was talking to a woman about the death of her father. She told me a few stories about the end, and I said, "It seems he was seeing beauty in everything." She laughed and said, "Yes, when I walked in the room, he said, 'You're so beautiful,' and I was flattered. Then when I brought him a glass of water, he looked at it and said, 'This is so beautiful.'"

The beauty, in my view, comes in the silence—and the mark of silence is the absence of thought, and the absence of thought is the presence of peace and joy and love.

THE OTHER SIDE OF THOUGHT

There are many approaches to peace, but one very distinctive feature of peace: the stillness of thought. It's thought that constructs the self-image. It's thought that keeps secrets. The end of thought means the end of secrets, the end of self-image, the end of suffering.

The peace on the other side of thought is the opposite of the illusory peace of the self-image model. It's not merging the image of who you are with the image of who you want to be. It's *dissolving* the image of who you are—and dissolving the image of who you want to be.

This is mysticism. You can hear it in these verses from the *Diamond Sutra*, a discourse by the Buddha that is one of the most influential texts in Buddhism.

"Incalculable is the merit attained by Bodhisattvas
who act generously without attaching to the
concept that they are acting generously."

"The mind should be kept independent of any
thoughts that arise within it. If the mind depends
upon anything, it has no sure refuge."

"The world is not what we name it or think it,
and . . . there is no such thing as a self or an other."

This domain beyond thought is where many wise people of the past would not go. But today, as people are more urgently seeking peace, it's becoming clearer that these insights align with truths from other cultures and other times, with the insights of mystics and scientists and poets and playwrights, both ancient and recent, who talk to us of our human reality, our search for peace, and what it's like on the other side.

DEMYSTIFYING MYSTICISM

On September 11, 2001, Eckhart Tolle had an interview scheduled with Tami Simon, the founder of Sounds True, the organization Simon founded in 1985 to "disseminate spiritual wisdom."

After the planes hit the towers, Simon called Tolle and offered him a chance to reschedule, but Tolle kept the appointment, doing one interview that day and another later in the week. Sounds True released both under the title *Even the Sun Will Die,* a line Tolle used on September 11.

Tolle's insights on the madness of the attacks, which he gave in the first interview, are worth listening to more than twenty years later. But Simon's second interview with Tolle is the one I cherish more. As a collection of Tolle's insights on the relationship between thoughts and awakening, it is the mother lode.

When Simon asked Tolle what changed with his awakening, he said that he wouldn't have been able to explain it when it happened, except that he had been anxious and depressed for many years, and suddenly he was at peace. Only later did he come to understand that, as he put it that day, "My thought processes had become reduced."

Thoughts were still there, he said, and he could still use thought. But he was no longer "trapped" in thought or in the emotions that accompany it. Thought was no longer a tool for seeking or enhancing his identity, and he said he found that there is "a vast realm of consciousness beyond thought."

Then, halfway into the interview, Tolle offered the most succinct description of a spiritually awakened state that I've ever heard.

"A while ago," he said, "somebody asked me, 'What is your greatest achievement in life?' And I couldn't think of very much. But what suddenly came to me was, well, 'I don't need to think.'

"That's why I couldn't think of it," he said laughingly. "I don't need to think anymore unless I want to think." He chuckled again and said, "That's not really an achievement because it's a negative thing. It's a 'non'—'I don't need to think.' So, I haven't achieved, really, and I wouldn't get a job if I put that on my résumé: 'I don't need to think anymore.' But really that's what it is. The very power of the teaching comes from that state of awareness."

Tolle added in the same interview that his thought processes were reduced by 80 percent. So it wasn't that all thoughts were gone, but that he was liberated from compulsive thinking, from identification with thinking. Thinking still happens for him. He needs to think to give a talk, for example. "But ever since then," he said, "no thought has made me unhappy."

On several occasions after that interview, I've heard Tolle repeat that point, "I don't have to think if I don't want to think," including during a Tolle retreat I attended in Phoenix in May 2022. It's an artful way of putting thought in its place. Thought can help us solve practical problems, build bridges, and cure diseases. Thought can even help people report to others of the world beyond thought—but thought is not a path to peace; it's a barrier to peace.

With about fifteen minutes left in the interview, Simon said: "I've heard you a couple times quote Ramana Maharshi, the great sage of India. How do we measure spiritual progress? And you attribute to him the saying that we measure spiritual progress by the absence of thought."

"Yes, yes," Tolle confirmed. "The degree of absence of thought. Yes, that's right."

CONVERGENCE

It's possible that the quote Tolle had been citing came from the book *Be As You Are*, a collection of statements from Sri Ramana Maharshi, the spiritual teacher whom Philip Novak, the writer on world religions, called one of the "greatest mystic-sages of the Hindu tradition."

Ramana was born in the Indian state of Tamil Nadu in 1879. He experienced a dramatic enlightenment at the age of sixteen, then left his home and traveled to the holy mountain Arunachala, where he lived and taught for fifty-four years until he died in 1950 at the age of seventy.

Ramana didn't write down his teachings. The books that bear his name are his responses to seekers who came to see him. In *Be As You Are,* Ramana was asked, "How can I tell if I am making progress with my enquiry?" And he responded, "The degree of the absence of thoughts is the measure of your progress towards Self-realisation."

Thought and ego are the same for Ramana. He calls the ego the "I"-thought.

"After the rising up of this 'I'-thought," he says, "all other thoughts arise. The 'I'-thought is therefore the root thought. If the root is pulled out, all the rest is uprooted at the same time."

There is a deep alignment between the practice taught by Ramana and the practice taught by Byron Katie, which is striking because Katie created her method without any awareness of Ramana or his teaching. Katie calls her approach "Inquiry" and says, "Question the thought." Ramana calls his approach "Self-enquiry," and says, "Ask who thinks that thought."

What's especially intriguing about these two practices is that they both slip the trap that tricks us into activating the ego in the effort to dissolve the ego.

Ramana points out the trap: "How can 'I' eliminate itself? . . . The mind is only a bundle of thoughts. How can you extinguish it by the thought of doing so? . . . The mind is simply fattened by new thoughts.

"Therefore," he says, "seek the root 'I'; question yourself: 'Who am I?'; find out the source of the 'I.' Then all these problems will vanish and the pure Self alone will remain."

Ramana insisted that the ego—the "I"-thought—exists only because we fail to question its reality. And he tells a parable that makes his point:

> In Hindu marriage functions, the feasts often continue for five or six days. On one of these occasions a stranger was mistaken for the best man by the bride's party and they therefore treated him with special regard. Seeing him treated with special regard by the bride's party, the bridegroom's party considered him to be some man of importance related to the bride's party and therefore they too showed him special respect. The stranger had altogether a happy time of it. He was also all along aware of the real situation. On one occasion the groom's party wanted to refer to him on some point and so they asked the bride's party about him. Immediately he scented trouble and made himself scarce. So it is with the ego. If looked for, it disappears. If not, it continues to give trouble.

While Ramana strongly emphasized Self-enquiry as the direct method, he also taught other methods. He explained: "I approve of all schools. The same truth has to be expressed in different ways to suit the capacity of the hearer . . . [but] all other methods lead up to Self-enquiry."

Ramana is saying you can do any method you want, and they all can help you make progress, but they are all—with the exception of Self-enquiry—ego-driven: "I do this practice so I can get enlightened." So those practices, after eliminating every other obstacle, must eventually return and confront the obstacle of the ego—the thing that wants to get enlightened—which is the last barrier to enlightenment.

"In this method, the final question is the only question and is raised from the very beginning," Ramana says. "Keep the attention fixed on finding out the source of the 'I'-thought by asking, when any other thought arises, to whom it arises."

So, Self-enquiry requires getting better at the skills that allow us to turn our attention away from the *object* of thought and back toward the *subject* of thought—and asking, "Who thinks that thought?"

While the intelligence beyond thought is generally dismissed or ignored in Western religion, this teaching is at the heart of one of the most beloved passages in Christian scripture, from the Sermon on the Mount.

> [25] Therefore I say unto you, take no thought for your life, what ye shall eat, or what ye shall drink; nor yet for your body, what ye shall put on. Is not the life more than meat, and the body than raiment?

> [26] Behold the fowls of the air: for they sow not, neither do they reap, nor gather into barns; yet your heavenly Father feedeth them. Are ye not much better than they?

> [27] Which of you by taking thought can add one cubit unto his stature?

> [28] And why take ye thought for raiment? Consider the lilies of the field, how they grow; they toil not, neither do they spin:

> [29] And yet I say unto you, That even Solomon in all his glory was not arrayed like one of these.

> [30] Wherefore, if God so clothe the grass of the field, which to day is, and to morrow is cast into the oven, shall he not much more clothe you, O ye of little faith?

To my ears, Jesus sees "take no thought" as an act of faith. He implies that the fewer thoughts we have about our life, the greater faith we have—and the more faith we have, the less thought—like Mary compared with her sister, Martha. This teaching converges with Ramana's message that the fewer thoughts we have, the greater our spiritual progress. So "take no thought" is not only exhorting us to faith; it is the *triumph* of faith.

This was the interpretation of Howard Thurman, the African American mystic who was a spiritual advisor to Martin Luther King Jr. In his book *Meditations of the Heart,* Thurman wrote:

> Take no thought for your life. What a strange thing it is, this injunction! Up to this period of my life, I have seemed to survive by taking thought for my life. Upon deeper reflection, I begin to see that my life is not now, nor has it ever been, my own. I did not create nor have I sustained my life through the years. In so many ways, without my own plans and purposes, hard places have been made soft and rough places smooth. . . . Take no thought for your life—it is in God's hands and ever, when I am obeying the laws of life, it is God who works through me.

JOY

In 1965, the Catholic priest and Trappist monk Thomas Merton, likely the most famous American Christian monk and mystic, compiled and published a book called *The Way of Chuang Tzu,* a collection of poems and essays by the Chinese mystic from the fourth century BC who had written one of the foundational texts of Taoism.

Merton had written fifty books by the time he died three years later, and of this volume, he wrote, "I have enjoyed writing this book more than any other I can remember."

Why would Merton feel an affinity for Chuang Tzu? Merton said that the mystic "shares the climate and peace of my own kind of solitude and is my own kind of person."

Merton was a mystic. He gained insight outside of thought, and he saw the confusion in our conceptual thinking. In his introduction to the book on Chuang Tzu, Merton writes: "The problem with 'the hero of virtue and duty' is that he sees 'happiness' and 'the good' as 'something to be attained,' and thus he places them outside himself in the world of objects. In so doing, he becomes involved in a division from which there is no escape."

Merton uses an essay from Chuang Tzu to make this point about placing happiness outside ourselves. In this passage, titled "Perfect Joy," the Taoist master says:

> I cannot tell if what the world considers "happiness" is happiness or not. All I know is that when I consider the way they go about attaining it, I see them carried away headlong, grim and obsessed, in the general onrush of the human herd, unable to stop themselves or to change their direction. All the while they claim to be just on the point of attaining happiness. For my part, I cannot accept their standards, whether of happiness or unhappiness. I ask myself if after all their concept of happiness has any meaning whatever. My opinion is that you never find happiness until you stop looking for it. My greatest happiness consists precisely in doing nothing whatever that is calculated to obtain happiness.... If I cease striving for happiness,

the "right" and the "wrong" at once become apparent all by themselves. Contentment and well-being at once become possible the moment you cease to act with them in view.

This is happiness where there is no thought of happiness. This is happiness *because* there is no thought of happiness.

BRING IT UP

A few years ago, I asked my son Ben, "How's your meditation going?"

"A couple more days and I'll be happy," he said.

I laughed out loud, mostly at myself. His flip response exposed a silly conceit I still have about happiness. "If I can just get a little more of this and a little less of that, I'll be happy. I'm *almost* there."

It's a mirage. Contrary to the fervent creeds of our culture—peace and happiness are not found by creating a self-image and trying to be it. Peace comes with the end of the self-image and the thoughts that obsess over it.

But what's going to happen to me when I stop worrying about what's going to happen to me?

I'm going to be whatever grace makes of me.

That's what Eckhart Tolle said at the end of his 2001 interview with Tami Simon: "My life is . . . consciousness unfolding and it does what it wants. I'm not making any plans for it."

Byron Katie said in *A Mind at Home with Itself:* "I have no life of my own; my life is not my business. I'm following orders."

And Howard Thurman said in the passage quoted above: "Upon deeper reflection, I begin to see that my life is not now, nor has it ever been, my own."

This is what happens when we expose the false authority of thought. We lose our lives. And while these are the voices of three mystics, and mystics have always been marginalized in our culture, times are changing, we're impatient for peace, and we want to know what they know.

So, if a mark of peace is the stillness of thought, what makes thought still?

I believe that the answer—and the action that underlies every practice of profound healing I've seen—is bringing up the things we've been hiding. To do this, we need to question the thoughts we've been believing and face the feelings we've been avoiding.

From Annie Hopper, who says we must bring limiting beliefs to mind so we can expose them, to Byron Katie, who tells us to allow our feelings to express themselves as they arise, to Robert Johnson, who says that accepting one's shadow is whole-making and thus holy, to Patricia Coughlin, who says that full and direct experience of previously avoided feelings is the key to healing, to Howard Schubiner, who heals patients by teaching them to express their suppressed emotion, to James Pennebaker, who warns us about "the work of keeping secrets"—the theme repeats itself again and again: healing means becoming whole, and becoming whole means bringing up what we shove down. The things we hide are not harmful. Hiding them is harmful.

In his book *Breathing Underwater*, Richard Rohr writes:

> As any good therapist will tell you, you cannot heal what you
> do not acknowledge, and what you do not consciously ac-

knowledge will remain in control of you from within, festering and destroying you and those around you. Quote 70 in the Gospel of Thomas is many peoples' favorite. It has Jesus saying, 'If you bring forth that which is within you, it will save you. If you do not bring it forth, it will destroy you.'

THE OTHER SIDE OF FEAR

When I started work on this book, I believed that stillness of thought was the essence of peace. I now believe that stillness of thought is a *mark* of peace. The *essence* of peace is to be unafraid of any feeling. When we lose the fear of our feelings, we automatically lose our obsessive thinking—because obsessive thinking is a defense against feeling.

Feelings are never the problem—*resisting* our feelings is the problem. And the self-image is the fortress of resistance. We created the self-image to resist the feelings that cause us fear, and we can't dismantle the self-image until we master that fear. We all face this challenge in small ways. The challenge comes to spiritual teachers in dramatic ways.

In *The Teachings of Ramana Maharshi in His Own Words*, Ramana reflects on his moment of awakening: "I was sitting alone in a room on the first floor of my uncle's house. I seldom had any sickness, and on that day there was nothing wrong with my health, but a sudden violent fear of death overtook me. . . . The shock of the fear of death drove my mind inwards and I said to myself mentally, without actually framing the words, 'now death has come, what does it mean? What is it that is dying?'"

Eckhart Tolle wrote of his fear and awakening in *The Power of Now:*

> I was fully conscious, but there were no more thoughts. Then I felt drawn into what seemed like a vortex of energy. It was a slow movement at first and then accelerated. I was gripped by an intense fear, and my body started to shake. I heard the words 'resist nothing,' as if spoken inside my chest. I could feel myself being sucked into a void. It felt as if the void was inside myself rather than outside. Suddenly, there was no more fear, and I let myself fall into that void.

The spiritual teacher Adyashanti described his awakening to Tami Simon:

> I got to a point where I just felt completely defeated. . . . I just said to myself . . . "I just can't do this anymore' . . . and at that moment it was like a nuclear explosion went off inside of me. It was actually violent. . . . I really felt like my heart's going to explode . . . and a thought just came out of nowhere . . . "if this is what it's going to take for me to be free, if I'm going to die today, if I just let go to this' . . . [that's fine with me]. 'I've *got* to find out. I've *got* to know what happens.' . . . I was actually willing to die at that moment, and I just let go, and in a snap of a finger I was in a completely different dimension.

These are three spiritual masters in the midst of dramatic awakenings. Their stories would seem to have little relevance for us, except that the pattern is universal for breakthroughs large or small: a feeling comes up, unfamiliar, frightening—either we resist it, shove it down, and try to remain who we were, or we receive it, take it in, and become something new.

Tolle was given the internal guidance "resist nothing." Most of us may need some *external* guidance—skilled teachers who can show us how to disarm our defenses and ease our resistance so that when the feelings rise, we have the skill and presence and preparation to welcome them. Without this guidance, suppressed emotions can push up into consciousness and our resistance will push down just as hard. That's what I believe kept me stuck for so many years. My fear and panic at the Buddhist hermitage, for example, came when I was living in conditions that were perfect for stirring up suppressed feelings, but I didn't have the skill and experience to allow them in. Instead, the forces pushing the feelings up were met by fear that shoved them down—and my mind and body almost melted from the heat of the high-pressure standoff. So, I returned to my old life, where my suppressed feelings could settle back down and wait for another moment when they might rise up and be felt. It was not until I received the life-changing guidance from teachers in this book that I learned not only how to bring feelings up but how to take them in—and that has had a completely unexpected effect.

I wrote earlier in this chapter that my practice of Vipassana had not worked for me; that I felt I was one layer away from true leverage. A number of Vipassana teachers, after I came back from Sri Lanka, said to me, "There is something inside that doesn't want to come up." Actually, I think it was the opposite. The feelings wanted to come up, but I kept shoving them down—and without knowing it. I didn't know how to disarm my own resistance. This is a skill I've learned only as I've written this book, with the result that my lifelong Vipassana practice is now clearly working for me. When I'm in the midst of painful thoughts, I know the thoughts are a decoy, a diversion—a deception to distract me from feeling.

So, I don't take the bait. I question the thoughts and focus on the sensations—and I can now feel with icy precision the flesh-cutting pain deep inside, pain that can make me clench in resistance or flee in search of relief, but can only be relieved when I open up and feel it. It's as if the unrealized gains of forty years of meditation are now being redeemed by the insights of scientists. For me, this is a deeply personal example of the fruit of the convergence of ancient spirituality and modern neuroscience.

THE ERA OF SCIENCE AND GRACE

In the early pages of his book *Feeling & Knowing*, Antonio Damasio, one of the world's leading neuroscientists, writes, "Before we proceed, I need to say a few words about how I approach the investigation of mental phenomena.

"The approach begins," he says, "with the mental phenomena themselves, when singular individuals engage in introspection and report on their observations. Introspection has its limits," he says, "but it has no rival, let alone a substitute. It provides the only direct window in to the phenomena we wish to understand."

In brain science, then, we are in a unique domain of scientific inquiry that elevates the role of ordinary, nonspecialist human beings. What we see in our own mind matters—and not just for the reports we make to brain scientists. Seeing the movement of our own minds is the only approach that can awaken us. The insights of Buddhism that have become interesting to brain scientists came from meditators looking into their own minds and describing what they saw as the unconscious became conscious.

As we watch, we see things we didn't use to see. We see that as soon as our self-image is threatened, we feel pain. As soon as we feel pain, we rush to blame. We see how suffering rises with our own resistance. We see our self-image as our own creation that keeps us trapped. We see our thoughts *as thoughts* and not as a map of reality. And as we start to see this, we begin to go beyond it—because we cannot be the conscious authors of our own suffering. It is only when we "*know not what we do*" that we create suffering for ourselves and others. That's why spiritual practice is a process of making the un-conscious conscious, and introspection is not just essential to scien-tific inquiry; it is the heart of spirituality.

In the fall of 2023, I wrote an email to Dr. Damasio to ask him how modern neuroscience sees the unconscious. He wrote back, "The idea that there are non-conscious processes underneath the conscious ones is both profound and scientifically current."

It's in this area of nonconscious and conscious processes where I believe investigations in brain science and spiritual practice con-verge. These domains have in the past been kept resolutely separate. Science and religion. Reason and emotion. Thought and feeling. Body and mind. In many cases, experts still keep them separate, but more and more leaders in each of the spheres now see that they're working in the same domain.

Dr. Jeffrey M. Schwartz, a research psychiatrist at the UCLA School of Medicine, and a pioneer in applied neuroplasticity, writes in his book *You Are Not Your Brain*: "On its own, neuroplasticity is neither good nor bad. It simply is a brain mechanism that developed to help us adapt to our environment and survive changing condi-tions. The real power is in self-directed neuroplasticity, because it gives you a say in what happens to you and how your brain is wired."

Neuroplasticity means the brain can be conditioned to adapt to different environments. And, of course, if the brain can be conditioned, the brain can be deconditioned. If we believe and obey our thoughts, if we suppress and resist our feelings, we are more deeply conditioning our brains. If we start to question our thoughts, if we start to feel all our feelings, we are making the unconscious conscious. We are deconditioning our brains. And hatred is a conditioned response. Fear is a conditioned response. And love is a *de*conditioned response. Love is the underlying reality. When fear goes, what's left is love.

Today, neuroscientists can train *patients* to reduce their fear. Teachers of meditation can train *students* to reduce their fear. They're both deconditioning the brains of people who want to ease their suffering. They're both moving people toward peace. The scientists are doing it to support mental health. The mystics are doing it to support spiritual growth. They share a similar process. They invite the old stimulus. They practice a new response. Whether you're coming from science or spirituality, it's a race for the best practice with a common aim of ending suffering and finding peace.

None of us is seeking peace alone. There are so many trends and friends and forces working in our favor. We have better teachers, better students, and better techniques—grounded in neuroscience, taught by mystics, explained by experts, and tailored to the lives of ordinary people.

This is a prominent and hopeful feature of our age—the fruit of the epic convergence of two great systems of knowing that together have the power to make all things new.

CHAPTER TWELVE

The Endgame

All the inventing and discovering and experimenting and exploring we've done in the history of human beings has never uncovered one thing that is a greater mark of our progress than how we treat one another.

And while scholars have cataloged a decline in violence over time, none of this data can dim the present-day evidence that we, as a species, have never been closer to the edge. If we are getting better at how we treat one another, we're not getting better fast enough.

All around the world, political leaders and public figures are becoming heroes to the people whose hatred they express. They reassure their followers that their hatred is not a sin but a sign of their own virtue, a principled response to the evil of "the other." So as their hatred rises, so does their moral self-regard.

But we don't hate people because of their bad character. We hate them because of *our* bad character. We hate others because they are standing in the way of the goals we seek for our group, our people, our country, our views. We hate them because they are standing in the way of our story.

The states of breakdown that are playing out for each one of us *personally* are also playing out for all of us *collectively*, and for the same reasons: *the strategy of finding peace and happiness by seeking dominance for our story is collapsing, for individuals and for groups.*

This is traumatic because this is how we respond to difference and disagreements. This is how we find meaning and purpose and our place in the world—by telling good stories about ourselves and bad stories about others and by trying to defend our stories against rival stories in social, political, and military battles. This is all we know. This is who we are.

We all belong to groups with stories that say: "We're good people. We're smart. We know what we're doing. We deserve to be happy. We have earned success." But every story hides something, and when reality exposes what our story hides, we tell a second story to explain the failure of the first: "It's all your fault." Instead of saying, "Maybe we're not all the things we claim to be," we say, "It's your fault if we're not all the things we claim to be!" And we hurt the people we blame for our pain instead of changing our story to match the truth.

It's creating a crisis. And thank God for that—because the solution is something we would never consider *without* a crisis. We must surrender at least some part of our story or we're locked in a war we all will lose. I think that I'm good and you're bad. You think I'm bad and you're good. But we share this: our self-image is our religion. It's our most sacred belief. It makes any insult to the self-image a holy war—and to uphold my self-image, I must insult yours.

The only way for me to heal is to see in myself some of what I'm hating in you—and to see in you some of what I admire in me. This means shedding some of my self-image and opening to the truth that I may be a little worse than I think, and you may be a little better than I think, and we're not as different as we think. We need to surrender some of the beliefs that pit us against each other. If we surrender, we can win.

THE FATAL FLAW

If we want to give up part of our self-image, we should give up the part that does the most harm and creates the most hate. My self-image that "I'm an honest, honorable, reliable person who will do anything for a friend and never cheats at cards" is not a big problem. It's exaggerated, but it's not dangerous. The toxic part of the self-image comes into play when there is a conflict between my self-image and yours. Then, literally, "this town is not big enough for the two of us." That kicks us into the addictive, self-image-driven urge to create hierarchy.

I am not talking about a hierarchy of skill or talent or training. I'm talking about a hierarchy of human worth—the often denied but deeply embraced belief that some people are worth more than other people and that privilege and resources and respect and opportunity should be allocated along those lines. This instinct to create and honor hierarchy is entangled with our self-image, our need to feel safe, our urge to belong. The self-image requires hierarchy for its satisfaction.

This social impulse is summed up with merciless insight by

theologian James Alison, who described the mechanism to me in an email: "I create a false personality which learns how to fit in by looking down on whoever I need to look down on in order to belong."

This is the cause of hierarchy: our need to look down on other people. As long as I can look down on somebody, I feel a little bit better about myself.

We all look down on others in order to fulfill our self-image, to feel good about being a valuable member of our group. And while most of us in some way decry the cruelty of it, and say we are opposed to hierarchy, it may be truer to say that we are opposed to our place in someone else's hierarchy and that we each have in our own minds an alternative hierarchy that places people we like at the top and people we dislike below.

The people we place above are likely those who honor our story, and those we place below are those who challenge our story. At the very bottom are those we blame for the *failure* of our story. If not for those people, we would be great. That makes us into innocent victims and sometimes heroes too. We like to make innocent victims into heroes when it can throw a spotlight on the flaws of the people we hate. It gives us more cause to look down on them.

Many of us see the cruelty of hierarchy, and we have come up with a remedy. We call it "tolerance." But the very word *tolerance* shows how hopelessly embedded we are in hierarchy. We have to be arrogant to be tolerant. Tolerance is just a sanitized way of looking down on others. The one who tolerates is above the one who is tolerated. The word reinforces the divisions it presumes to remove. It even creates new divisions. We feel superior to people who aren't tolerant. In fact, we don't tolerate people who aren't tolerant.

We don't even have a word for tolerance that doesn't imply the presence of a difference of an inferior sort. Because our words and thoughts both reflect and create our reality, it's notable that the best we can do to describe an all-embracing approach to life is the word *tolerant*, which is full of self-conscious virtue and can't hide a tinge of scorn.

We need a stronger, more dramatic remedy for hierarchy.

DIGNITY

In 2006, Donna Hicks, the international conflict–resolution specialist from Harvard, joined Archbishop Desmond Tutu on a panel for a BBC documentary on the Troubles in Northern Ireland—the thirty-year violent confrontation between Catholics and Protestants that caused immense suffering on both sides. Dr. Hicks had spent three decades working in conflict zones around the world—from Israel and Palestine to Colombia, Sri Lanka, Cambodia, and the Balkans. As the two worked together, Hicks shared her "Dignity Model" of peacemaking with Tutu, and the archbishop encouraged her to write a book about it. When she did, bringing out her book *Dignity* in 2011, the archbishop wrote the foreword, saying, "In the concept of human dignity, we have in our hands, as it were, the key to the conundrum of the ages—how can peace on earth be found."

Dignity is the inherent worth we all have from birth, says Hicks. "Along with our survival instincts," she writes, "the yearning to be treated with dignity is the single most powerful force motivating our behavior. It transcends race, gender, ethnicity, and all the other social distinctions. If we violate someone's dignity repeatedly, we will get a divorce or a war or a revolution—because a desire for revenge is an instant response to a dignity violation."

A desire for revenge. That's what happens when we treat people as if they don't matter, when we insult someone's self-image to uphold our own. It leads to an escalating cycle of violence. The world is suffering a global pandemic of dignity violations right now. There is only one way to turn it around.

Just as a tree takes in carbon and puts out oxygen to save the earth, we must take in hatred and give out love to save humanity. This is the defining spiritual gift. We all have it in some degree—to love the person who hates us. If you've raised a toddler or a teenager, you've done it countless times. We can all learn to do it a little more—to be wounded and treat others well, to answer ill will with good will, to absorb pain without passing it on. It seems to go against our deepest instincts, but it's actually a call to our highest gifts.

We need to evolve to survive.

JUDGE NOT

The Sermon on the Mount, which Jesus delivered early in in his ministry, is a call to evolve to a higher spiritual understanding. Six times he cites the old law with some form of the construction "Ye have heard that it was said by them of old time," and six times, he says, "But I say unto you . . ."

In the last of the six teachings, he says:

> Ye have heard that it hath been said, Thou shalt love thy neighbour, and hate thine enemy.

But I say unto you, Love your enemies, bless them that curse you, do good to them that hate you, and pray for them which despitefully use you, and persecute you.

"Love your enemies" is perhaps both the most famous and least practiced teaching of Jesus. It is a categorical warning against hatred. He's not saying, "Use hatred sparingly." He's saying that even when we think hatred is not only acceptable but essential, "Do not hate."

It's an outrageous message. He is warning us against a habitual behavior wired deep in our human brains, important to the past survival of the species. Even now, among those of us who've heard this teaching our whole lives, we can't suppress a protest from inside: "Can't we at least hate the people who hate?"

No. Our hatred will harm us, no matter who it's directed against. (Augustine writes, "No enemy could be more dangerous to us than the hatred with which we hate him.")

If we can't hate our enemies, but must love them; if we can't hate people who curse us, but must bless them, then the teaching offers no exceptions and no excuses. The law is clear: "Don't hate anyone ever."

The instinctive rebuttal is, "Can't we at least hate evil people?"

The sermon answers, "Judge not." Jesus knows (and knows that we do not know) that judging others is a trap. As soon as we start making judgments of good and evil, our self-image says, "I'm good, and you're evil," and that claim becomes a *cause* of evil. As soon as we call another "evil," we give ourselves the right to inflict pain and feel virtuous about it. No genocide ever occurred without a story of good and evil that unleashed evil in the name of good.

There are a lot of people in the world inflicting pain on innocent victims. Why can't we judge *them*? Because we are not qualified to judge, because we have a beam in our eye. The self-image *is* the beam, the distorting filter. It is always scanning the landscape, seeking evidence for its stories, finding material to feed the narrative, "I'm good; you're evil." So, when we judge someone, it will be a false judgment, twisted to make ourselves feel virtuous, and that is the gateway to hatred.

But if we can't judge anyone, how can we form opinions, make decisions, and take action to make society safe and protect innocent people? The answer is to "first cast the beam out of thine own eye." Then we can hold others accountable, but with the purpose of helping others, not hurting them—to keep people safe, not to make anyone suffer.

When we're told not to judge, it's not amnesty for bad people. It's a compassionate teaching for us—to give us guardrails that lead us not into temptation but deliver us from evil.

Love your enemies has been seen as an impossible commandment intended only for monks and nuns and mystics and saints. But now it reads like practical advice for the survival of the species. The threat of extinction is a material problem, but it requires a spiritual solution.

CAN WE EVOLVE?

At the end of his landmark book *Sapiens*, Yuval Noah Harari reflects on the history of human happiness: "Unfortunately, the Sapiens regime on earth has so far produced little that we can be proud of. We have mastered our surroundings, increased food production, built cities, established empires and created far-flung trade networks. But did we decrease the amount of suffering in the world?"

He asks, "Was the late Neil Armstrong, whose footprint remains intact on the windless moon, happier than the nameless hunter-gatherer who 30,000 years ago left her handprint on a wall in Chauvet Cave? If not, what was the point of developing agriculture, cities, writing, coinage, empires, science and industry?"

Harari faults historians for not asking such questions, and then writes:

> In recent decades, psychologists and biologists have taken up the challenge of studying scientifically what really makes people happy. . . . The most important finding of all is that happiness does not really depend on objective conditions of either wealth, health or even community. Rather, it depends on the correlation between objective conditions and subjective expectations.
>
> You might say that we didn't need a bunch of psychologists and their questionnaires to discover this. Prophets, poets and philosophers realised thousands of years ago that being satisfied with what you already have is far more important than getting more of what you want. Still, it's nice when modern research—bolstered by lots of numbers and charts—reaches the same conclusions the ancients did.

In other words, peace and happiness depend not on our ability to get what we want but on our ability to want what we get. This, as I wrote at the start of the book, is the difference between chasing peace and finding it. And it means getting beyond the evolutionary instruction that directs our attention to what we lack.

Rick Hanson, in *Hardwiring Happiness*, says, "In your subcortex and brain stem, connected but separate circuits handle liking and wanting. This means you can like something without wanting it."

The brain's distinction between liking and wanting is at the heart of Hanson's project to help people build up "the bone-deep ongoing sense that core needs are already met." When you experience that your core needs are met, Hanson says, your brain returns to its resting state, its "green," responsive mode.

"Imagine a world," Hanson writes, "in which a critical mass of human brains—100 million? a billion? more?—spend most if not all of each day in the responsive mode. Eventually there would come a tipping point, a qualitative alteration in the course of human history."

Hanson is not the only one who believes in a tipping point. Eckhart Tolle says that "something is pushing forward, the transformation wants to happen," and that our survival "depends probably on the number of humans who are open now to a transformation."

Mystics and scientists—drawing on science and grace—believe that the evolution is possible, even underway, and that if it happens for enough of us, it can happen for all of us.

But we can't evolve as a species unless we evolve as individuals. The evolution has to happen within us. It has no way to express itself except through us.

MY ENDGAME

In a webcast he did in 2016, Richard Rohr said, "We have narrowed and cheapened the Gospel to make it about private individuals going to heaven, as if you could go without the rest of us—as if there could *be* a heaven if we all didn't go there together."

Before I heard his words, my attitude was "This is a house on fire; how can I get out?" After I heard his words, it became "This is a house on fire; how can we *all* get out?"

If we're going to get out, we must acquire the skills to curb hatred. And we can't curb hatred with suppression and willpower. We've tried that. It blows up on us. We have to find a way to get the hateful thoughts out of our heads, and we can only do the work on ourselves. We can't operate on anyone else.

This challenge recalls the words spoken by Macbeth to the doctor who came to treat his wife, who'd been suffering grief and guilt over the murder of King Duncan. Macbeth asks, "How does your patient, doctor?" and the doctor replies, "Not so sick, my lord, / As she is troubled with thick-coming fancies / That keep her from her rest."

Macbeth answers:

> Cure her of that.
> Canst thou not minister to a mind diseased,
> Pluck from the memory a rooted sorrow,
> Raze out the written troubles of the brain,
> And with some sweet oblivious antidote
> Cleanse the stuffed bosom of that perilous stuff
> Which weighs upon the heart?

The doctor replied, "Therein the patient / Must minister to himself."

But he doesn't say how.

A hateful thought gets planted in my head when I tell myself the story of someone ruining my dream or insulting my self-image. And the hatred deepens when I repeat the story.

I am the author of my self-image. I am the author of the story about someone insulting my self-image. I am the author of my hatred and my suffering. So, what if I start practicing methods that dissolve the thoughts that create my self-image—that dissolve the story that makes me hateful?

We will never overcome group hatred until we soften our group self-image, and we will never soften our group self-image until we surrender our personal self-image. That's the work. And it takes the moral courage that one modern writer ascribed to Saint Augustine, the "willingness to risk being a fool for the truth." That's as good a description as I've heard for shedding the self-image—and it requires tremendous faith.

When I was a child, my faith involved a set of beliefs and practices I trusted would get me into heaven. Today, my faith is not a belief in dogma or doctrine or scripture or ritual but instead believing that grace is working to heal me, that every breakdown is leading to breakthrough, and that if I can ever lose my need for comfort and control, I will drop into the lap of God.

That faith grows stronger with a practice that works—and works *much* stronger with a practice that works on its own. When I started with neuroplastic approaches, I began the process of defying, not obeying, my fears, and I worked hard at it. But I realize now that I was setting in motion new habits in my brain that after a time began to work on their own.

In the beginning, I would notice a thought coming, carrying a huge negative feeling, and I would take steps to weaken the thought, to steal its fuel. But today, I see a thought rising and I feel its dark-

ness, as if it were about to blast fear and depression in all directions—
but before it explodes, it dissolves, like a flaming bomb hitting the
water. Over and over, waves of thoughts and feelings come, hit the
water, and are gone. I do nothing. I just watch. It seems that I assist
the process if I pay attention. But it's not my doing. It's not practice.
It's witness.

Perhaps it's what Katie calls the wordless questioning alive inside
of us. In any case, the witness is a loving presence that is powerfully
indifferent to the beliefs and instructions of my self-image, which
not only wants to be better than others, and better than itself, but
wants to live forever and never die.

THE SCIENTIFIC AND THE
SPIRITUAL—THE SYNTHESIS

In the opening chapter of this book, I wrote that what thrills me
most about neuroscience-based approaches is that they unify the
scientific and the spiritual. I believe that the neuroplastic practices
in *Chasing Peace* are forms of spiritual practice.

The University of Colorado back-pain study—and others I have
cited—apply the practice of "pain reprocessing therapy." As I practice, I no longer interpret the pain as a sign of danger; I feel it as a
neutral sensation. Of course, I've had my medical tests done, and I
know there's no tissue damage, so I have physical evidence for the
argument that I'm not in danger. That lets me let go of the fear, and
when the fear goes, the pain goes with it.

This is the same basic process for spiritual practice—with one
distinction. In the back-pain treatment, I can feel the sensations

without fear because my mind knows the body's not in danger. But what if I'm dying of cancer? What can the neuroplastic approach do for me when my body *is* in danger? How can I convince my brain that I'm not in danger when I'm dying? This is the spiritual question.

The answer is, I *cannot* convince my brain that I'm not in danger when I am the thing that is dying. But if I keep questioning this belief that I am my body, and that belief begins to let go, then my body can be dying, and my brain isn't sending out danger signals, because even the brain has understood what the mind already knows—that I am not my body. And while my body is dying, I am not dying, and thus, there is no danger and no reason to fear.

THE FEAR THAT TESTS THE FAITH AND THE PRACTICE

When I was going through the most intense phase of my health concerns, moving out of my home to ease my symptoms, a friend said to me, "You're more afraid of death than anyone I know." That didn't sing a harmonious duet with my self-image, and I pushed back.

I wasn't afraid of death, I argued, just dementia. When I visited dozens of doctors and spent thousands of dollars and moved out of my home, the fear of dementia is what drove me. The anxiety and panic and depression and brain fog and neuropathy all played a role, but the biggest motivator was the fear that my brain would die before my body did, and I would be living in a facility at age ninety-one with dementia as my father was. That's the thought that created the anxiety that turned to fear that bordered on panic.

I suspect a lot of us keep track of signs that we're decaying and dying, or just nearing some point of diminishment or embarrassment. For some people it could be their weight, or their cholesterol, or their hearing, or their wealth, or some other measure. Martha Beck calls them "Do Not Mention Zones," where the mention of anything near those topics can feel alarming.

For me, the Do Not Mention Zone was not only dementia but fading memory. Every memory slip or lapse stirred my fear of fading away—losing my family and friends even as I stood in front of them. How will they know that I love them if I can't remember their stories?

As I began the self-directed neuroplasticity, I had hoped the practice would improve my memory, but it didn't. Six years on, my life is happier and more productive and more exciting than ever. My relationships are warm and honest and fun. My work has never been more interesting. I'm physically fit. I enjoy working out. I feel young. I have a lot of energy. My sense of humor keeps expanding. My anxiety and depression keep fading. I keep doing things I've never done before.

But my memory is not better.

That is frustrating. I wanted to write this book to tell the story that "I figured it out!" I wanted a storyline that would be a ringing testament for my practice without complications and caveats and counterexamples. This stubborn memory thing wrecked my story. But if I embrace my full story—including the part that I want to leave out—then what has happened to me is more precious than what I'd hoped for.

If I had gotten the story I wanted—a complete and total restoration of the health of youth—I would not have gotten what I *really* wanted, which is the growing ability to find peace and joy in any situation, even when my body and brain, and the abilities I rely on to make my way in the world, begin to give way.

Today, when I forget an appointment, when I can't remember something my son tells me he just told me, when I flip through my travel photos and say, "Where did that dog come from? I don't remember a dog!"—whenever any of these things happen to me, I feel an echo of the fear that drove me to find a protocol that would save me.

But today I don't try to save me. I stop. I get still. I become loose. I open up to the excruciating feeling without clenching or flinching. Then, if a fearful thought is still there, I question it: "Is it true?" "How do I react when I believe that thought?" "Who thinks that thought?"

Underneath all those thoughts and feelings is the end of the urge to fix things; even more, it's the end of the person who sees things as broken and wants them fixed. It's the end of being stuck in the story that my fate is tied to the fortunes of this fading body. If I believe this story, then I need to believe the story that "I'm getting better": my health is getting better, my emotions are getting calmer, my memory is getting clearer, my cholesterol is getting lower. I must believe I'm getting better because if I'm not getting better, I'm dying. And I'd rather be lying than dying.

And once I start lying, I must keep lying. If the first lie is "I'm getting better," one of my next lies leaves out the fading memory. And that's missing an opportunity—because somewhere in the slipping memory is an invitation to drop the story. A fading memory is a nudge into the now.

I'm not against stories. I have made my living by telling stories. But I need to be mindful of what my story leaves out and keep trying to add it back in. This is one of the joys of getting older. To see the truth—and sometimes to tell it.

To hide from the whole story at this stage of my life may be the silliest cost-benefit calculation in the universe—clinging to the lie that "I'm getting better" and sacrificing the reality that I am not the thing that dies. If I believe I need to get better, then I have bought into my self-image, which means, even with all my embellishments, that I'm just a guy in the fourth quarter of life who, because I look younger than my age, am closer to the grave than my photos would suggest.

Why is that something to cling to?

Any line I draw between who I am and who I'm not, what must happen and what must not, is doomed to be thrown down by life. The shadow will emerge to unsettle the self-image; the scary story will pierce the soothing story until we give it all up, let it all in, and say goodbye to ourselves.

But even in this pre-awakened state, while still longing to be whole and still forcing things out, I am so much happier than I've ever been, with the kind of joy I've always secretly doubted could exist for me.

How did this happen? Even though, as Richard Rohr said, my effort to engineer my own enlightenment is ego-driven, my ego is not the only force in play. Grace rushes in to fill the gaps and set the traps that break me down and wake me up.

This is why we should never devalue the work we do before the breakthrough—because the work *prepares* the breakthrough. The self-image is doomed. Only the divine is real and will prevail. That is the good news and the great promise: that one day soon, forced by merciful, remorseless grace, I will drop my story, embrace my shadow, and surrender the urge—embedded deep in my finite brain—to rage, rage against the dawning of the light.

At Savatthi. Standing to one side, the devata
recited this verse in the presence of the Blessed One:

"Life is swept along,
short is the life span;
No shelters exist
for one who has
reached old age.
Seeing clearly
this danger in death,
One should do
deeds of merit
that bring happiness."

The Blessed One [responded]:
"Life is swept along,
short is the life span;
No shelters exist
for one who has
reached old age.
Seeing clearly
this danger in death,
A seeker of peace
should drop
the world's bait."

Acknowledgments

In January of 2020, I submitted an article to Maria Shriver's *The Sunday Paper*, and Maria wrote back to me in her "email-haiku" style:

> There is a line in here
> Where you write that your mood turned to darkness . . .
> It seems like we walked over a big part of the story right here
> What occurred in you that led you to darkness . . .
> What pushed you down
> So that you could find your teachers
> I don't mean to pry . . .
> But I feel you have a book in here
> I'm starting an imprint of books
> that speak to hearts and minds
> Just a thought

With that message, Maria brought *Chasing Peace* to life. For that, I'll be forever in her debt.

Luck—or karma or grace or synchronicity, or any of the many words we use to explain the happy things that happen for us—has been an engine of this book from the start.

There's no explaining how I would end up with an editor of the stature of Brian Tart. He was a dream guide, bringing his experience with masters in my field to the advice he offered me. He let me write my heart out on the early drafts, then made artful interventions to lead me back to the point of the book. "Get to the insights faster" is a comment of Brian's that is immortalized on a note card and taped to my wall.

I want to thank the team at Penguin Life, including Ivy Cheng and Rebecca Marsh for publicity, Claire Vaccaro for art, Mary Stone for marketing, Eric Wechter for production, and Jenn Houghton for everything. I want to give special thanks to my gracious copyeditor who had to deal with my low IQ on antecedents and other subtleties. She did her best with a weak student.

I owe enormous thanks to my literary agent, Rafe Sagalyn. When I sent him my proposal, he called and said: "*Chasing Peace* is about breaking down and breaking through—can you make your case in a Kübler-Ross–style framework by creating stages of breakdown?" I had been looking for a way to use the Jungian themes of self-image and shadow to explain the process of breakdown, and then carry the theme through the book. Aligning the chapters with states of breakdown let me do that, and that was Rafe's idea.

When I set out to write *Chasing Peace,* I thought it would be a matter of writing what I knew. Then I found it was a matter of writing what I was learning—and the manuscript always needed updating. I owe a lifetime debt to Nathaniel Frank, the science writer and social historian who wrote the *Washington Post* article I cite in chapter 1. Nathaniel gave me an ongoing, long-form tutorial on mind-body medicine and connected me to other experts in the field. He's now writing a book on mind-body pain for Mayo Clinic Press. I can't wait to read it.

I want to thank Doctor Howard Schubiner for his pioneering work in the field of mind-body medicine and his generosity in sharing his knowledge with me. He is my ideal of what a doctor should be, and I wish him well as he strives to bring his breakthroughs into the mainstream of medical practice.

Patricia Coughlin is a marvel. Her books on intensive short-term dynamic psychotherapy pushed me to find a therapist to work with me on this approach. It sounded too good to be true—and turned out to be better than it sounded. Dr. Coughlin's work is a gift to the world.

When I met Annie Hopper at her Austin workshop, I gave her a hug of thanks and told her, "I had no path." I found her book when I was on the edge of losing everything, and her guidance took me from the lowest point in my life to the highest, and set in motion the forces that would take me higher.

I'm profoundly grateful to Stephen Mitchell, Byron Katie's husband, who is a collaborator on Katie's books and a translator of some of the world's great spiritual works. Stephen responded instantly and generously when I asked him to review the chapter on Katie. I was fortunate to have his authoritative input.

I feel a special sense of love and gratitude for Father Richard Rohr, whose spiritual writings convey insights that make me gasp, and often weep. He generously found time to read extensive portions of my manuscript and gave me, with his blessing, the confidence I needed to finish the work.

I imposed heavily on the time of many friends as I looked for signs that my words would connect. For reading drafts and offering feedback and encouragement, I want to thank Paul Gralen, who had a much more intimate view of the ultimate than I had, Mike

McCurry, Jenny Aguilar, Bill Peterson, Jane Prelinger, Molly Bing-ham, Rhonda McCrory, Marianne Viray, Les Boney, and Ret Boney. And I want to thank Suzy King for creating an occasion for a reunion with Matt.

Rose Shriver has been a partner in *Chasing Peace* from the begin-ning, when I asked her to critique my book proposal through the eyes of a Jungian therapist. I reached out to her repeatedly over the next three years, testing out ideas and insights, and asking for feedback. Rosie met every request, guiding me like a guardrail along a narrow mountain pass, keeping me safely on the road, climbing higher.

Tami Pyfer has spent more time working on *Chasing Peace* than anyone but me, often receiving and turning around chapters on the same day. She was my sounding board, and when I wandered into abstractions, she would pull me back, saying "Huh?" in just the right places. She has a deep unerring sense of what is true and clear—and she never failed to share it when I needed it. Without her sup-port, *Chasing Peace* would have arrived later, run longer, and been a lesser work.

Killian Noe is a spiritual teacher hiding out as a social justice warrior. She reviewed many drafts of my manuscript with love, speed, and insight. Killian's own books have been an inspiration for this one—as have been her everyday words of prophetic wisdom.

Donna Hicks, who brings peace to war-torn corners of the world, gave me—with her book *Dignity*—a lens for understanding the world and a point of leverage for making it better. Her insight and scholarship are the foundation for the final chapter of my book. Donna's help in reviewing *Chasing Peace*, especially those pages, was indispensable.

Maria DeLiberato, my friend John's attorney, helped me with the background on John's life and guided me in what I could safely write about his life in prison. Maria is my hero for defending the dignity of some of the world's most demonized people.

Beth Giudicessi, my fellow Notre Dame philosophy major, had the background to see what I was trying to say and helped me say it better. She talked me out of some of my longer wanderings while still helping me end up where I'd wanted to go. More than once, when I thought the book was a mess, I called Beth, who heard me out, calmed me down, and sent me back to work.

Olivia Eggers—who told me when she was fifteen years old that she wanted to be a speechwriter in a presidential administration and achieved that aim by the age of twenty-four—read the manuscript in a day and told me that the message works for young people, as heartening an endorsement as I've heard.

Annie Robinson, a relentless seeker of peace, has been pushing me to write a book for the past ten years, all the while sending me teachers, insights, and ideas that became ingredients of *Chasing Peace.* Annie is a brilliant teacher and collaborator, and a deeply intuitive friend.

James Alison is perhaps the humblest, most humorous and generous wise person I know. I was constantly sending him ideas that came to me in meditation that I never would have published without the approval of a scholar. I owe my understanding of scapegoating and its role in human suffering almost entirely to his books, emails, and personal conversations. I want to repeat what Richard Rohr whispered to a few of us about James over dinner back in 2016: "He really is a genius."

I want to thank my partners Jeff Shesol and Paul Orzulak, whose key interventions at crucial moments kept me improving as a writer and a person. Without their friendship, encouragement, and example, I could not have written this book.

I want to thank Halcy Bohen and my partners in my Thursday morning therapy group—whose candor always made it clear there was more work for me to do, and whose encouragement made that work lighter and friendlier.

Brooke Anderson, my White House colleague and longtime friend, took all my questions and responded in ways that were never exactly what I wanted to hear and always exactly what I needed to know. I've worked with Brooke on hundreds of projects—*Chasing Peace* is just one. But on this one, even more than on all the others, she supported me on the project itself, and on the chaotic events that occur when one is "overbooked." Brooke is the friend of a lifetime.

I want to acknowledge my teacher Sayadaw U Jagara, the Buddhist monk who received me in his hermitage in Sri Lanka and also guided me thirty years later at a retreat in Massachusetts. His light-hearted approach to the eightfold path has been a steadying influence in my life. I thank him also for pointing me years ago to the scriptural passage that closes *Chasing Peace* and summarizes the book in a few lines.

I want to thank Linda Potter for her feedback on the manuscript. I long ago learned to my delight that Linda's warmth and kindness will not keep her from delivering a candid edit—and not just on my writing. Her house has long felt like a second home for me, a place where I've enjoyed some of the most honest, astonishing, and boisterous conversations of my life.

I want to acknowledge what I owe to Tim Shriver, but I'm afraid if I admit my debt, he might ask me to pay him back. Tim turned me from a writer into an activist and wants me to be done with this book so I can get back to work. He read drafts of *Chasing Peace* with depth and care and pushed me toward a deeper synthesis—his passion and specialty. Tim is a leader for the coming age when politics, social justice, and spiritual insight converge. It's impossible to measure the benefits of spending time in his company.

I want to thank my brothers: John, for being home base for us after Mom and Dad died; Dan, for being the most sure-footed, fun-loving, and reliable one of us; and Dave, for being a deep spiritual seeker with a brilliant mix of respect and irreverence for things the world calls sacred. If I ever die of laughter, it will be from something Dave had just said. I'd like to thank all of them for reading this manuscript, reviewing my version of our family's stories, and asking for no edits—an astounding act of generosity. I also want to thank my sisters-in-law Sharon and Jean for opening their homes to me without limit.

Finally, and primarily, I want to thank Molly and the boys. To Nick and Ben, who've done a good job raising me—your pride and independence proved early to me that pressure in relationships backfires. That crucial lesson—which I wouldn't have had the love or patience to learn from anyone else—is the basis of everything I'm striving to learn more deeply now. I can't imagine who I would have become without you, but I wouldn't want to be him.

To Molly, who is so smart in ways I am not—thank you for listening to my ideas, for being my loving skeptic, and for taking a mad gamble thirty-five years ago and marrying the man who wanted to read you his essays when we were out on a date. You've shown me what it's like to feel absolutely at home on earth—with no desire to be anywhere but where I am. You, and the sound of your laughter, bring me joy.

Notes

Epigraph

ix not necessarily accord with the truth: Antonio Damasio, *The Feeling of What Happens: Body and Emotions in the Making of Consciousness* (New York: Harcourt Brace, 1999), 187.

ix learn to lie to ourselves: Michael Gazzaniga, *The Mind's Past*, (University of California Press, 1998), p. 26. Thanks to Stephen Mitchell for identifying the two quotations that serve as epigraphs and citing them in Byron Katie's book *Loving What Is*, where I first learned of them.

Chapter One: The Self-Image Model of Happiness

2 "he was the wisest and justest": Plato, *Phaedo*, loc. 645.

5 "the steps you take": Covey, *Seven Habits*, 111–12.

7 "If we seek spiritual heroism": Rohr, *Falling Upward*, 65.

8 "Love your enemies": James Alison, "Jesus: Forgiving Victim: A webcast with James Alison and Richard Rohr," Center for Action and Contemplation, Albuquerque, New Mexico, July 12, 2016. The video is not publicly available.

9 "I am human": Terence, *Heauton Timorumenos (The Self-Tormentor)*, trans. Henry Thomas Riley (London: Stage Door, 2019), 2. The preface of this book cites the line "I am human . . ." as I've cited it in this book. It notes that it is Terence's most famous line and includes the Latin, "Homo sum, humani nihil a me alienum puto," but in the play itself, this famous line is rendered in language that doesn't have the clarity, simplicity, and depth of the more famous translation I've cited—namely, "I am a man, and nothing that concerns a man do I deem a matter of indifference to me."

15 "Your mind can change your brain": Jeffrey M. Schwartz and Rebecca Gladding, *You Are Not Your Brain: The 4-Step Solution for Changing Bad Habits, Ending Unhealthy Thinking, and Taking Control of Your Life* (New York: Penguin, 2011), xv.

16 **the power of a neuroplastic approach:** Yoni K. Ashar, PhD; Alan Gordon, LCSW; Howard Schubiner, MD, "Effect of Pain Reprocessing Therapy vs Placebo and Usual Care for Patients with Chronic Back Pain," *JAMA Psychiatry* 79, no. 1 (2022; original investigation, September 29, 2021): 13–23, jamanetwork.com/journals/jamapsychiatry/fullarticle/2784694; Nathaniel Frank, "Chronic Pain Is Surprisingly Treatable—When Patients Focus on the Brain," *Washington Post*, October 15, 2021.

18 **"If we can disrupt":** Neuroscientist Antonio Damasio uses this phrase the "two-way network" in his book *Looking for Spinoza*: "Associative learning has linked emotions with thoughts in a rich two-way network. Certain thoughts evoke certain emotions and vice versa. Cognitive and emotional levels of processing are continuously linked in this manner." Antonio Damasio, *Looking for Spinoza: Joy, Sorrow, and the Feeling Brain* (New York: Harvest, 2003), 70.

Chapter Two: The Beginning of Breaking Down

19 **"So to all of you":** Daniel K. Inouye, "Democratic National Convention Keynote Address," August 26, 1968, Chicago, Illinois, transcript, dkii.org/speeches/august-26-1968.

20 **"Even the sanest of people":** Celia W. Dugger, "Clinton Fever: A Delighted India Has All the Symptoms," *New York Times*, March 23, 2000, nytimes.com/2000/03/23/world/clinton-fever-a-delighted-india-has-all-the-symptoms.html.

28 **an article appeared:** Bob Davis, "Gore Hopes New AIDS Pact Will Help Shake Protestors," *Wall Street Journal*, August 12, 1999.

29 **He read to me:** Jane Perlez, "U.S. Asks Russia to Play Mediating Role in the Kosovo Crisis," *New York Times*, April 7, 1999, archive.nytimes.com/www.nytimes.com/library/world/europe/040799kosovo-diplo.html.

33 **raising your children in freedom:** Clinton speech, "Remarks by the President to the People of Ukraine," June 5, 2000, St. Michael's Square, Kyiv, transcript, clintonwhitehouse5.archives.gov/WH/New/Europe-0005/speeches/20000605-1830.html.

33 **"beloved national poet, Taras Shevchenko":** Associated Press, "Clinton Speaks Ukrainian," June 5, 2000, nytimes.com/aponline/i/AP-Clinton-Native-Tongue.html.

33 **"I heard there is freedom":** Associated Press, "Clinton Speaks Ukrainian," June 5, 2000, nytimes.com/aponline/i/AP-Clinton-Native-Tongue.html.

37 **"ego surrenders to those depths":** Singer, *Boundaries of the Soul*, 216.

37 **only word in the English language:** Johnson, *Owning Your Own Shadow*, 40.

Chapter Three: Anxiety

41 "all that we are ashamed of": Singer, *Boundaries of the Soul*, 165.

42 "everyone immediately understands what is meant": C. G. Jung, *The Quotable Jung*, ed. Judith Harris (Princeton, NJ: Princeton University Press, 2016), 47.

42 The prophetess at the temple: Plato, *Apology*, 11

44 "Not being welcome": Nouwen, *Inner Voice of Love*, 101.

53 "No one can become conscious": Jung, *Quotable Jung*, 39. I'm quoting Jung saying that "no one can become conscious of the shadow without considerable moral effort" just after I quote him saying that "everyone immediately understands what is meant by 'shadow.'" I mean here to note the difference between knowing that shadow means our "inferior personality" and acting to hide it or deny it—and being aware of the power and presence of the shadow in the moment as it influences our thoughts, feelings, and behavior.

53 "looking for happiness": Thomas Keating, *The Daily Reader for Contemplative Living*, ed. S. Stephanie Iachetta (London: Bloomsbury, 2013), 70.

55 "a strong emotional experience": Rohr, *Falling Upward*, 132–33.

61 "a judge had published the reasons": Karla Adam, "Prince Philip's Will Can Be Kept Secret for 90 Years, U.K. Court Rules," *Washington Post*, September 17, 2021.

62 "a lady and a flower girl": George Bernard Shaw, *Pygmalion* (New York: Dover, 1994), 47.

Chapter Four: Depression

70 "In my right mind": Mike Gerson, "Sunday Sermon," February 17, 2019, Washington, DC, transcript, cathedral.org/sermons/michael-gerson.

79 "I have prayed for years": Rohr, *Falling Upward*, 128.

81 "This is pure poison": Robert A. Johnson, *He: Understanding Masculine Psychology* (New York: HarperCollins, 1989), 49.

Chapter Five: Addiction

88 Johann Hari highlights research: Johann Hari, "Everything You Think You Know about Addiction Is Wrong," July 9, 2015, TED video, youtube.com/watch?v=PY9DcIMGxMs.

95 "if I wanted to make things right": Shaka Senghor, *Writing My Wrongs: Life, Death, and Redemption in an American Prison* (New York: Convergent Books, 2016), 2.

97 doing handfuls of downers: I was rebellious in many ways but naively obedient in others. I remember coaching third base as a high school baseball player and relaying the steal sign to a base runner on first. He didn't steal, and at the end of the inning, I asked him why. "It was muddy," he said. "I couldn't get a jump." I thought, "Wow, you can *do* that?"

100 "Many very sensitive people": Eckhart Tolle, *Freedom from the World: Bridging the Dimensions of Form and Formlessness* (Louisville, CO: Sounds True, 2014), Audible audio ed., ch. 65, 1:12–1:40. After the line I quote in the book, Eckhart continues, "But often hiding behind the external appearance of the so-called addict, which is another mental label, lies a spiritual being that perhaps is . . . ready for awakening, often more ready than the well-adjusted humans."

104 "I shall go down to history": Alan Bullock, *Hitler: A Study in Tyranny*, 281. I read this book in my early twenties, and it completely engrossed me. Speech after speech after speech followed the same exact pattern. "Wow," I thought "this isn't genius. It's robotic; it's formulaic." And it's also very effective. C. S. Lewis, writing to his brother in July 1940, mentioned that he had just heard a speech of Hitler's on the radio, and he wrote, "I don't know if I'm weaker than other people: but it is a positive revelation to me how while [Hitler's] speech lasts it is impossible not to waver just a little. . . . Statements which I know to be untrue all but convince me, at any rate for the moment, if only the man says them unflinchingly." Alan Jacobs, *The Narnian: The Life and Imagination of C. S. Lewis* (New York: HarperOne, 2009), 104.

106 These four concepts: In my own AA experience, the most helpful of the Twelve Steps has been Step Eleven, which reads, "Sought through prayer and meditation to improve our conscious contact with God as we understood Him, praying only for knowledge of his will for us and the power to carry that out." This, to me, seems to synthesize the concepts cited in the exchange between Jung and Bill W.—spiritual experience, union with God, and ego collapse.

Chapter Six: Illness

109 "Keeping up personas": Walker, *Unapologetic Guide to Black Mental Health*, 155.

116 The ongoing inflammation: Website of The Virginia Center for Health and Wellness, vc4hw.com/chronic-inflammatory-response-syndrome -cirs.html#:~:text=Chronic%20Inflammatory%20Response%20 Syndrome%20(CIRS)%20is%20a%20progressive%2C%20multi, if%20left%20untreated%20becomes%20debilitating.

120 **"When our brains are on high alert"**: Frank, "Chronic Pain Is Surprisingly Treatable—When Patients Focus on the Brain."

125 **"Do not be perceived as what?"**: Brené Brown, "Listening to Shame," March 16, 2012, TED video, ted.com/talks/brene_brown_listening _to_shame/transcript?hasProgress=true, 14:47–16:38.

Chapter Seven: Crisis

136 **"Suffering is the only thing"**: Richard Rohr, "Suffering Love," *Daily Meditations*, Center for Action and Contemplation, April 28, 2017, cac .org/daily-meditations/suffering-love-2017-04-.

136 **"Probably the worst damage"**: Johnson, *Owning Your Own Shadow*, 34.

140 **the Cicero Speechwriting Awards:** Pro Rhetoric's Cicero Speechwriting Awards, vsotd.com/cicero-awards.

140 **"original definition of courage"**: Brené Brown, "The Power of Vulnerability," June 2010, TED video, ted.com/talks/brene_brown_the_power _of_vulnerability.

141 **"The most accurate measure"**: Brown, "Listening to Shame."

141 **"the birthplace of joy"**: Brown, "Power of Vulnerability."

141 **the idea jumped at me:** I met Brown in July 2015 after a talk she gave in Seattle, and I asked her about vulnerability and trust. "Vulnerability is absolutely the birthplace of trust," she said. In that talk, she had just given further proof that she is the master of clarity. She said, "Anyone sick of the word *boundaries*? I've got the simplest definition in the world: 'Saying what's okay and what's not okay.'"

141 **The speech was Neil's story:** A transcript of Neil Colomac's speech can be found on the website of the US Department of Veterans Affairs: va.gov /wholehealthlibrary/docs/10-neil-colomac-speech-use.pdf. A video of the speech can be found on YouTube: "Neil Colomac, Grassroots Speech, June 4, 2012," youtube.com/watch?v=SbNoZT0h0O8.

146 **when the psychiatrist told me:** "Highly abnormal" was just the last of the dire medical "diagnoses" I received on my journey—which included "Your mercury levels are off the charts"; "You are smart to have come. Eventually you would have developed Alzheimer's"; and "I'd support disability because it's not looking that healthy." These messages are strikingly at odds with the guidance of psychology professor Ellen Langer, the first woman ever to be tenured in psychology at Harvard and the author of *The Mindful Body: Thinking Our Way to Chronic Health* (New York: Ballantine, 2023). In her book, Langer describes the dangers of scary diagnoses, and says: "The language of illness, which for the most part is rooted in a biomedical model of the body (and thus ignores the power of the

mind), creates an illusion of symptoms as stable and unmanageable. As a result, people quickly adopt stereotypical responses and behaviors . . . without questioning their diagnosis and acting differently. . . . The key is to question those things we mindlessly accept, to mindfully interrogate all of the descriptions and diagnoses that can hold us back. When we do, we can get better. We can learn to heal ourselves" (26–27). If I had read Ellen Langer sooner, I might have turned the corner more quickly.

147 **"the arrogance beaten out"**: Johnson, *He*, 76.

147 **"Letting go"**: Bourgeault, *Meaning of Mary Magdalene*, 104.

Chapter Eight: Grace

156 **"Who knows how long I've loved you?"**: "I Will," on The Beatles, *The Beatles* ("White Album"), Apple Records, 1968.

158 **"Anglican priest and a man of God"**: Glenn Frankel, "Desmond Tutu, Exuberant Apostle of Racial Justice in South Africa, Dies at 90," *Washington Post*, December 26, 2021, washingtonpost.com/local/obituaries /desmond-tutu-archbishop-south-africa-apartheid/2021/12/26/ 9fef6f0c-661e-11ec-a7e8-3a8455b71fad_story.html; Stephen Martin, "Seeing the Impossible as Possible," *Messenger*, Anglican Diocese of Edmonton, January 11, 2022, edmonton.anglican.ca/news/seeing-the -impossible-as-possible.

159 **established Damien Ministries**: damienministries.org.

159 **"hug and pick up babies"**: Lois Romano, "The Hug That Says It All," *Washington Post*, March 22, 1989, washingtonpost.com/archive/lifestyle /1989/03/23/the-hug-that-says-it-all/7a1ca11b-51cc-453f-bc0d-8cd923 92aba2.

160 **"a person with the virus"**: Barbara Bush, *Barbara Bush: A Memoir* (New York: Scribner, 2010), 273.

162 **"Spirituality is always"**: Richard Rohr, "Transforming Our Pain," *Daily Meditations*, Center for Action and Contemplation, July 3, 2016, cac.org /daily-meditations/transforming-our-pain-2016-07-03. Richard makes the same point in a piercing way in *Dancing Standing Still* "If we do not transform our pain, we will always transmit it. Always someone else has to suffer because we don't know how to suffer; that's what it comes down to" (87).

162 **trained in Somatic Experiencing**: In *Waking the Tiger*, Levine describes Somatic Experiencing in part with these words: "You initiate your own healing by re-integrating lost or fragmented portions of your essential self. In order to accomplish this task, you need a strong desire to become

whole again." Peter A. Levine with Ann Frederick, *Waking the Tiger: Healing Trauma* (Berkeley, CA: North Atlantic Books, 1997), 61.

163 **"this poor widow":** Mark. 12:41–44, KJV.

164 **an especially moving example:** Doyle, *Untamed*, 309–11.

172 **"in our own despair":** Arthur M. Schlesinger Jr., *Robert Kennedy and His Times* (New York: Houghton Mifflin Harcourt, 1978), 618, 874–75.

173 **"whose law it is":** Edith Hamilton, *The Greek Way* (New York: W. W. Norton, 2017), 62. In her book, Hamilton introduces these lines of poetry that Kennedy would make famous in our time by saying, "Aeschylus too had his conception of the price of wisdom." RFK was given Hamilton's book by Jackie Kennedy the first Easter after President Kennedy was killed. They were with friends in Antigua, and according to Schlesinger's account, "Jacqueline, who had been seeking her own consolation, showed him Edith Hamilton's *The Greek Way*. 'I'd read it quite a lot before and I brought it with me. So I gave it to him and I remember he'd disappear. He'd be in his room an awful lot of the time . . . reading that and underlining things.'" Schlesinger Jr., *Robert Kennedy and His Times*, 617.

Chapter Nine: Breakthrough

176 **Annie has been using her approach:** Here is a testimonial from a patient who was cured from long COVID through DNRS: "Covid Recovery Stories: How Long-Hauler Sandra Regained Her Mobility, Energy & Taste," Dynamic Neural Retraining System, December 10, 2023, retrainingthebrain.com/success-stories/sandra-covid-recovery-stories -how-long-hauler-sandra-regained-her-mobility-energy-taste.

177 **"the enduring weakness":** John Sarno, *Healing Back Pain: The Mind-Body Connection* (New York: Balance, 1991), 14. The full passage from Sarno reads: "It may be hard to believe that highly sophisticated twentieth century medicine cannot properly identify the cause of something so simple and common as these pain disorders, but physicians and medical researchers are, after all, still human and, therefore, not all-knowing, and, most important, subject to the enduring weakness of bias."

177 **"induce physiologic change":** Sarno, *Healing Back Pain*, 14.

177 **"leave the emotional dimension out":** Sarno, *Healing Back Pain*, 16.

180 **"Through my own experience":** Hopper, *Wired for Healing*, loc. 434.

181 **"this body of research":** Hopper, *Wired for Healing*, loc. 1011.

181 **"One man's migraines":** Nichole Sachs, "Overcoming Intense Fibromyalgia and Nerve Pain with Catherine Oxenberg," August 25, 2023, in *The Cure for Chronic Pain with Nicole Sachs, LCSW*, produced by Lisa

Eisenpresser, podcast, podcasts.apple.com/us/podcast/the-cure-for-chronic-pain-with-nicole-sachs-lcsw/id1439580309?i=1000625645999.

181 **"Every time a specific encounter"**: Hopper, *Wired for Healing*, loc. 937.

181 **"limiting core beliefs"**: Annie Hopper, *Dynamic Neural Training System Workshop Manual*. Not publicly available.

182 **"what I came to understand"**: Hopper, *Wired for Healing*, loc. 1269.

187 **"This is how we increase"**: Rohr, *Universal Christ*, 64.

187 **"historically unprecedented intersection"**: Rick Hanson and Richard Mendius, *The Buddha's Brain: The Practical Neuroscience of Happiness, Love, and Wisdom* (Oakland, CA: New Harbinger, 2009), 1.

187 **"The brain is the organ"** Hanson, *Hardwiring Happiness*, 9.

187 **"My focus is on increasing"**: Hanson, *Hardwiring Happiness*, 15.

191 **"What is the seal of liberation?"**: Brown, *Rising Strong*, 204.

193 **our brain actually generates**: In her book *How Emotions Are Made* (New York: Houghton Mifflin Harcourt, 2017), Lisa Feldman Barrett writes, "Scientific evidence shows that what we see, hear, touch, taste, and smell are largely simulations of the world, not reactions to it. Forward-looking thinkers speculate that simulation is a common mechanism not only for perception but also for understanding language, feeling empathy, remembering, imagining, dreaming, and many other psychological phenomena. . . . Simulation is the default mode for all mental activity" (27–28).

193 **"Mind Body symptoms"**: Schubiner, *Unlearn Your Pain*, 436.

194 **"the false messages"**: Schubiner, *Unlearn Your Pain*, 424–25.

195 **of the Colorado study**: Michael W. Donnino, Garrett S. Thompson, Shivani Mehta, Myrella Paschali, Patricia Howard, Sofie B. Antonsen, Lakshman Balaji, Suzanne M. Bertisch, Robert Edwards, Long H. Ngo, and Anne V. Grossestreuer, "Psychophysiologic Symptom Relief Therapy for Chronic Back Pain: A Pilot Randomized Controlled Trial," *PAIN Reports* 6 no. 3 (September/October 2021): e959, doi.org/10.1097/PR9.0000000000000959.

195 **PSRT can decrease symptoms**: Michael Donnino, MD; Patricia Howard, BS; Shivani Mehta, BA; Jeremy Silverman, BA; Maria J. Cabrera, BA; Jolin B. Yamin, PhD; Lakshman Balaji, MPH; Katherine M. Berg, MD; Stanley Heydrick, PhD; Robert Edwards, PhD; and Anne V. Grossestreuer, PhD, MSc, "Psychophysiologic Symptom Relief Therapy for Post-Acute Sequelae of Coronavirus Disease 2019," Mayo Clinic *Proceedings: Innovations, Quality & Outcomes* 7, no. 4 (May 19, 2023), 337–48, mcpiqojournal.org/article/S2542-4548(23)00028-0/fulltext.

195 **Intensive Short-Term Dynamic Psychotherapy**: The bibliography in Sarno's book *The Divided Mind* cites a book edited by Davanloo: *Basic*

Principles and Techniques in Short-Term Dynamic Psychotherapy (New York: Spectrum, 1978).

196 **"Full and direct experience"**: Malan and Coughlin Della Selva, *Lives Transformed*, 47.

196 **"Use of visualization and imagery"**: Malan and Coughlin, *Lives Transformed*, 65

196 **"speak the words"**: Schubiner, *Unlearn Your Pain*, 199.

197 **"dreaming while awake"**: Malan and Coughlin, *Lives Transformed*, 319.

197 **"liberation of positive emotion"**: Malan and Coughlin, *Lives Transformed*, 61.

197 **"experienced an outpouring of love"**: Malan and Coughlin, *Lives Transformed*, 61.

199 **"My migraines have"**: Schubiner, *Unlearn Your Pain*, 427.

199 **a reduction of pain scores**: H. Schubiner, A. Burger, and M. Lumley, "P02.147. Emotions Matter: Sustained Reductions in Chronic Non-Structural Pain after a Brief, Manualized Emotional Processing Program," *BMC Complementary Alternative Medicine* 12, suppl. 1 (2012), doi.org/10.1186/1472-6882-12-S1-P203.

199 **the first large-scale study**: Mark A. Lumley, Howard Schubiner, Nancy A. Lockhart, Kelley M. Kidwell, Steven E. Harted, Daniel J. Clauwd, and David A. Williams, "Emotional Awareness and Expression Therapy, Cognitive Behavioral Therapy, and Education for Fibromyalgia: A Cluster-Randomized Controlled Trial" *PAIN* 158, no. 12 (December 2017): 2354–63, dx.doi.org/10.1097/j.pain.0000000000001036.

199 **a trial with military veterans**: Brandon C. Yarns, MD, MS; Mark A. Lumley, PhD; Justina T. Cassidy; W. Neil Steers, PhD; Sheryl Osato, PhD; Howard Schubiner, MD; and David L. Sultzer, MD, "Emotional Awareness and Expression Therapy Achieves Greater Pain Reduction Than Cognitive Behavioral Therapy in Older Adults with Chronic Musculoskeletal Pain: A Preliminary Randomized Comparison Trial," *Pain Medicine* 21, no. 11 (November 2020): 2811–22, doi.org/10.1093/pm/pnaa145.

200 **"the fact that she's gone"**: *The Crown*, season 6, ep. 5, "Willsmania," written by Jonathan Wilson, Peter Morgan, Meriel Baistow-Clare, and Daniel Marc Janes, produced by Peter Morgan, aired December 14, 2023, on Netflix.

201 **chronic neck or back pain**: Howard Schubiner, William J. Lowry Marjorie Heule, Yoni K. Ashar, Michael Lim, Steven Mekaru, Torran Kitts, and Mark A. Lumley, "Application of a Clinical Approach to Diagnosing Primary Pain: Prevalence and Correlates of Primary Back and Neck

Pain in a Community Physiatry Clinic," *Journal of Pain* 25, no. 3 (March 2024): 672–81, doi.org/10.1016/j.jpain.2023.09.019.

201 **"most diagnoses cite a physical cause"**: Nathaniel Frank, "That Pain in Your Back? It's Really a Pain in Your Brain," *Los Angeles Times*, January 29, 2024, latimes.com/opinion/story/2024-01-29/chronic-pain-health -wellness-mind-body.

202 **need for healing lie**: Rohr, *Dancing Standing Still*, 106.

203 **"your whole view of the world"**: Rohr, *Dancing Standing Still*, 26.

203 **"nothing really changes"**: Rohr, *Breathing Under Water*, loc. 162.

203 **"changing the direction"**: Keating, *Daily Reader for Contemplative Living*, 70.

Chapter Ten: Breakthrough after Breakthrough

205 **something called The Work**: thework.com.

207 **Schubiner directs his readers**: Schubiner, *Unlearn Your Anxiety*, 394.

210 **And Michael Gazzaniga writes**: Katie and Mitchell, *Loving What Is*, xii–xiii.

211 **"absolute dread"**: Tolle, *Power of Now*, 3–5.

212 **"Laughter welled up"**: Katie and Mitchell, *Loving What Is*, x.

215 **"the happiest she had ever been"**: Katie and Mitchell, *Loving What Is*, 231.

219 **"a totality more real"**: Johnson, *He*, 64.

219 **parts of ourselves we've denied**: The shadow is what we disown, but we are drawn to the shadow even as we disown it—because it's the only path to wholeness. Theologian Henri Nouwen wrote this in his book *The Return of the Prodigal Son*:

All my life I have harbored a strange curiosity for the disobedient life that I myself didn't dare to live, but which I saw being lived by many around me. I did all the proper things, mostly complying with the agendas set by the many parental figures in my life—teachers, spiritual directors, bishops, and popes—but at the same time I often wondered why I didn't have the courage to "run away" as the younger son did. It is strange to say this, but, deep in my heart, I have known the feeling of envy toward the wayward son. It is the emotion that arises when I see my friends having a good time doing all sorts of things that I condemn. I called their behavior reprehensible or even immoral, but at the same time I often wondered why I didn't have the nerve to do some of it or all of it myself. The obedient and dutiful life of which I am proud or for which I am praised feels, sometimes, like a burden that was laid on my shoulders and continues to oppress me, even when I have accepted it to such a degree that I cannot throw it off.

A fascination for the defiant life many of us don't dare to live can also be seen in the popularity of country music legend Merle Haggard. When Johnny Cash performed at San Quentin prison on January 1, 1959, Haggard was there—as an inmate. It's true, as his famous song "Mama Tried" says, that he "turned 21 in prison." And when he died, the lead of his *New York Times* obituary read: "Merle Haggard, one of the most successful singers in the history of country music, a contrarian populist whose songs about his scuffling early life and his time in prison made him the closest thing that the genre had to a real-life outlaw hero, died at his ranch in Northern California on Wednesday, his 79th birthday." Bill Friskics-Warren, "Merle Haggard, Country Music's Outlaw Hero, Dies at 79," *New York Times*, April 6, 2016.

A few years earlier, *GQ* magazine had written, "Merle Haggard stands as country's remaining black-hat rebel, the last man singing for the underdog," and quoted Haggard as saying: "They don't want to hear about the easy part, the good days that you did. They want to hear about the places they haven't been. The pain they haven't felt." (In the same article, Haggard is reported as saying backstage to guitarist Les Paul, then 89, "By the time you get close to the answers, it's nearly all over.") Chris Heath, "Merle Haggard: The Last Outlaw," *GQ*, August 7, 2012, gq.com/story/merle-haggard-profile-chris-heath.

219 "honor and accept one's shadow": Johnson, *Owning Your Own Shadow*, x.
219 "to pay out that shadow": Johnson, *Owning Your Own Shadow*, 21.
220 "Culture can only function": Johnson, *Owning Your Own Shadow*, 52.
220 "low-grade short story": Johnson, *Owning Your Own Shadow*, 23.
222 "Don't try to be wiser": Katie and Mitchell, *Loving What Is*, 14. Katie's counsel here gets support from Jung, who writes: "When one tries desperately to be good and wonderful and perfect, then all the more the shadow develops a definite will to be black and evil and destructive. People cannot see that; they are always striving to be marvelous. . . . The fact is that if one tries beyond one's capacity to be perfect, the shadow descends into hell and becomes the devil. For it is just as sinful from the standpoint of nature and truth to be above oneself as to be below oneself." Jung, *Quotable Jung*, 35.
222 "without any fear of consequences": Katie and Mitchell, *Loving What Is*, 14.

Chapter Eleven: What Works?

226 **"Keeping secrets is physical work":** James W. Pennebaker and Joshua M. Smyth, *Opening Up by Writing It Down: How Expressive Writing Improves Health and Eases Emotional Pain* (New York: Guilford, 2016), 8–10.

227 **"to have to wander about":** Nouwen, *Life of the Beloved*, 38.

228 **"Bewail and lament":** Thomas à Kempis, *The Imitation of Christ*, 183.

233 **I had a much better dad:** Have you ever nursed a grievance against someone and then suddenly seen them as a human being struggling to do their best? This feeling overcame me as I watched Jewel sing "My Father's Daughter" (youtube.com/watch?v=2TYepdbTI0g), which she performed with Dolly Parton. Jewel talks about the song in her book, *Never Broken: Songs Are Only Half the Story* (New York: Blue Rider Press, 2015), which was such an intimate read, especially toward the end, that when I finished it, I walked around the house thinking: "Jewel just *dropped* me. She just totally stopped talking to me!" Jewel had moved me to tears with stories of the work her dad did to overcome his abusive upbringing, and knowing that background, her song did me in. The lyrics alone on the page are amazing, but still won't convey the experience. Go watch the video.

234 **three books by Patricia Coughlin:** The three Patricia Coughlin books were Coughlin, *Facilitating the Process of Working Through in Psychotherapy*; Malan and Coughlin Della Selva, *Lives Transformed*; and Coughlin Della Selva, *Intensive Short-Term Dynamic Psychotherapy*.

235 **"primitive murderous rage":** Malan and Coughlin Della Selva, *Lives Transformed*, 259.

236 **"Feelings do not cause problems":** Malan and Coughlin Della Selva, *Lives Transformed*, 106, 141. I love hearing a truth from one domain expressed in another. In *The Book of Forgiving*, which Archbishop Desmond Tutu wrote with his daughter Mpho, the archbishop says: "When I am hurt, when I am in pain, when I am angry with someone for what they have done to me, I know the only way to end these feelings is to accept them. I know that the only way out of these feelings is to go through them. We get into all sorts of trouble when we try to find a way to circumvent this natural process" Tutu and Tutu, *The Book of Forgiving*, 138.

241 **"no such thing as a self":** Byron Katie with Stephen Mitchell, *A Mind at Home with Itself: How Asking Four Questions Can Free Your Mind, Open Your Heart, and Turn Your World Around* (New York: HarperOne, 2017), 29, 139, 277. The three verses of the Diamond Sutra are interpretive adaptations by Stephen Mitchell, working with existing translations.

242 "My thought processes": Tolle, *Even the Sun Will Die*, ch. 2, 2:40.

242 "a vast realm of consciousness": Tolle, *Even the Sun Will Die*, ch. 2, 7:35.

242 "power of the teaching": Tolle, *Even the Sun Will Die*, ch. 2, 42:55–43:45.

243 "no thought has made me unhappy": Tolle, *Even the Sun Will Die*, ch. 2, 12:00.

243 "The degree of absence": Tolle, *Even the Sun Will Die*, ch. 2, 59:32.

243 "greatest mystic-sages": Novak, *The World's Wisdom*, 40.

244 "the measure of your progress": Ramana, *Be As You Are*, 73.

244 "all the rest is uprooted": Ramana, *Teachings of Ramana Maharshi*, 102.

244 effort to dissolve the ego: This is the paradox that the Jesuit in Japan warned me of in 1982 when he said, "But you're activating your dynamic side to cultivate your passive side," or as he might have put it, "You're activating the ego to dissolve the ego."

244 "The mind is simply fattened": Ramana, *Be As You Are*, 70.

245 "So it is with the ego": Ramana, *Be As You Are*, 80.

245 "The same truth has to be expressed": Ramana, *Teachings of Ramana Maharshi*, 124–25.

246 "the final question": Ramana, *Be As You Are*, 72.

246 "Keep the attention fixed": Ramana, *Be As You Are*, 95.

246 "O ye of little faith": Matt. 6:25–30, KJV.

247 "it is God who works": Thurman, *Meditations of the Heart*, loc. 1364–71.

248 "I have enjoyed writing": Chuang Tzu, *Way of Chuang Tzu*, 9.

248 "shares the climate and peace": Chuang Tzu, *Way of Chuang Tzu*, 11.

248 "there is no escape": Chuang Tzu, *Way of Chuang Tzu*, 22.

249 "Contentment and well-being": Chuang Tzu, *Way of Chuang Tzu*, 101.

249 "consciousness unfolding": Tolle, *Even the Sun Will Die*, ch. 2, 58:21.

249 "I have no life": Katie and Mitchell, *Mind at Home with Itself*, 251.

251 "If you bring forth": Rohr, *Breathing Under Water*, 38–39. Robert Johnson makes this point in his book *Inner Work:*

If we don't go to the spirit, the spirit comes to us as neurosis. This is the immediate, practical connection between psychology and religion in our time. Every person must live the inner life in one form or another. Consciously or unconsciously, voluntarily or involuntarily, the inner world will claim us and exact its dues. If we go to that realm consciously, it is by our inner work: our prayers, meditations, dream work, ceremonies, and Active Imagination. If we try to ignore the inner world, as most of us do, the unconscious will find its way into our lives through pathology: our psychosomatic symptoms, compulsions, depressions, and neuroses.

251 "I was sitting alone": Ramana, *Teachings of Ramana Maharshi*, 3.
252 "there was no more fear": Tolle, *Power of Now*, 4.
252 "I was actually willing": Adyashanti, interviewed by Tami Simon, *Waking Up: Over Thirty Perspectives on Spiritual Awakening* (Louisville, CO: Sounds True, 2015), Audible audio ed.; "Waking Up: What Does It Really Mean?—Adyashanti on Insights at the Edge," March 21, 2022, YouTube video, 15:50–18:00, youtube.com/watch?v=cArhYkYkfZg.
254 "the only direct window": Damasio, *Feeling and Knowing*, 7–8.
255 "The real power is in self-directed neuroplasticity": Schwartz and Gladding, *You Are Not Your Brain*, 38.

Chapter Twelve: The Endgame

260 "I create a false personality": Father Alison is an expert on the work of René Girard, whose research has pointed to the habit of scapegoating as both a tool for creating false belonging and as foundational to human civilization. Alison, in scholarship singled out by Girard for its theological application of his own anthropological insight, uses Girard's concepts of mimetic desire and scapegoating to open doors to the meaning of original sin. Father Alison's insights were on display in a conversation we had with a small group in the summer of 2019, when he said, "To be able to refer to somebody as a scapegoat, you're saying they are falsely accused. That is an extraordinary cultural acquisition, to be able, in the same sentence, in the same breath, to perceive that somebody is accused, that they're being accused holds the group together, but that they have been falsely accused, and therefore, the group's unity is based on a lie. That's what the word scapegoat means, and it's astounding. I mean it's been incomprehensible to the vast majority of human societies."
261 international conflict–resolution specialist: *Facing the Truth*, BBC three-part television series, aired March 4–6, 2006.
261 "the key to the conundrum": Hicks, *Dignity*, x.
261 "Along with our survival instincts": Donna Hicks, "Opinion: In Marriage, Politics, and Cultural Clashes—This Is the Root of Conflict," *Deseret News*, September 26, 2022, deseret.com/opinion/2022/9/26/23365894/opinion-cause-of-conflict-human-dignity.
261 "all the other social distinctions": Hicks, *Dignity*, 18.
263 "Love your enemies" is perhaps: Matt. 5:21–44, KJV.
263 "No enemy could be more dangerous": Augustine, *Confessions*, 19.
265 "decrease the amount of suffering": Harari, *Sapiens*, 415.
265 "the point of developing agriculture": Harari, *Sapiens*, 376.

265 "objective conditions and subjective expectations": Harari, *Sapiens*, 380, 382.

265 "reaches the same conclusions": Harari, *Sapiens*, 382.

265 "like something without wanting it": Hanson, *Hardwiring Happiness*, 87.

266 "the bone-deep ongoing sense": Hanson, *Hardwiring Happiness*, 221.

266 "there would come a tipping point": Hanson, *Hardwiring Happiness*, 221.

266 "humans who are open now": Tolle, *Even the Sun Will Die*, ch. 2, 1:10:57.

266 "narrowed and cheapened the Gospel": Alison, "Jesus: Forgiving Victim."

267 "Must minister to himself": William Shakespeare, *Macbeth*, eds. Barbara A. Mowat and Paul Werstine, Folger Shakespeare Library (New York: Simon & Schuster, 2013), act 5, sc. 4, 171, 173.

268 "a fool for the truth": Augustine, *Confessions*, xxii.

271 "Do Not Mention Zones": Martha Beck, *The Way of Integrity: Finding the Path to Your True Self* (New York: Penguin Life, 2021), 70.

275 "drop the world's bait": *The Connected Discourses of the Buddha: A Translation of the Samyutta Nikāya*, trans. Bhikkhu Bodhi (Boston: Wisdom, 2000), loc. 1562–72, Kindle.

Bibliography

This is a list of bibliographic sources. To me, they are acknowledgments. Many of these books are cited in *Chasing Peace*, some are not, but all contributed to the insights and practices that led me to write this book. Each author either put forward ideas or practices I'd never heard of before or wrote truths I'd never seen written with such clarity and beauty. I'm indebted to all of them.

Alison, James. *The Joy of Being Wrong: Original Sin through Easter Eyes*. New York: Herder and Herder, 1998.

Augustine. *Confessions*. Translated by F. J. Sheed. Indianapolis: Hackett, 2006.

Bourgeault, Cynthia. *The Meaning of Mary Magdalene: Discovering the Woman at the Heart of Christianity*. Boston: Shambhala, 2011.

Brooks, Arthur. *Love Your Enemies: How Decent People Can Save America from the Culture of Contempt*. New York: Broadside Books, 2019.

Brown, Brené. *Daring Greatly: How the Courage to Be Vulnerable Transforms the Way We Live, Love, Parent, and Lead*. New York: Avery, 2012.

Brown, Brené. *Rising Strong: How the Ability to Reset Transforms the Way We Live, Love, Parent, and Lead*. New York: Random House, 2015.

Buddha. *The Dhammapada*. Translated by Irving Babbitt. New York: New Directions, 1965.

Bullock, Alan. *Hitler: A Study in Tyranny*, abridged ed. New York: Harper-Collins, 1971.

Carter, Dan T. *The Politics of Rage: George Wallace, the Origins of the New Conservatism, and the Transformation of American Politics*. New York: Simon and Schuster, 1995.

Chuang Tzu. *The Way of Chuang Tzu*. Edited by Thomas Merton. New York: New Directions, 2010.

Coughlin, Patricia. *Facilitating the Process of Working Through in Psychotherapy: Mastering The Middle Game*. New York: Routledge, 2023.

Coughlin Della Selva, Patricia. *Intensive Short-Term Dynamic Psychotherapy: Theory and Technique*. New York: Routledge, 2018.

Covey, Stephen. *The 7 Habits of Highly Effective People*. New York: Simon and Schuster, 2013.

Damasio, Antonio. *Feeling and Knowing: Making Minds Conscious*. New York: Pantheon, 2021.

Doyle, Glennon. *Untamed*. New York: Dial Press, 2020.

Feldman Barrett, Lisa. *How Emotions Are Made: The Secret Life of the Brain*. New York: Mariner Books, 2017.

Frankl, Viktor E. *Man's Search for Meaning*. Boston: Beacon Press, 2006.

Glasser, William. *Choice Theory: A New Psychology of Personal Freedom*. New York: HarperCollins, 1998.

Goenka, S. N. *The Discourse Summaries of SN Goenka*. Edited by William Hart. Onalaska, WA: Vipassana Research Publications, 2012.

Gottschall, Jonathan. *The Story Paradox: How Our Love of Storytelling Builds Societies and Tears Them Down*. New York: Basic Books, 2021.

Hanson, Rick. *Hardwiring Happiness: The New Brain Science of Contentment, Calm, and Confidence*. New York: Harmony, 2013.

Harari, Yuval Noah. *Sapiens: A Brief History of Humankind*. New York: HarperCollins, 2015.

Hicks, Donna. *Dignity: The Essential Role It Plays in Resolving Conflict*. New Haven, CT: Yale University Press, 2011.

Hopper, Annie. *Wired for Healing: Remapping the Brain to Recover from Chronic and Mysterious Illnesses*. Altona, Canada: Friesens, 2015. Kindle.

Horney, Karen. *Our Inner Conflicts: A Constructive Theory of Neurosis*. Abingdon, UK: Routledge, 1946.

Ignatius of Loyola. *Personal Writings: Reminiscences, Spiritual Diary, Select Letters—including the Text of the Spiritual Exercises*. Translated with introductions and notes by Joseph A. Munitiz and Philip Endean. New York: Penguin, 1997.

John of the Cross. *The Dark Night of the Soul.* In *Wellsprings of Faith.* New York: Barnes & Noble Books, 2005.

Johnson, Robert A. *Inner Work: Using Dreams and Active Imagination for Personal Growth.* New York: HarperOne, 1989.

Johnson, Robert A. *Owning Your Own Shadow: Understanding the Dark Side of the Psyche.* San Francisco: HarperOne, 1991.

Jung, C. G. *Memories, Dreams, Reflections.* Translated by Richard and Clara Winston. New York: Vintage, 1989

Jung, C. G. *Modern Man in Search* of a *Soul.* New York: Harcourt Brace, 1955.

Katie, Byron, with Stephen Mitchell. *Loving What Is: Four Questions That Can Change Your Life.* New York: Harmony Books, 2002.

Katie, Byron, with Stephen Mitchell. *A Mind at Home with Itself: How Asking Four Questions Can Free Your Mind, Open Your Heart, and Turn Your World Around.* New York: HarperCollins, 2017.

Katie, Byron, with Stephen Mitchell. *A Thousand Names for Joy: Living in Harmony with the Way Things Are.* New York: Harmony Books, 2007.

Keating, Thomas. *Open Mind, Open Heart.* London: Bloomsbury, 2006.

Keating, Thomas. *Intimacy with God: An Introduction to Centering Prayer.* New York: Crossroad, 2009.

Kegan, Robert. *The Evolving Self: Problem and Process in Human Development.* Cambridge, MA: Harvard University Press, 1982.

Kopp, Sheldon. *If You Meet the Buddha on the Road, Kill Him: The Pilgrimage of Psychotherapy Patients.* Palo Alto, CA: Bantam, 1976.

Jayakar, Pupul. J. *Krishnamurti: A Biography.* New Delhi, India: Penguin, 1986.

Lao Tzu. *The Way of Life: Tao Te Ching.* Translated by Raymond B. Blakney. Dublin, Ireland: Mentor Books, 1955.

Malan, David, and Patricia Coughlin Della Selva. *Lives Transformed: A Revolutionary Method of Dynamic Psychotherapy.* New York: Routledge, 2018.

Merton, Thomas. *Conjectures of a Guilty Bystander.* New York: Image, 2014.

Noe, K. Killian. *Descent into Love: How Recovery Café Came to Be.* Seattle: inward/outward, 2015.

Noe, K. Killan. *Finding Our Way Home: Addictions and Divine Love.* Scottsdale, PA: Herald Press, 2003.

Nouwen, Henri J. M. *The Inner Voice of Love: A Journey through Anguish to Freedom.* New York: Doubleday, 1998.

Nouwen, Henri, J. M. *Life of the Beloved: Spiritual Living in a Secular World.* New York: Crossroad, 2002.

Nouwen, Henri, J. M. *The Return of the Prodigal Son: A Story of Homecoming.* New York: Doubleday, 1992.

Nouwen, Henri J. M. *The Way of the Heart: Desert Spirituality and Contemporary Ministry.* New York: Seabury Press, 1981.

Novak, Philip. *The World's Wisdom: Sacred Texts of the World's Religions.* San Francisco: HarperOne, 2011.

Nozick, Robert. *Anarchy, State, and Utopia.* New York: Basic Books, 2013.

Pennebaker, James W., and Joshua M. Smyth. *Opening Up by Writing It Down: How Expressive Writing Improves Health and Eases Emotional Pain.* New York: Guilford Press, 2016.

Piyadassi Thera. *The Buddha's Ancient Path.* Onalaska, WA: Buddhist Publication Society, 2020.

Plato. *The Apology.* In *Plato: The Complete Works.* Translated by Benjamin Jowett and George Buress. Copenhagen, Denmark: Titan Read, 2015. Kindle.

Plato. *Phaedo.* In *Plato: The Complete Works.* Translated by Benjamin Jowett and George Buress. Copenhagen, Denmark: Titan Read, 2015. Kindle.

Ramana. *Be As You Are: The Teachings of Sri Ramana Maharshi.* Edited by David Godman. London: Penguin, 1988.

Ramana. *The Spiritual Teaching of Ramana Maharshi.* Edited by Joe and Guinevere Miller. Boston: Shambala, 1972.

Ramana. *The Teachings of Ramana Maharshi in His Own Words.* Edited by Arthur Osborne. Tamil Nadu, India: V. S. Ramanan, 2013.

Rohr, Richard. *Breathing Under Water: Spirituality and the Twelve Steps.* Cincinnati: St. Anthony's Messenger Press, 2011.

Rohr, Richard. *Dancing Standing Still.* New York: Paulist Press, 2014.

Rohr, Richard. *Eager to Love: The Alternative Way of Francis of Assisi.* Cincinnati: Franciscan Media, 2014.

Rohr, Richard. *Everything Belongs: The Gift of Contemplative Prayer.* New York: Crossroad, 2003.

Rohr, Richard. *Falling Upward: A Spirituality for the Two Halves of Life.* San Francisco: Jossey Bass, 2011.

Rohr, Richard. *The Universal Christ: How a Forgotten Reality Can Change Everything We See, Hope for, and Believe.* New York: Convergent Books, 2019.

Sabatier, Paul. *The Road to Assisi: The Essential Biography of St. Francis.* Edited by Jon M. Sweeney. Brewster, MA: Paraclete Press, 2014.

Sarno, John E. *The Divided Mind: The Epidemic of Mindbody Disorders.* New York: HarperCollins, 2006.

Schmidt, Amy. *Knee Deep in Grace: The Extraordinary Life and Teaching of Dipa Ma.* New York: BlueBridge, 2005.

Schubiner, Howard. *Unlearn Your Anxiety and Depression: A Self-Guided Process to Reprogram Your Brain.* Pleasant Ridge, MI: Mind Body Publishing, 2016.

Schubiner, Howard. *Unlearn Your Pain: A 28-Day Process to Reprogram Your Brain.* Pleasant Ridge, MI: Mind Body Publishing, 2019.

Shriver, Maria. *I've Been Thinking . . . : Reflections, Prayers, and Meditations for a Meaningful Life.* New York: Pamela Dorman Books, 2018.

Shriver, Timothy. *Fully Alive: Discovering What Matters Most.* New York: Sarah Crichton Books, 2015.

Singer, June. *Boundaries of the Soul: The Practice of Jung's Psychology.* New York: Anchor Books, 1994.

Suzuki, Shunryu. *Zen Mind, Beginner's Mind: Informal Talks on Zen Meditation and Practice.* Boston: Weatherhill, 1970.

Taylor, Stephen. *The Leap: The Psychology of Spiritual Awakening.* Novato, CA: New World Library, 2017.

Teresa of Avila, *The Interior Castle.* In *Wellsprings of Faith.* New York: Barnes & Noble Books, 2005.

Thomas à Kempis. *The Imitation of Christ.* In *Wellsprings of Faith.* New York: Barnes & Noble Books, 2005.

Thurman, Howard. *Jesus and the Disinherited.* Boston: Beacon Press, 1976.

Thurman, Howard. *Meditations of the Heart.* Boston: Beacon Press, 2014. Kindle.

Tolle, Eckhart. *Even the Sun Will Die: An Interview with Eckhart Tolle.* Louisville, CO: Sounds True, 2003. Audible audio ed., 2 hr., 26 min.

Tolle, Eckhart. *A New Earth: Awakening to Your Life's Purpose.* New York: Penguin Life, 2006.

Tolle, Eckhart. *The Power of Now.* Novato, CA: New World Library, 2010.

Tutu, Desmond, and Mpho Tutu. *The Book of Forgiving: The Fourfold Path for Healing Ourselves and Our World.* New York: HarperCollins, 2014.

Walker, Rheeda. *The Unapologetic Guide to Black Mental Health: Navigate an Unequal System, Learn Tools for Emotional Wellness, and Get the Help You Deserve.* Oakland, CA: New Harbinger, 2020.

Welwood, John. *Journey of the Heart: The Path of Conscious Love.* New York: HarperCollins, 1996.